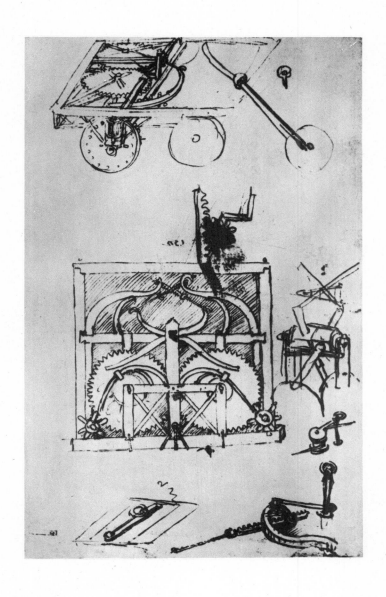

Leonardo da Vinci's self-propelled cart (from the Codex Atlanticus).

History of the MOTOR CAR

MARCO MATTEUCCI

Motoring Correspondent of *Corriere della Sera* Milan.

CROWN PUBLISHERS, INC.

NEW YORK

First published in the United States of America by
Crown Publishers, Inc. 419 Park Avenue South, New York, N.Y. 10016
ISBN 7064 0000 3 Printed in Italy
Reprinted 1975

CONTENTS

COLOUR PLATES

1915 Ford model "T"

INTRODUCTION

This brilliant book, lavishly illustrated in full colour, covers in detail the amazing development of the motor car from its most primitive beginning over 2,000 years ago in the minds of scientists and philosophers to the fulfilment of their prophetic dreams in the 20th Century. Written in clear, non-technical language, this is a book to delight everyone. The absorbing sections on the great inventors and manufacturers reveal the magnificent human endeavours behind the machine we all now unthinkingly accept as a necessary part of life, and the simple yet comprehensive approach to the technical and mechanical aspects of automobile development through the years, makes what is usually a subject reserved for specialists into enjoyable and instructive material for readers at all levels of interest.

1899 Fiat 3½ H.P.

Cugnot's three-wheeled, steam-driven tractor

For the majority of historians the vital starting point, the basis of the modern car, was Cugnot's fantastic three-wheeled, steam-driven gun tractor, completed in 1765 and, as is fully emphasised in this book, it was steam that made the motor car possible (in the same way as it had made the whole industrial revolution possible) but although France may claim Nicholas Joseph Cugnot as the inventor of the motorised vehicle, he in fact based his work on the principles of locomotion discovered by the Scotsmen, Watt and Murdock, and the Englishmen, Savery and Newcomen. However, it is ironic that in the two ensuing decades it was Britain that effectively pioneered steam public service vehicles, while Cugnot's clumsy invention led to his ruin.

Development of the wheel

Many of these early machines had carriage wheels, others had metal ones, and consequently the early history and development of the wheel is fundamental to the entire story of the motor car. It is a crucial subject and is given fascinating treatment in the book, and there are many other examples in this work of such individual studies of allied subjects, ranging from such light-hearted topics as Count Zborowski and his immortal Chitty-Chitty-Bang-Bang, to more serious matters which include the histories of braking systems, lighting and starting, the dynamo and alternator, and technical achievements such as the invention of turbine and rotary engines; there are features on hovercraft and hot-rods, on styling, safety and comfort and there are engrossing profiles of famous men and the cars with which they were associated.

The "Red Flag Act"

Inevitably, the history of the motor car and of motoring through the ages is deeply influenced by contemporary political and economic events, and their importance is not overlooked. This vital aspect is well illustrated by the unfortunate Locomotives on Highways Act of 1865, which has been misnamed the "Red Flag Act". Thus, while other countries were rapidly developing bigger and better motor cars, it was still illegal to drive in Britain without a man walking in front of the car. Consequently, Britain lost years of leeway in automobilism, which were not made up until the "Emancipation" Act of 1896 was passed, and that is why Daimler and Benz had a significant advantage over Simms, Lanchester and Austin.

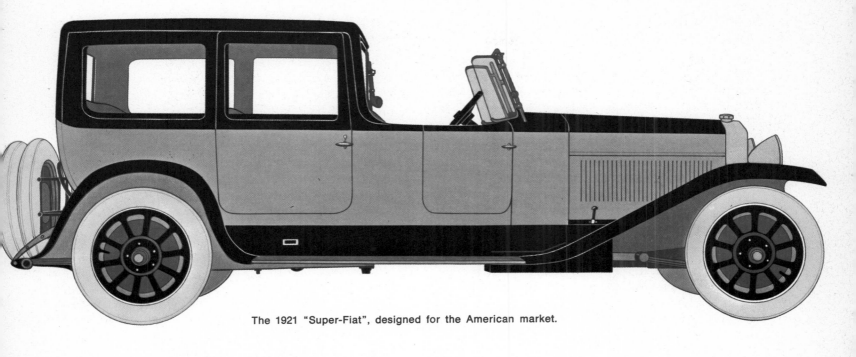

The 1921 "Super-Fiat", designed for the American market.

Henry Ford

The last quarter of the 19th Century saw the beginnings of the great motor manufacturing corporations, the rise of the brilliant Henry Ford; it also produced many strange inventions. Those who now hope for cheap electric commuter cars will see in this series that the electric motor reached its zenith in France and America in the 1890's, yet it became obsolete shortly afterwards. But if the last years of the 19th Century were the formative ones, the beginning of the 20th Century showed clear evidence of the crystallisation of design and of organised effort. The wild scrambles to earn colossal fortunes were nicely balanced by the need to produce increasingly efficient machines, and this situation survives today — to the benefit of the consumer.

Historic road races

From the very early days the "horseless carriages" and the real cars that evolved from them, bred a spirit of friendly rivalry among enthusiasts. To read the dramatic accounts of the early classical events — the epic long-distance runs and the historic road races — is to share this feeling and to understand the heavy odds stacked against these pioneers. Safety lay only in the sheer bulk of the larger machines and in the restricted speed of the lighter ones. Punctures happened by the mile, dense dust clouds obscured the vision, burning tar was a hazard in hot weather, and brakes were unreliable. Enthusiasts will be stirred by the incredible Pekin-Paris trial of 1907 and the equally heroic 1908 race from New York

to Paris via Alaska and Siberia. Indeed, today's international formula racing originated from the first French Grand Prix which was held at Le Mans in 1906. It was in this era, too, that the famous, but now defunct, Brooklands track was opened. Evidence of the influence of early racing on the development of the modern car can be seen in the detachable wheel rim, which brought victory to those who used it and revolutionised motoring.

The foundation of the Industrial Giants

The historic period from 1905 to 1920 also saw the inception of Britain's world famous Tourist Trophy Races in 1905, the Vanderbilt Cup Series in America and in 1911 the first of the fabulous Indianapolis 500-mile Races. After the First World War, British manufacturers were among the first to recognise the general public's growing demand for motor cars, and it was during this period that William Morris, the genius of the British motor industry, made his millions and laid the foundations for the British Motor Corporation/Leyland colossus of today.

However, it was America which led the world in the manufacture of popular cars. The Ford empire produced more than 15 million Model T cars in the 19 years from 1908 on. But despite the First World War, manufacturers throughout the world, and particularly in Europe, made tremendous progress. In France, Andre Citroen presented a new challenge to the ancient, brilliant Renault concern, which is now state controlled, and in Italy no other manufacturer ever matched the business acumen and enthusiasm of Fiat.

9

Royal enthusiasts

Many enthusiasts of today consider that the most exciting years of motoring were the 1920's, and it must be acknowledged that some of the finest designs and technical innovations stemmed from this era. It was between 1920-1925 that car makers finally settled down to a standard technique of manufacture and this was to influence car building for many decades to come. While it must be remembered that such features as overhead camshafts, epicyclic gear boxes and coil ignition were far from new even in the 'twenties, the fact remains that these improvements began to impress a wider public. In Britain, public interest in motoring was continually stimulated by the enthusiasm of the Royal Family, which has continued to the present day, and there are many delightfully nostalgic photographs of cars and their various owners from this colourful period. It was at this time that many of the great names and records were made. In 1926 a 9-litre single seater Renault broke the 24-hour record at Montlhery, covering 2,600 miles at over 107 mph; a Duesenberg, the car that was the status symbol in the great days of Hollywood, won the 1924 Indianapolis contest; Bentleys also achieved spectacular success, and a brief revival of the steam car produced the Doble, which travelled at speeds of more than 100 mph. Many fascinating and heroic exploits are recounted, among them those of Gaston Chevrolet, Parry Thomas and Ettore Bugatti, whose cars are now among the most coveted of collector's pieces.

The Great Depression and the Second World War

But on the industrial side the manufacturers were beginning to feel the economic slump, and this affected America's production first of all. Then, during the Second World War private motoring ceased. The great motor companies made military vehicles, and even these were almost exclusively based on pre-war designs for civilian cars and lorries. Ironically, it was Germany that produced at this time the basis of a family car that was later to gain enormous popularity as the Volkswagen.

Post-war intrigue

In the first year of peace the 50th anniversary of the motor car was celebrated, on the basis that 1895-1896 was the time when the first practicable car was produced. British manufacturers were among the first to resume production after the war, but the trade generally was disturbed by the world-wide political upheaval. A classic example of the tragic results of post-war intrigue was the arrest of Louis Renault, who was accused of collaboration with the Nazis. He died in prison under mysterious circumstances; his vast automobile empire was then taken under state control, and expanded to meet global demand for its popular products.

The national racing car

With the improvement in the international situation there was a resurgence in the motor industry. America's greatest technological contribution was the perfection of automatic transmissions and, in more recent years, the American manufacturers have successfully invaded the international competition field with racing cars and land speed record machines, whilst their large, powerful engines are in great demand by European producers of GT cars. The French and Italians were also quick to see that competitions and track work were good for sales as well as development, but it took longer for British manufacturers to concern themselves with sport. Even the much publicised "national" B.R.M. racing car was the product of a small group of men with little financial backing; it took 15 years for the name to attain success. However, the Jaguar was supreme in the sports-racing category and the racing world owes a great debt to the remarkable Sir William Lyons.

The exciting future

This great book offers everyone the thrilling experience of living through those vital years of pioneering endeavour, of sharing the excitement and fun of those colourful eras, and of taking a look at an even more exciting future with the industry's most advanced designers and technicians. The range of this work is immense, its scope is encyclopaedic, and with its beautiful appearance it is a collector's piece.

The "Scarabeo" experimental saloon built by OSI of Turin and based on the Alfa Romeo "Giulia 1600". It has a transverse engine, four carburettors and all-round independent suspension — one of the world's present-day dream cars. In less than a century, the motor car has progressed from angular freak to a masterpiece of shape and design.

CHAPTER ONE
THE ANCIENT DREAM

The dream of the motor car, of the "horseless carriage", self-propelled and capable of extraordinary speeds, is perhaps as old as man himself. Even if this book were limited to the story of the car as we know it today, we have to go a long way back through the centuries to find the first signs of what was to become one of the greatest adventures in the history of man.

A 1915 Buick "dream car".

Some people have even identified the first hints of the history of the car in Homer's Iliad — to be precise in the section in which are described the fantastic creations built by Vulcan in preparation for the Council of the Gods, among which was a magic wheel of solid gold which obeyed the gods' commands. Others have found indications of what was in future to become the motor car in the prophecies of Nahum and Ezekiel in the Old Testament, in which are described marvellous carriages capable of self-propulsion along the roads, and fantastic mechanical monsters which were perhaps even able to fly.

Traces of legends probably originating from these prophecies are also found in Greek and Roman bas-reliefs, showing mythical chariots drawn by invisible horsemen.

Jet of steam

Ideas rather more technical and somewhat less fantastic are first encountered in the studies of Hero of Alexandria, who describes a machine of his own invention which moved under its own power by means of a device — a hollow sphere out of which was expelled a strong jet of steam — which seems in some ways to anticipate the modern jet engine.

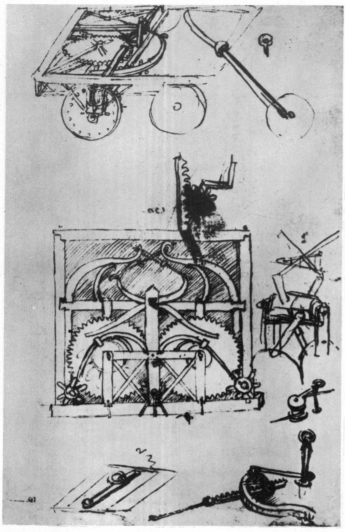

Leonardo da Vinci's self propelled cart (from the Codex Atlanticus).

The first truly self-propelled vehicles however, probably date from the time of Alexander the Great, when fearsome chariots were introduced bristling with scythes and lances. Depending on gravity, these were hurled down steep slopes against the enemy ranks. Such weapons were to be re-invented in the Middle Ages, and used with great effect by the Swiss in their battles against the Austrian overlords.

Philosopher's prophecy

It has been held by some people that the motor car was foreseen by Roger Bacon.

Even if untrue, the unique gifts of prophecy of this great 13th century scientist and philosopher must be recognised. Bacon, in fact, wrote the following, "One day we shall construct machines capable of propelling large ships at a speed far superior to that of an entire crew of oarsmen and needing only a pilot to steer them. One day we shall endow chariots with incredible speed without the aid of any animal. One day we shall construct winged machines able to lift themselves into the air like birds". Such farsighted forecasts could only arouse

suspicion in those times, and Bacon spent ten years of his life in prison, accused of magic and of pacts with the devil. The treatise containing the above passage was not published until three hundred years after his death. In 1472 Robert Valturio described a vehicle designed for use in war which drew power for its movements from large windmill sails, transmitted through a mechanism of cranks and gears. This was no more a practical proposition than many other devices studied and described at that time, all of them characterised by a total, and understandable, lack of consideration for the effects of friction. Some of these mechanisms were intended to use the muscular power of their passengers. Leonardo da Vinci, among others, occupied himself with such a design.

All these devices, powered by other than thermal or chemical energy, constitute a chapter of their own in the story of technical development.

A clockwork vehicle

Among them figured a marvellous machine built in 1649 by the German Johannes Hautsch, of Nuremberg, a vehicle whose bodywork was in the form of a dragon. A number of men concealed in the interior constituted the "engine" and the device so aroused the enthusiasm of the Crown Prince of Sweden that he bought it.

In 1748 another strange vehicle appeared, built by

Leonardo — sketch for a vehicle powered by a falling weight.

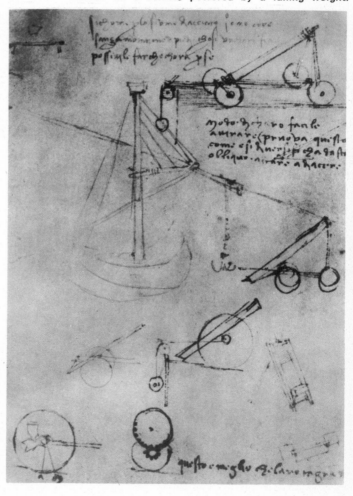

Roberto Valturio's wind-driven machine

the Frenchman, Jacques de Vaucanson. He modified a 58-year-old design by his fellow countryman Richard, who had the idea of using a series of steel springs similar to those used in church clocks. A chronicler of the time reports "The driver was able to set the carriage in motion or to stop it without horses". The monarch congratulated the ingenious inventor and ordered a similar machine for his own use, to be added to the royal stables. The Duke of Montmar, the Baron of Avenac and the Count of Bauzum, who saw the experiment, could hardly believe their eyes. In spite of this, various members of the Académie Française issued a statement that such a vehicle would never be able to travel the roads of any city.

Mounted boiler

It cannot be said that this pessimistic opinion was wrong. The failing, however, was certainly not in the concept of a self-propelled vehicle, but in the means chosen to power it, as history was to demonstrate.

But the time has come to consider the first powered vehicle in which men tried to harness the hidden forces of nature. The first man to consider using steam for propelling a carriage was probably Giovanni Battista Della Porta, an Italian scientist from Pesaro, who in 1589 invented a pump capable of raising water by means of steam pressure. He actually suggested the possibility of using such a mechanism for locomotion. Later how-

ever, when his pupil, Solomon de Caous, tried to put this idea into practice, the experiment aroused such alarm among the French clergy that the man was put in a lunatic asylum.

It was to be another Italian, Giovanni Branca, who was to turn the efforts of Della Porta and Caous into reality, building the first practical steam engine. The principle of this engine was, of course, simple — steam produced by a boiler passed through a nozzle and struck holes bored around the circumference of a wheel. Thus the wheel turned, and through a train of gears caused the alternate raising of two weighted arms. In this way the ingenious inventor succeeded in replacing the manual labour necessary to use a pharmacist's mortar.

A new chapter in the long story of the predecessors of the motor car derives from the experiments of Fernando Verbiest, a Jesuit missionary in China, who succeeded in building a model vehicle which actually worked. It was powered by steam produced in a boiler mounted in the carriage. In this case, too, the principle was of a perforated wheel moved by steam pressure, which transmitted motion through a gear train to the front wheels (it was a four-wheeler).

Principle of reaction

The name of Sir Isaac Newton is often mentioned as one of the pioneers if not the outright inventor of the idea of steam jet propulsion. But this does not seem

Newton's idea — a vehicle driven by a crude reaction engine.

to survive the light of a close examination and, in fact, probably arises from a surprising misunderstanding. In one of Newton's texts, published during the author's lifetime, there is a drawing of a carriage moved by steam. In this drawing is seen a boiler installed in a crude wheeled chassis, with a nozzle connected directly to the boiler itself and directed to the rear of the vehicle. It now seems certain that this drawing was meant to be only a visual illustration of the principle of reaction and does not represent a design for steam locomotion. It is just possible that from this drawing, most likely by an unknown draughtsman, was born the idea of the steam driven vehicle which was to have such a vigorous growth particularly in Great Britain — the home of every practicable invention for the use of steam. It is necessary to say at once, however, that the inventor and constructor of the first true steam driven vehicle was not English but French — Captain Nicolas Joseph Cugnot, builder of a tractor for towing artillery. This is rightly considered a milestone in the prehistory of the motor car.

Secret trials

On the oposite page there is a description of Cugnot's powerful vehicle: it may seem laughable by today's standards, but it was revolutionary when it appeared. It is important to note that Cugnot's studies certainly derived from the earlier invention of the Englishman Thomas Savery, who in 1698 had produced a somewhat complicated machine powered by steam energy and capable of raising a substantial quantity of water by means of what may be called a crude steel lung. The machine was actually built to pump the water which continually seeped in through the underground seams of a coal mine and it worked satisfactorily until it eventually blew up. Savery's steam engine was improved by another Englishman, Thomas Newcomen, who was the first of these

pioneers to design a version for locomotion. It concerned a simple railway for the transport of coal inside the mine, but was never actually built. It was to be the great physicist James Watt who was to apply himself, from 1765 onwards, to the scientific study of the application of the steam engine (for which he had in the meantime designed important improvements) to the movement of road vehicles. Watt did not bring his studies to a successful conclusion.

He was heavily engaged in the large-scale production of stationary steam engines for the mechanisation of the textile industry which was in rapid development at the time.

It was one of his competitors, the London merchant Francis Moore, and one of his keen supporters, his own workshop manager, William Murdock who were to take positive steps along the way to the steam road carriage. It was a similar path that Cugnot was treading in France at the same time. Moore succeeded in building a vehicle of this kind and demonstrated it in front of the King, obtaining the royal approval. Later however he disappeared from the scene, probably due to Watt's lively protests in which he maintained that Moore had infringed his patents. As for Murdock, he at first conducted all his experiments secretly by night, probably to keep them secret from his employer. The matter became public knowledge due to accidents during the first trials on the deserted roads. Thus, in a short time, everyone knew of his vehicle which, however, was never to become more than an interesting curiosity and was to end up in the British Museum.

Londoners' joy-rides

This chapter in the story of the ancestors of the motor car now contains a list of names, all British, of engineers responsible for an ever-improving series of steam vehicles. Among the first was William Symington, who

STEAM GOES TO WAR

Nicolas Joseph Cugnot's artillery tractor is perhaps the most important vehicle in the whole history of the motor car. It is generally accepted as being the first vehicle capable of self-propulsion that man constructed, excluding all those carriages built at various times which achieved short journeys by rolling down slopes, by muscular force applied directly or stored in springs, or by means of atmospheric phenomena.

Mammoth tricycle

Its inventor, a Captain of French artillery, had unusual ability considering the small progress made with mechanisms using steam power at the time when, about 1763, he began to study the possibility of experimenting with a means of locomotion. The most credible reconstruction of his studies — there are few documents — maintains that around 1765 Cugnot had already finished a steam vehicle capable of carrying four passengers at a speed of around two miles per hour. Having the idea of using the principles of this extraordinary vehicle for towing heavy artillery pieces, he obtained permission from the then Minister of War, the Marquis of Choiseul, to conduct the necessary experiments.

No trace remains of the vehicle and it is not known if the large, heavy, self-propelled carriage which came out of these experiments and which can be seen today in partially rebuilt form in the Conservatoire des Arts et Métiers in Paris, was constructed like its predecessor in the engineering workshop of Brézin at Brussels. It is certain, however, that its construction was made possible by a device for machining cannon bores which the French General Gribeauval had invented and built a short time before and which made possible the construction of precision cylinders for Cugnot's carriage. This had not been previously possible.

Towards the end of 1769 or in 1770 the mammoth brainchild of the ingenious officer was ready. It consisted of a huge tricycle entirely built of wood, over the front of which was hung a double-walled boiler, with the fire grate in the space between the inner and outer vessels. It was connected by a copper tube to two vertical cylinders which received steam under pressure. Inside the cylinders slid pistons connected through two con-rods and two cranks to the single, powered front wheel for steering. It is not known exactly how the transmission functioned, because the reconstruction of the model preserved in Paris would not work, though rack and pinion seem likely.

Economic crisis

Things must have been different at the time however, for the first trials held at Vincennes in the presence of a number of high ranking officers were successful. Some time afterwards this monster, which could haul five tons and travel at three miles per hour, ran into and demolished a wall, turning itself over. This unfortunate accident discouraged the Minister who, faced with the economic crisis which preceded the French Revolution, withdrew the funds necessary for Cugnot to continue his experiments. No more was heard of the historic machine and the new regime was not favourably inclined towards the inventor, from whom it even withdrew the pension of 600 francs awarded to him by the royal government. In the end, Cugnot died unknown in Brussels in 1804.

Cugnot's artillery tractor.

built a vehicle very similar to Murdock's. This carriage created an understandable curiosity, some enthusiasm not to mention considerable fear among the inhabitants of 18th century England. Then followed Richard Trevithick, an enthusiastic inventor, who among the activities was to build the first vehicle to run on rails (designed to carry coal in the Pen y Darren mine in Wales), and the first steam threshing machine.

Trevithick built between 1796 and 1801 various tricycles for the transport of light goods and in 1802 the first vehicle for passenger transport. He built, in fact, a new mechanical carriage weighing all of eight tons, with which he organised public shows within a circular arena where the more spirited spectators could race the puffing monster in return for a small payment. The machine, which could do 10 m.p.h. on the level and 3½ m.p.h. up a hill, was adapted for towing horseless carriages for Londoners' joy-rides. They were however, quick to forget this great engineer when Trevithick was refused a grant in recognition of his ability. He died in solitude in 1833.

Era of the steam coach

Parallel with the development of the first British steam vehicles, the prehistory of the motor car records somewhat similar development in America where, however, the different state of the road network directed the inventors more towards marine applications of the steam engine. The reports of this pioneering period contain the names of Nathan Read of Brompton, who designed a particularly advanced engine with a view to road vehicle application, and of John Fitch who founded the first company to build steam engines although none went into production.

Oliver Evans, a keen scientist and Pennsylvania businessman, spent a large part of his life in fighting the ignorance of his contemporaries in order to obtain the right to patent his steam engine for road propulsion and for the mechanisation of flour milling. Among other achievements, Evans succeeded in building a strange amphibious vehicle which he demonstrated publicly at Philadelphia, amidst the understandable curiosity of the crowd.

In the meantime in England there had exploded, almost without warning, what may justifiably be called the era of the steam carriage. The first name which is found in

Trevithick's three wheeler.

Trevithick's carriage.

Church's steam coach.

the history of these public vehicles, powered by much more efficient engines than those of the self-propelled vehicles of the early years of the century, is that of Julius Griffiths. He was the inventor and builder of the first real bus to be put into regular public service for passenger transport.

This bus dates from 1822, during the time Stephenson was beginning to operate the first steam railway in history. This competition in means of transport, in fact, was to remain for some decades. The development of the two systems in Great Britain was more or less parallel and gave rise to an active battle, not only on a technical basis, but also in the fields of commerce and finance due to the powerful interests which attached themselves to one side or another.

More or less contemporary with Griffiths, whose carriage had an efficient tubular boiler of a new type, were two other English inventors — James, inventor of four different steam buses fitted with such unheard of devices as cylinders with different pressures to give a steering effect and a gear change by means of chains, and John Scott Russell who began a regular steam coach service between Glasgow and Paisley. Another important name of the period is that of Sir Goldsworthy Gurney, builder of an improved steam coach which, beginning in 1825, supplied a regular public service between London and Bath. Before designing this vehicle, Gurney had interested himself for some time in strange projects for carriages moving on mechanical legs, inspired by the original ideas of a predecessor, David Gordon, who held that natural friction would be insufficient and that therefore designs of his type were necessary. The London-Bath steam coach could carry eighteen passengers (six inside and twelve outside) at a speed of 12½ m.p.h. It weighed two tons and had the boiler mounted at the back with the cylinders under the chassis. Coke was used as fuel. For ease of steering, Gurney had designed a front axle controlled by two steering wheels which moved the heavy tiller.

Another constructor, Walter Hancock, some years later put into service further improved vehicles on various routes which he ran in company with Francis Maceroni, a businessman of Italian origin. But parallel to this technical progress went that of the railways, whose expansion was undoubtedly due to the greater comfort and speed which they offered. Self-propelled road vehicles always suffered from boiler weaknesses, and even improved models required frequent stops for refilling. The competition between locomotive and steam coach gradually became more bitter. Ranged against the steam coach proprietors, already targets for the owners of bridges and toll rights who demanded ever-increasing payments, were the stage coach owners who created an association specifically to combat the establishment of the steam coach.

Passing of 'Red Flag Act'

The years between 1834 and 1839 saw numerous hostile acts against steam buses, particularly after the effect on the public of the first major accident in which one of these vehicles crashed into a pile of stones in the middle of the road just round a bend, causing the boiler to explode with consequent deaths and injuries. In 1839 another accident, in which a steam coach ran down two people at a cross road, killing one, triggered off a public reaction against mechanically-propelled road vehicles. This led to the passing of legislation which seems incredible today. This imposed a blanket speed limit of 7 m.p.h. on such vehicles.

In 1865 these regulations were made more onerous by the conditions of the "Locomotives on Highways Act", or "Red Flag Act", which required drivers of mechanical vehicles to be preceded by a man on foot.

This requirement, coupled with the general inferiority of road vehicles in relation to the railway at that time, started the rapid decline of the British steam coach, which finally disappeared within a few years. A similar decline took place in France with the end of the first coach service, begun in 1835 by Charles Dietz, between

Wheel used at Ur in 4000 B. C.

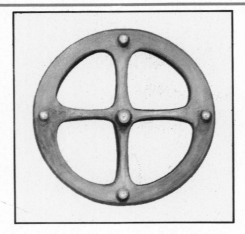

from the necessity to lighten wheels came the idea of spokes. The picture shows a Greek wheel of the 7th century B. C.

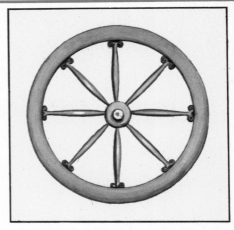

Light, elegant and modern-looking — a 4th century B. C. wheel.

WHEEL COMES OF AGE

A six-spoked wheel of the 3rd century B. C.

The story of the wheel is either thousands of years old or very short depending upon which part of the world is considered. It is known, for example, that while the Sumerian civilisation which flourished on the banks of the Euphrates circa 6000 years ago knew its use (as is recorded by the bas-relief of Ur, from which is taken the first wheel shown on this page) and while the Egyptians showed familiarity with it from 1700 B. C., the wheel was unknown in Oceania before the arrival of the first Europeans. Even the pre-Columbian American civilisations had found no practical use for it, though aware of it in principle.

First device

It is thought that the wheel was developed originally from the roller (a tree trunk) which probably represented the first device used by man to overcome sliding friction by turning it into rolling friction. After the roller became a disc, it was probably the need to get a hand inside to lubricate the axle which caused man to cut large holes in the disc. At some time someone thought of protecting the hub from shocks by means of a cap, and this was the forerunner of modern car hubcaps which have a more or less functional purpose. The evolution of the motor car wheel, as was the case also with bodywork, developed directly from that of the horse-drawn carriage with which it was at first identical. Almost from the beginning, car wheels had rims shod with rubber — solid and therefore long-wearing but also too hard. In the second half of the 19th century, John Boyd Dunlop, a Scottish veterinary surgeon, made his son's tricycle more comfortable by

inventing the pneumatic tyre — a cover for the rim which consisted of a rubber tube containing air under pressure. In 1888 the invention was patented in Great Britain, but Dunlop thought it unwise to abandon his profession and sold all his rights in it for a small sum. The idea proved unsuitable for motor cars, however, which continued to use solid tyres until someone thought of substituting the Dunlop tyre for another in two parts, an inner tube and a cover.

To Charles Goodyear is owed the innovation of vulcanising by which rubber acquires durability and elasticity. Until 1920, tyres were made by fixing rubber under pressure on to a body of cotton. The whole was then shaped and the exterior vulcanised. The tyres so built had a high-pressure inner tube and on average lasted about 4500 miles.

Return to past

In the 1920s low-pressure tyres were introduced and many of these had more than five times the life of the high-pressure tyres.

Beginning in 1955, tubeless tyres became common, particularly in the United States. These are tyres without an inner tube and are a return to the past in a sense, except that they are largely resistant to punctures or self-sealing. The tyre must fit the rim perfectly, in order to be air-tight.

a) A wheel built with wooden rim and spokes. It was with wheels of this type that Prince Scipione Borghese won the Pekin-Paris race in 1907. It is true that one of the wheels broke when the car turned over as a bridge collapsed b). But it is also true that a simple Siberian craftsman could build a replacement that took the car all the way to Paris c).

b

c

a

A wheel with metal spokes and rubber-lined rim.

A special electron wheel.

A spoked wheel typical of sports and racing cars of the 1930's.

Bordino's steam carriage, built in the Arsenal in Turin in 1854.
Consuming 66 lbs. of coke an hour, the horizontal twin cylinder
engine gave it a speed of 5 m.p.h. on the level.

Paris and Versailles. The service was held to be particularly comfortable due to the coaches' "elastic"
wheels, which had a strip of felt and rubber between
the rim and the tyre.

Revival of steam

In fact there were to be several further revivals of the
steam carriage in France thereafter, starting with the
interesting enterprise of Lotz and Albaret, respectively
in 1860 and 1865, designers of somewhat advanced
vehicles, and later Amedée Bollée's original vehicle,
"L'Obéissante". Bollée, a bell founder in Le Mans,
designed and built a vehicle capable of 25 m.p.h.
fitted with new devices such as a gear change and
independent front wheel suspension. Later he built
even more advanced vehicles, "La Mancelle" and the
"Rapide" in which it is even possible to see certain
features of the modern car, such as a front engine,
rear driving wheels connected to the engine by a propeller shaft and a differential. The Bollée family made a
small fortune with these machines, which were accepted
with enthusiasm in Germany and Austria. But it was
all a flash in the pan, as was the only Italian excursion
into the field. This was a steam coach, built by Virgilio
Bordino, an engineering officer in the Sardinian army

and constructor of three such vehicles inspired by the
English models.

So closes the glorious era of the steam coach, glorious
above all for the passion with which certain far-sighted
engineers fought for the success of their inventions,
clearly too advanced for the world in which they lived.
At this point however, it is necessary to return in time
to trace the origins of what is today — as it has been
ever since the true beginnings of motoring in the last
quarter of the 19th century — the standard prime
mover, the internal combustion engine.

Internal combustion engine born

It is possible to see the conception of such engines in
the studies of Christian Huygens, who in 1678 described,
if only in theory, the first internal combustion engine
in history. In essence, it consisted of a piston sliding in
a cylinder, at one end of which was placed a small
quantity of gun-powder whose subsequent ignition and
explosion caused the displacement of the piston. At the
end of the 18th century a similar idea was studied, and
this time was actually built, by the Swiss De Rivaz who
succeeded in building a crude vehicle which used the
energy of exploding gas. In this case, ignition was by
means of a "Volta's pistol", or in other words, a method
relatively similar to that in use today.

Meanwhile an Englishman, Robert Street, was experimenting with the use of inflammable gas in cylinders, and in France an engineer named Le Bon was making the first experiments with the ignition of gases by means of an electric spark. Another enthusiastic experimenter in the early years of the 19th century was the American, Peter Cooper, whose efforts to build an efficient internal combustion engine were dramatically interrupted by an explosion which unfortunately blinded him. Cooper's experiments seem to have been very ambitious as he also hoped to build a flying machine powered by his engine.

An important step forward was made in 1825 when Michael Faraday, the author of fundamental studies in many other branches of human science, discovered benzene in tar derived from coal. It was among the first liquid fuels capable of being used successfully in i.c. engines and was quickly accepted by various scientists.

Gas replaced by liquid

At this period between 1850 and 1870, when the motor car was to appear on the distant horizon, two Italians were pioneering the building of the first true internal combustion engine: Eugenio Barsanti, a scientist and doctor of physics, and Felice Matteucci, a landowner who moved to Florence to work with him. Their experiments in the College of San Giovannino were inspired by the theoretical studies of the Milanese aristocrat De Cristoforis, who also planned to extract mechanical power from the burning of an explosive mixture.

The first engine which came out of the joint efforts of the two Italians was born in 1856, built on the basis of Italian and English patents previously taken out. It used the explosion in two cylinders of a mixture of air and inflammable gas and worked on a three-stroke cycle, without compression. From the beginning the use of petrol or benzene was foreseen in place of gas. The prototype of 1856 was followed by a second engine in 1858, and two years later a third engine was ordered from Escher and Wyss in Zurich and shown at the first National Exhibition in Florence in 1861.

In France, Etienne Lenoir's first gas engine had been patented in 1859, and the Italians secured recognition only in their own country for their work. Barsanti's sudden death from typhus in 1864 at Liege, where he had gone to arrange the series production of low-powered engines, was a deathblow also for Matteucci, who was seriously ill. A few years later their enterprise was forgotten. The gas engine designed and built by Etienne Lenoir in 1860 thus passed into history as the first, even though it was built later than that of the two Italians.

In fact this engine differed very little from that of the Italians. Both used the explosion of a mixture of air and inflammable gas inside a cylinder without compressing it. While Barsanti and Matteucci's engine had an intermittent connection between piston and crankshaft (a sort of "freewheel" permitting the piston to be hurled freely upwards by the explosion, re-establishing connection when it was drawn backwards by gravity and the vacuum behind it), Lenoir's engine had two pistons in the same cylinder, permanently connected to the crankshaft. Introduction of the mixture was by means of a distributor and ignition was by battery and Ruhmkorff coil.

Commercial success

There has been much discussion as to the effective power developed by the two engines, and their practical value. There are those who are in favour of the Italian engine and they may be right. Certainly the French one had much greater commercial success. It was used for the mechanisation of machine tools in small workshops, but it seems that one such engine was installed in a wheeled vehicle in 1862 or 1863. This derives from a note left by Lenoir himself. According to this, the vehicle — which seems to have had sparking plugs similar to those of today and even an embryonic distributor —

Rickett's steam vehicle.

made a number of journeys between Paris and Joinville-le-Pont, a distance of 12 miles.

The doubts that exist arise from the complete absence from the press reports at the time of any news of the public appearance of such an unusual vehicle. In any case, even if Lenoir's vehicle was only an intention, the years 1854 to 1862 are of fundamental importance in the story of the motor car. It was then that the internal combustion engine, "our" engine, was born. The form in which it came into the world however, was extremely crude. It is not easy to see in that trembling, romantically simple machine, the forebear of today's descendant. It was from two Germans, Nikolaus Otto and Eugen Langen, and another Frenchman, Alphonse Beau de Rochas, that were to come the first wonderful improvements that directed technical progress along the right road.

From that day onwards technical progress was almost headlong, apart from a few pauses.

THE DETERMINED EXPERIMENTERS

The official story — so to speak — of great men hides a second story, the private one, which is often dramatic, always full of interest. Their professional battles lead to ever more difficult personal decisions, often to sacrifices and poverty.

All this was true in the case of the three major figures in the development of the i.c. engine, the Germans Nikolaus August Otto, Gottlieb Daimler and Karl Benz. Otto was 28, and employed in a shop in Cologne, when in 1860 he learned from a newspaper of the existence of Lenoir's engine. He was enthusiastic and at once conceived the idea of an engine similar, but burning liquid fuel. He drew his brother Wilhelm into the affair, but when his request for a patent was rejected by the Prussian government — which saw no difference between his engine and Lenoir's — the latter dropped out. Otto passed through a critical period which would have made most people give up, but which led him to a dramatic decision — to give up his job and to concentrate entirely on experiments with his engine, despite his limited means.

In 1862 the engine was ready, though fuelled by gas. It worked for a while and then blew to pieces. Although it was impossible to repair it, Otto did not weaken but instead went to England to see Barsanti and Matteucci's model. When he returned to Cologne he built a new engine and tried to sell it and patent it, but failed in both respects.

His meeting with Eugen Langen, a businessman and engineer, another enthusiast for the work of Barsanti and Matteucci, was the piece of good fortune he needed to revive him from a series of setbacks. Langen, through his friend Franz Reuleaux, examiner for the Prussian patents commission, succeeded in getting the much desired patent for his partner Otto.

Ideas workshop

But the difficulties were not over. A year after production began, sales were down to zero because of technical weaknesses discovered by clients. Yet another effort of will was necessary to put the enterprise back on its feet and only in 1871 did the Deutz factory become possible, the future "ideas factory" for the basic progress of the i.c. engine.

August Otto's later work as theoretician and manufacturer is probably far more important. But his early struggles reveal that progress depends not only on creative energy, but also on determination.

These considerations hold true for the other two pioneers of the time, Daimler and Benz. Both for example were men of humble origin, the first being the son of a baker in Schorndorf, and the second the son of an engine-

driver in Karlsruhe, and they both had to fight hard to establish themselves. Daimler began as a mechanic in a gunmaker's and took his degree in engineering by alternately working and studying in Germany, France and England. Before settling in the Otto factory in Deutz he acquired wide experience in various German machine-tool factories. Benz, after having been a workman in a machine factory in his native city and subsequently a draughtsman in Mannheim, met with economic misfortune in his first private venture, an engineering workshop opened in partnership with August Ritter. In spite of this he presevered with his old studies on gas engines and to carry them to a successful conclusion, building his first two stroke.

There are two episodes in the story of these two great men that are remarkably similar and which demonstrate

Nikolaus August Otto (1832-1891).

Gottlieb Daimler (1834-1900).

Karl Benz (1844-1929).

3 H.P. Benz "Velo" of 1893. The rear-mounted horizontal single-cylinder engine has a bore and stroke of 110 × 120 mm., giving a capacity of 1,140 c.c. Output was 3 b.h.p. at 400 r.p.m., and other features are the belt transmission with two forward speeds, and the coil ignition.

the atmosphere of hostility in which they had to work most of their lives. Both were subject to attacks by the press of the cities in which they worked. The "Cannstatter Zeitung" in 1885 made bitter complaints against the motor tricycle that Gottlieb Daimler was testing on the streets of Cannstatt, talking of a "repugnant, diabolical device dangerous to the life and well-being of the citizens", and it called for drastic intervention by the local police. Confronted with this declaration of war, Daimler did not feel able to continue his experiments with the tricycle and turned to the study of a motorboat, the "Marie", fitted with a 1½ H.P. i.c. engine. When the time came for trials on the waters of the Neckar he disguised the boat with wires and insulators and announced that it was electrically powered. After his tests had proved successful, he revealed the truth, and the psychological battle was won.

'Useless invention'

About the same time Karl Benz was the object of a violent attack by the "Mannheimer Zeitung", which described as "useless, ridiculous and indecent" the horseless carriage on which he was working. The newspaper asked, "Who is interested in such a contrivance so long as there are horses on sale?"

Benz was probably inclined to bow before such attacks and to withdraw from the field, but his wife Bertha decided that they had suffered enough and that it was time to counter-attack.

Thus one day, in the summer of 1888, the astounded farmers of the area saw one of Benz's snorting mechanical carriages advancing down the road, occupied by a delicate woman with her two children, one of whom was driving. It was Frau Benz who had insisted on taking her husband's machine and refused to stop until she had reached her own home, and had made the return journey without serious mishap. The adversaries had been dealt with and Benz too had won his battle, by proxy.

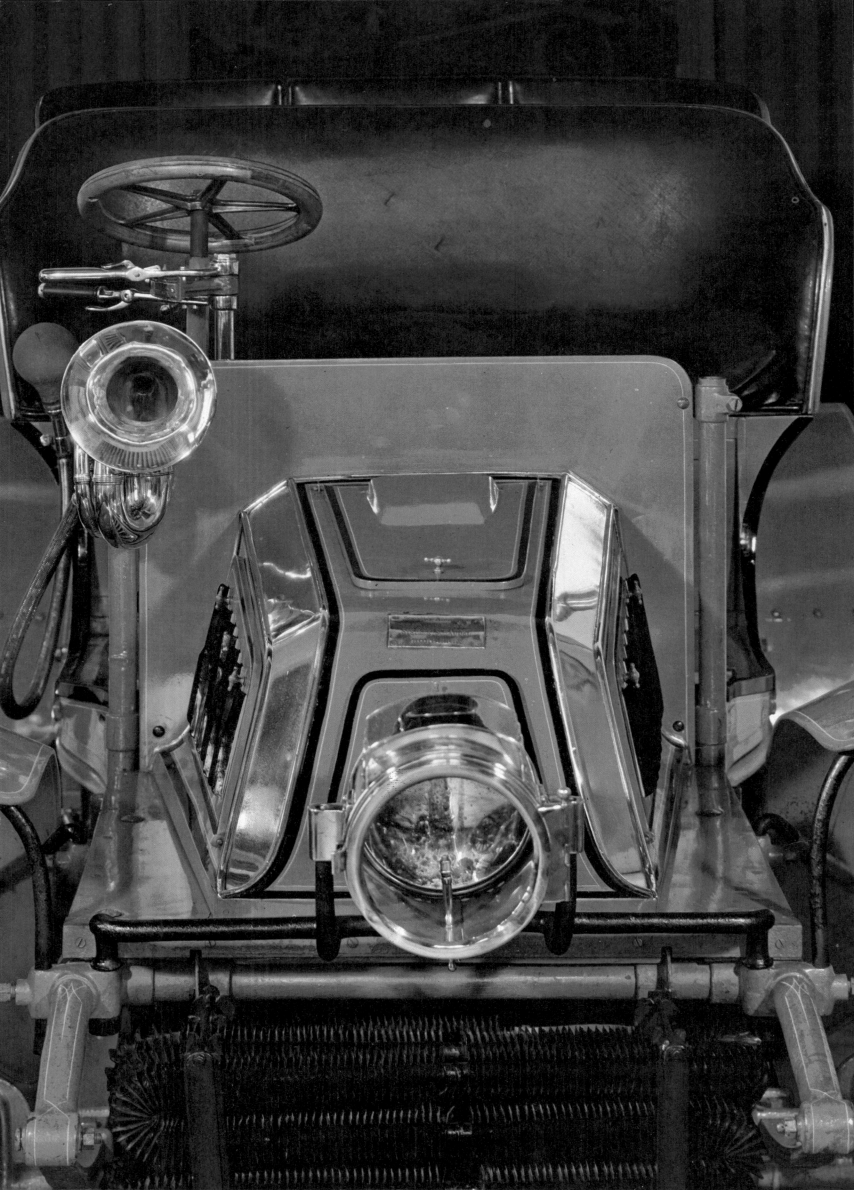

A modern Alfa-Romeo 1300 G.T. The vast difference in power between this and the Darracq shown on this page reflects sixty years of progress.

CHAPTER TWO
THE YEARS OF DISCOVERY

The year 1862 is an important one in the history of the motor car, for it was in that particular year that Alphonse Beau de Rochas, a Frenchman and civil engineer in retirement at the relatively early age of 45, propounded the "four stroke explosion cycle" in a memorandum. Three hundred copies were distributed to the press explaining the principle on which almost all internal combustion engines function to the present day. The engines of Lenoir and of Barsanti and Matteucci exploited only the kinetic effects of the explosion of the mixture and used a three stroke cycle — induction, explosion and expansion. Beau de Rochas added the fourth stroke, compression, which represented the key to the effective exploration of the potential of the i.c. engine.

As we have seen, Otto persevered in his experiments based on Lenoir's principles, despite frustration from official sources, and one of the results of his partnership with Langen was a four-stroke engine built and patented

1906 A.L.F.A. - Darracq made under licence from the famous French factory by the predecessors of to-day's Alfa-Romeo concern.

This is the world's first true motor car. It was built by Siegfried Marcus in 1875 and was driven by a 4 H.P. engine. The photograph was taken at the Stockholm International Exhibition. Note the steering.

in 1866-7. This had considerable defects, and unfortunately he abandoned this line of experiment. For more than ten years, even after his partnership with Langen, his experiments and his industrial activity were concentrated on the Lenoir, Barsanti - Matteucci type of "atmospheric" (without compression) engine.

It should be mentioned that the first true and proper four-stroke engine, using the Beau de Rochas cycle, was to be built in 1872 by a certain Reithmann, a Munich watchmaker, but it had no subsequent industrial development.

Emotion and experience

The early atmospheric engines, which arose in 1866 out of the association between Otto and Langen, though still very noisy and heavy, had many improvements compared with those of Lenoir. For instance, the fuel consumption was a half. But a few years later the Otto-Langen engines were much improved and regular series production (if the term can be used) was begun in the factory at Deutz near Cologne. It should be emphasised that these engines were still gas engines and were for stationary use.

When Gottlieb Daimler, a capable engineer with experience of production methods, joined Otto and Langen, the firm took an even keener interest in research. Daimler had previously approached the aging Lenoir,

proposing to build an improved version of his engine, but they were not able to come to an agreement. Later, reading the writings of Beau de Rochas, he was deeply impressed.

Silent and reliable

With the collaboration of Wilhelm Maybach, for some time his assistant and who had moved with him to Deutz, Daimler first applied himself to reorganisation in order to increase production.

By 1875 over 2000 engines had been sold in Europe and a number of manufacturers had obtained permis-

A 1894 Peugeot/Daimler car, built at Saronno, Italy, under licence from the Valentigney factory. It had a two-cylinder engine of 1,206 c.c. which developed 2½ H.P. at 400 r.p.m. Ignition was by burner and platinum wire; there was a leather cone clutch. The car had a gearbox with four speeds and reverse. It weighed 880 lbs.

THE DRIVING FORCE

On August 27 1859 an American prospector named Edwin Drake drilled a primitive well at Titusville, a small town in Pennsylvania, and struck oil at a depth of 69 feet.

Since that eventful day an industry has grown up that now supplies more than half the world's total energy. It was not petrol, however, that the early pioneers were thinking about; the internal combustion engine had yet to be invented. They were looking for a better kind of lamp oil than could be manufactured from sperm or whale oil — a principal illuminant in the first half of the 19th century before the invention of the gas mantle.

Seepages in mine

As early as 1850 James Young, a Glasgow chemist, had noticed oil seepages in the coal measures of north Derbyshire from which he made a primitive paraffin; he went on to develop oil-bearing shales in the Scottish Lothians. But nobody had yet drilled a well with the object of finding oil.

This honour belongs to the otherwise bogus "Colonel" Drake, a half-educated train conductor from the New York and New Haven Railroad. Long before he arrived on the scene American settlers had been skimming an oily liquid they had named petroleum (or "rock oil") from little springs along Oil Creek, in north-western Pennsylvania. Its medicinal properties were highly prized and bottles of the stuff were sold by itinerant quacks who claimed it to be a cure for all ailments, human or animal. Ill-health compelled Drake to give up his job with the railroad and a certain James M. Townsend, President of the City Savings Bank of New Haven, Connecticut, sent him to look for oil in Pennsylvania on behalf of a company he had founded. On the site of the principal oil spring at Titusville, Drake built an engine house, set up a wooden derrick on which to swing the primitive drilling tools, and installed an engine and boiler.

Cradle of industry

His driller, a blacksmith by the name of William Smith, drove an iron pipe 32 feet through the quicksands and clay into bedrock. The drilling tools were placed inside the pipe, and about the middle of August 1859 drilling began averaging about three feet a day. On the afternoon of Saturday, August 27, just as Smith and his workmen were about to finish for the weekend, the drill dropped into a crevice at 69 feet and slipped down six inches. The men pulled out the tools and went home. Late on

Drake's original oil well.

BP's barge Sea Quest, which began exploration drilling in the North Sea in 1966.

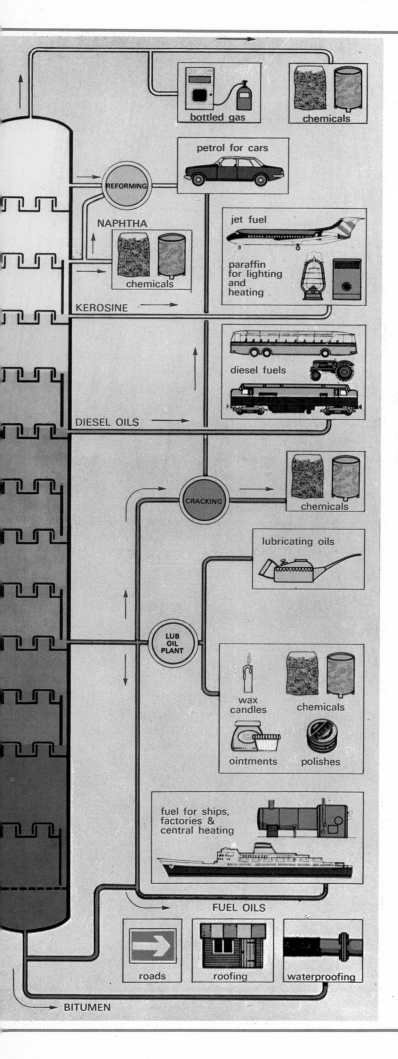

bottled gas

chemicals

petrol for cars

REFORMING

NAPHTHA

chemicals

jet fuel

paraffin
for lighting
and
heating

KEROSINE

diesel fuels

DIESEL OILS

CRACKING

chemicals

lubricating oils

LUB
OIL
PLANT

wax
candles

chemicals

ointments

polishes

fuel for ships,
factories &
central heating

FUEL OILS

roads

roofing

waterproofing

BITUMEN

Sunday afternoon "Uncle Billy", as the bearded black-smith was affectionately called, visited the well, peered down the pipe, and saw oil floating on top of the water within a few feet of the derrick floor.

They had struck oil. The well was to produce 25 barrels a day. Drake had tapped a large reservoir — and founded a new industry of incalculable potential. The United States was thus the cradle of the oil business, although in the next 20 years oil was discovered and began to be produced in Russia and Rumania.

The great paradox

The irony of the oil business is that, ever since Drake's time, oil has rarely been found in a form in which it can be immediately used. It is generally not available in the places where it is mainly wanted, being in inaccessible areas of the earth or under the sea. Oil has become, therefore, the largest single commodity in international trade, and tankers carry more than half the total cargoes (by weight) sailing the seven seas.

The costs of getting oil to market are far higher than the costs of finding and producing it. Today oil is moved in tankers with a carrying capacity five times greater than ten years ago to refineries that become steadily more complex to meet the demand for more varied and sophisticated products required by the market. To ensure that the finished products reach the customer in the most efficient way, modern distribution centres, larger diameter pipelines, and bigger road tankers and rail tank cars are needed.

When we think of oil we still think first of transport, for the vast majority of modern vehicles depend on petroleum for their motive power.

Into the future

In the early days of refining, petrol was burned to waste as a dangerous by-product for which there was no commercial use. Today more petrol is used than any other oil product: a world total of nearly 100,000 million gallons a year.

The prime task of the industry over the next 30 years will be to provide for the vast quantities of energy the world will need.

Although nuclear power is of growing importance, oil and natural gas will still be supplying more than half of total requirements at the turn of the century. Between now and the year 2,000 the industry must find nearly twice the reserves so far discovered.

Natural gas will gradually take over a growing proportion of Britain's public gas supplies. Petroleum is the basic "building block" for a vast chemical industry, which has changed our daily lives by providing a host of new and useful products ranging from plastics and detergents to agricultural fertilizers and pesticides.

Oil, from its chance beginnings a century ago, has become the most versatile of raw materials available to man.

Products of the refinery.

sion to build under licence. At the same time, Daimler and Maybach conducted a series of studies on the four stroke cycle, at the end of which they obtained the first European patent of this type in 1876.

A year later the first example of this revolutionary prime mover was ready and working. It represented enormous progress over the 1867 model and was already silent and reliable. The ignition of this engine, which had a single horizontal cylinder, was by means of two jets of flame which were alternately exposed by a distributor. The Otto-Daimler engine was exhibited in 1878 at the Paris exhibition and may be regarded as the basis on which all subsequent experiments were founded and improvements made, not only in Europe but also in America.

Secret vehicles

Though the progress of the i.c. engine at this period was largely associated with Otto and Daimler, that does not mean that others had not been trying in the meantime. Hugon in France and Bischop in Germany had built engines similar to Lenoir's, in some respect improved, but there was no commercial outcome.

In 1865 an original vehicle had appeared in Vienna, built by Siegfried Marcus, chemist, electrician and mechanic, who applied an i.c. engine to a hand cart. He was understandably afraid of official intervention, so he tested it by night, in a deserted street near the cemetery. Unfortunately the machine was so noisy that it attracted the attention of the police who stopped the experiment. It seems that Marcus was satisfied with this experience. His second experimental car, built in 1875, can still be seen in the Vienna Museum. It should not be thought, however, that the story of the "glorious years" of the i.c. engine was an exclusively European achievement. It could be maintained that the motor car — the vehicle powered by an i.c. engine — was an American invention. A young Boston engineer, George Brayton, before exhibiting his own i.c. engine at the Philadelphia Centennial in 1876, had already put on the streets of Providence a self-propelled vehicle powered by an earlier, cruder version of that engine. It was the encouragement he received with this vehicle, of which the technical specifications are unknown, that caused him to exhibit at Philadelphia. European industry was represented at the exhibition by no fewer than six Otto gas engines. Nevertheless, Brayton's sole U.S. example showed some advantages over the European engines. For example, the explosive mixture was obtained by forcing small drops of inflammable liquid along a narrow tube into an annular chamber filled with felt. Here the petrol came into contact with compressed air and was vaporised

The exhibition at Philadelphia represented the beginning of the rapid conversion of the Americans to the i.c. engine. Up to that time, it may be said that steam powered vehicles had dominated the transatlantic scene almost without opposition. Otto's and Brayton's eng-

The 1894 Daimler with the executives of the company. To the left are Maybach and Gottlieb Daimler. On the right are Bernhard and the manager of the Esslinger factory, Gross. Note the wheel for braking.

ines were reproduced in quantity from one shore of the continent to the other — legally, under licence, or without — and were quickly in use for the widest variety of industrial and agricultural applications. Even small fishing boats were powered — the first transport application in America.

The same exhibition caught the imagination of George Baldwin Selden, a young Rochester lawyer. Taken by the mechanical bug, Selden went home and set to work to adapt Brayton's engine to drive a land vehicle and thus applied in 1879 for a patent which, as will be seen, had an interesting effect on the American motor industry for some years to come.

End of a partnership

The alliance between Otto and Daimler was not destined to last for ever. Technical difference between the two became increasingly acute. In 1882 Daimler left Cologne, and on his estate at Cannstatt near Stuttgart, began a series of studies aimed at improving the Otto engine, especially as regards its weight, speed of rotation and ignition. This last represented the greatest problem. A year later the first Daimler-Maybach engine was born, with "hot-tube" ignition. This was yet another major step forward compared with the engines produced in collaboration with Otto.

Speed of rotation was raised from 200 r.p.m. to 900 r.p.m.; above all, an unusual and reasonably satisfactory system of ignition was developed, based on the continuous heating, by means of a burner mounted outside the cylinder, of a platinum tube, one end of which entered the combustion chamber.

The first tricycle

While Daimler and Maybach were busy with the first major technological problems created by the i.c. engine, in another city, Mannheim, another experimenter and designer, Karl Benz, was applying himself to similar work. In 1885 he completed the construction of a tricycle powered by a petrol engine and tested it on the streets of Mannheim just at the time when Daimler was testing an i.c. engined motorcycle. The significance of this parallel development is clearly more than the possible influence of one experimenter on the other, or the hypothetical passing of information between them. It was a measure of the progress already made in research in the field of the motor car, with the consequent nearness of success, that caused the simultaneous appearance on the still rudimentary world motoring scene of two radically new vehicles of such fundamental importance.

In identifying a common influence, the work of Otto must be considered.

Daimler's bicycle was fitted with a new version of the first "hot tube" engine of 1883. It was in fact the ancestor of the motorcycle. Benz's tricycle was driven

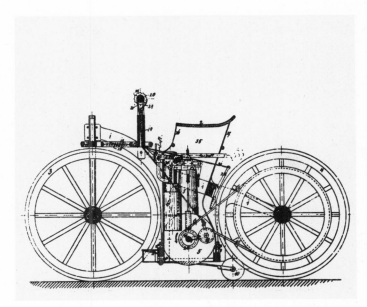

The design for a motor bicycle built by Daimler in 1885.

The 1885 Daimler motor bicycle.

A very early Daimler single cylinder.

Benz display. The three cars shown here were all built before 1895 but are still in working order and take part in veteran rallies.

by a horizontal single cylinder engine which developed under one horsepower at 200 r.p.m. and was capable of driving the vehicle at 10 m.p.h. There was water cooling by means of the vaporisation of water, ignition was by high tension magneto and sparking plug, and transmission was by chain to spoked wheels.

In the two successive four wheeled vehicles built by the same two manufacturers, that of Benz had the mechanical components laid out in practically the same way as those of the tricycle, with a rear engine of

1½ H.P. Maximum speed was 12½ m.p.h. This four wheeler was immediately put into production, because of the great interest it had inspired in technical circles.

Three to four wheels

Daimler was also involved in the manufacture of stationary engines and too dissatisfied with the state of his vehicles to begin production at once. By 1887 however, he had already made considerable improvements to his engine and began to grant licences for its construction abroad. Two years later he began commercial production in his own factory, after building a third version which solved his ignition and carburation problems. As regards the former, after some attempts at an electrical system, Daimler returned to the platinum hottube in improved form. As far as carburation was concerned the invention of a carburettor by his colleague Maybach, which functioned by bubbling air through the fuel, made possible a more regular and richer mixture. The 1889 engine was a narrow V, two cylinder type, with single acting pistons on a common crankshaft. Inlet and exhaust were through valves, the latter being positively actuated; the inlet valve was "automatic", being opened by the vacuum created in the combustion chamber. Maximum speed of rotation was 770 r.p.m. and cooling was through the circulation of water by means of a pump, the water passing through a radiator of small bore finned tubes. Even by 1890 Daimler's engine, born out of major technical rethinking, was an immediate success due to the excellence of its technical solutions. It reached an annual production of 350. In the same year, Daimler granted about 1,900 licences for manufacture abroad.

Out of the negotiations for the concession of one of

these licences arises the romantic story of the birth of the firm of Panhard and Levassor, which was to become one of the most important concerns in the first decades of the development of the motor car. Indeed, it may be considered the most important as it was due to these two courageous Frenchmen that at the beginning of the last decade of the century, the motor car, already satisfactorily developed so far as its major mechanical elements were concerned, began to assume a shape of its own, gradually moving away from that derived directly from the horse-drawn carriage.

Courageous wife

It was the engineer Sarazin, an old friend and school-mate of Daimler, who initiated the first contacts for the exploitation of the latter's patents in France.

As agents he chose two friends, René Panhard and Emile Levassor, both engineers with whom he had studied at the Ecole Centrale. Panhard and Levassor had been partners for some years in a business specialising in the construction of woodworking machinery, founded by a certain Périn in 1845. When Sarazin died in the midst of the negotiations, his courageous wife took them up and carried them to a successful conclusion. From this agreement was born not only a commercial-technical collaboration of fundamental importance in the history of the motor car, but also a marriage as in 1890 Sarazin's widow married Emile Levassor. In 1889 Panhard and Levassor entered the motor car field on their own account, having first completely re-equipped their factory. From these works there first issued a "vis-à-vis" (face to face) which was little more than experimental; then, in 1894, a second vehicle with a twin cylinder engine that was one of the most significant European creations.

1896 Bernardi. An enthusiastic pioneer, Bernardi, who had already constructed the i.c. engines "Pia" and "Lauro", in 1894 built the first Italian car with an i.c. engine. The light car shown here had the following characteristics: single horizontal cylinder 624 c.c. engine developing 4 H.P. at 800 r.p.m. Platinum mesh ignition, spiral metal cable clutch, three-speed gearbox, and chain transmission.

The car which was born out of the early years of Panhard-Levassor production had a number of interesting features both in function and layout, and especially the controls — clutch, gearchange, differential and transverse axle. Though the transmission was by sprocket and chain, it does not detract from the substantial similarities of the layout of the basic components of that ancient vehicle and those of today. It was, in fact, the first "modern" car. The term "automobile", used in many countries, is applied to early vehicles more for convenience of expression than for historical accuracy. It only came into use in Europe towards the end of the 19th century. There were indeed high level literary disputes in France on the matter, particularly because it was formed from words derived from two different languages — Greek and Latin. However, the word had already appeared in a French dictionary issued in 1877, and in 1895 the Académie Française gave its official approval.

Above and on the right, two 1895 Panhard-Levassors. Below a rebuilt 1901-1902 Bardon with a single-cylinder 2,000 c.c. engine. All three are still used.

FACE-TO-FACE REVOLUTION

The cover and two drawings from the Panhard-Levassor catalogue published in Paris around 1895.

One of the reasons that the second car produced by Panhard-Levassor in 1894, five years after the formation of the company, is significant in the story of early years of motoring is that this machine represented the first serious attempt to get away from the construction methods of the horse-drawn carriage.

The new ideas which indicated this revolutionary trend consisted in the location of the engine, which in the first "vis-à-vis" of 1891 was placed not centrally but over the front wheels, thus improving roadholding; in the adoption of an enclosure for the engine itself, which could function for the first time protected from dust and atmospheric pollution; and in substituting a gearbox for belt transmission.

The second Panhard-Levassor model was to represent the ideal for many keen motorists in France and other countries, in the years immediately before the end of the century, despite being in more or less direct competition with the first cars built by Peugeot. In both cases the engine was a Daimler, or more precisely was produced under Daimler licence. Even in those days there existed the same divergence of opinion on the position of the motor that was to divide into two groups the manufacturers today. Peugeot's cars were rear-engined. The engine of the 1894 Panhard-Levassor car was no longer single cylindered like that of the "vis-à-vis", but a 15° Vee twin, of 80 mm × 120 mm bore and stroke, which developed about 3½ H.P.

Steam tricycle built in 1891 by Enrico Pecori at Caslino d'Erba in Italy. There is a vertical fire-tube boiler with central fire-box.

The work of Otto, Daimler, Benz, and the Panhard-Levassor partnership overshadows that of other pioneers. Their ideas were not necessarily less valid, but for one reason or another, they never produced engines or vehicles in quantity and for this reason had little influence on the development of the motor car.

Bernardi, prophet and manufacturer

Among these, a place in the foreground is occupied by Count Enrico Bernardi of Verona who, after devoting himself enthusiastically to the study of the i.c. engine even before 1880, built such an engine based on the Lenoir cycle and demonstrated it to the Royal Venetian Institute of Science in 1883. In 1884 his first experimental vehicle, with an engine developing only a third horse power, appeared on the roads driven by his son Lauro.

Bernardi made his greatest contribution to motor car progress with a new engine built in 1889 exhibiting a series of impressive and farseeing technical innovations. These included a cylinder with detachable head, overhead valves actuated by a camshaft and rockers, a centrifugal governer on the inlet valve, a constant level carburettor with a float and hand control, a filter for air and petrol,

automatic lubrication of all moving parts by means of a revolving distributor, cooling by water circulation and tubed radiator, and a silencer. The tube ignition was of Bernardi's own design.

Bernardi built successively in 1892 and 1893 two interesting vehicles with respectively two and three wheels, and in 1894 demonstrated an improved version of his old car in which he succeeded in covering 15 miles in one hour. This vehicle had further ingenious novelties such as roller bearings for the transmission and the wheel hubs, and had properly designed steering layouts for the first time.

Engines and canals

In the following years two companies were formed, Miari and Giusti of Padova and the Società Italiana Bernardi, for the exploitation of the inventions of the ingenious aristocrat. The commercial failure of Bernardi's cars was probably due paradoxically to the fact that they were too fast. They raised too much dust and subjected their occupants to too much bumping on the roads of the time.

Another interesting Italian venture was that connected

with the name of Giuseppe Murnigotti, an engineer born at Martinengo in the province of Brescia. For a long time he lived in Milan, where he had managerial jobs in technical fields; among other things he was active in the field of canal construction. In a patent granted in 1879 at the end of some years of study, Murnigotti described an engine with two single-acting cylinders, fuelled by gas and having an ignition device. The power of this engine was low as it was only intended to drive a "velocipede" and it is not known if it was ever built. But the study, whatever its value, preceded those of Daimler.

Gas tank

In the same year, 1879, Dugald Clerk designed and built in England the first two-stroke engine, little different in principle from those in use today. The name derives from the fact that the entire cycle takes place in only two strokes of the piston, which, almost at the end of the power stroke, uncovers a series of holes in the cylinder out of which most of the exhaust gases pass before the piston reaches bottom dead centre. In the meantime, a jet of gas enters through other holes and occupies the place of the burnt residual gas, both clean-ing out and refilling the cylinder, which is thus ready for a new cycle. It is interesting to note that Clerk's ideas, which were based on those expressed in 1838 by his fellow Englishman Barnett, were developed prin-cipally to avoid infringement of Otto's four-stroke patents. Some years later it was the turn of the French mathematician, Edouard Delamarre-Deboutteville who in collaboration with a certain Malandin, in 1883 built first a tricycle (which blew up) and later a car powered by an i.c. engine driven by town gas compressed to 10 atmospheres in an appropriate tank. This was yet an-other abortive venture destined to have no further development in spite of the patent granted to the inventor in 1884. The failure to develop the ideas of Delamarre-Deboutteville, some of which were promising, was mainly due to his early death in 1901.

Another pioneering attempt of the time was represented by Butler's petrol tricycle built in England in 1885, whilst Roots, Knight and Bersey were other British pioneers.

There was a parallel development on the other side of the Atlantic. In America, the tardiness in the years before 1860, with the almost total absence of the heavy steam vehicles that were widely distributed in Europe, was remedied by 1876, the year of the Philadelphia Cen-tennial.

SPORT FOR ALL COMERS

"The competition is open to all types of vehicle, provid-ing that they are not dangerous, are easily controllable by the driver and do not cost too much to run!" Probably no other motoring competition has had its regulations written so widely as those of the Paris-Rouen race, run on Sunday, 22 July, 1894.

The motoring enthusiasts of the time took advantage of this lack of restriction, turning up at the offices of the "Petit Journal", where entries were accepted, with the most fantastically assorted means of locomotion. Some would-be entrants arrived simply with a design in their pockets, seeing that the eliminating trials were to be held two months later. From the records of the competition it can be seen that at the closing date for the entries, these included vehicles powered "by grav-ity", and in particular "by the weight of the passengers" (Rousset, Leval and Mansart); vehicles with "hydraulic" propulsion (Berthaud, Barriquand); compressed air ve-hicle (V. Popp, G. Peraire, Plantard, Roge-Andrillon); vehicles propelled "by levers"; vehicles with "automa-tic (?)" propulsion; vehicles driven "by a system of pendulums"; pedal vehicles; vehicles propelled by "combining liquids"; electric and semi-electric vehicles; and "compressed gas" vehicles.

Naturally most of these strange mechanical vehicles did not even make their appearance at the preliminary rally on 18 July at Neuilly. The reduced numbers that did arrive (26 out of 102 entered) were further reduced to 17 when they had to perform in the eliminating trials arranged for 22 July on five different routes in the suburbs of Paris. On this occasion a further four were eliminated, but by virtue of the successive re-runs 21 presented themselves for the "off" of the race itself.

The programme of the race — this too was unique rather than rare in the history of motor racing — provided for an hour's pause for lunch at the half-way mark at Nantes. The start signal was given at 8 a.m. and at once the Marquis De Dion's huge and powerful steam tractor went into the lead. It was followed by Peugeot and Panhard, whose direct rivalry supplied the real interest of the race which the Parisian newspaper had organised because of the frequent arguments between keen

A racing Panhard-Levassor was evidently not superstitious — it carried number 13.

supporters of one or other of the two new companies. The retirements soon began: many of the steamers overheated, a common fault of these vehicles when pressed to the limit.

Several retirements were due to mechanical breakages caused by the roughness of the road surface, then in a far different state from those today. Many competitors kept going after early breakdowns, thanks to enthusiastic assistance from spectators.

The results of the race are relatively unimportant as the criteria of classification were very different from those used today. The significant thing about the Paris-Rouen race was the intense interest exhibited by the crowd, which reached mob proportions in the city of arrival.

A De Dion-Bouton steam "Victoria" was the first vehicle to finish the race, but was disqualified.

Arrival in triumph

The exhausted but elated pioneers, their faces masked by dust and oil (ejection of oil in all directions and without pause being one or the characteristics of all cars of the time) were received in triumph. They were hoisted on the shoulders of their delighted supporters, after their vehicles' unsteady, banging and rattling appearance. The "équipes" of Peugeot and Panhard, equally triumphant in the great adventure, celebrated success in traditional champagne. For the record however it should be added that the official winner was a Peugeot driven by Lemaître, to whom went the attractive first prize of 5000 francs put up by the "Petit Journal".

In fact, the first to cross the finishing line was De Dion's "steamer" but the jury decided to disqualify him from the classification in view of the competition requirements of economy and manoeuvrability. They can hardly be blamed. This mammoth weighed two tons, consumed 16 cwts of water and fuel, and two people — driver and fireman — were necessary to keep it going!

The "type 1894" Peugeot, equal winner with the Panhard-Levassor.

Jenatzy's "Jamais Contente" which was the first vehicle to exceed 100 k.p.h. (62 m.p.h.). It had an electric motor.

70 YEARS OF RECORDS

With the introduction of jet planes, the holder of the land speed record could no longer claim to be the fastest man in the world, even though a land vehicle can now reach over 600 m.p.h. This is a speed that an air pilot of 30 years ago might well have considered unattainable.

But the first 600 m.p.h.-plus of Craig Breedlove in 1965 was probably no more exciting than the experiences of the pioneer drivers at the end of the last century — the 40 m.p.h. in 1898 of Chasseloup-Laubat and the 65 m.p.h. of Jenantzy a year later. The table alongside is a record of the more important dates in the steady raising of the record over the years.

DATE	DRIVER AND VEHICLE	M.P.H.
1898	Chasseloup-Laubat in Jeantaud (Acheres, France)	39.3
1899	Jenatzy in Jenatzy (Acheres, France)	41.42
1899	Chasseloup-Laubat in Jeantaud (Acheres, France)	43.69
1899	Jenatzy in Jenatzy (Acheres, France)	49.42
1899	Chasseloup-Laubat in Jeantaud (Acheres, France)	57.6
1899	Jenatzy in Jenatzy (Acheres, France)	65.75
1902	Serpollet in Serpollet (Nice, France)	75.06
1902	Fournier in Mors (Dourdan, France)	76.60
1902	Augières in Mors (Dourdan, France)	77.13
1903	Duray in Gobron-Brillie (Ostend, Belgium)	84.21
1903	Henry Ford in Ford "999" (Lake St. Clair, U.S.A.)	91.378
1904	W. K. Vanderbilt in Mercedes (Daytona Beach, U.S.A.)	92.307
1904	Rigolly in Gobron-Brillie (Nice, France)	93.20
1904	De Caters in Mercedes (Ostend, Belgium)	97.26
1904	Rigolly in Gobron-Brillie (Ostend, Belgium)	103.56
1904	Baras in Darracq (Montgeron, France)	104.53
1905	Arthur MacDonald in Napier (Daytona Beach, U.S.A.)	104.651
1905	Hémery in Darracq (Arles-Salon, France)	109.65
1906	Marriott in Stanley (Daytona Beach, U.S.A.)	121.512
1909	Hémery in Benz (Brooklands, G.B.)	125.947
1910	Barney Oldfield in Benz (Daytona Beach, U.S.A.)	131.724
1922	K. L. Guinness in Sunbeam (Brooklands, G.B.)	133.75
1924	René Thomas in Delage (Arpajon, France)	143.31
1924	E. A. D. Eldridge in Fiat (Arpajon, France)	145.90
1925	M. Campbell in Sunbeam (Pendine Sands, G.B.)	150.869
1926	H. O. D. Segrave in Sunbeam (Southport, G.B.)	152.336
1926	J. G. Parry-Thomas in Thomas Special (Pendine Sands, G.B.)	169.23
1926	J. G. Parry-Thomas in Thomas Special (Pendine Sands, G.B.)	171.09
1927	M. Campbell in Napier Campbell (Pendine Sands, G.B.)	174.883
1927	H. O. D. Segrave in Sunbeam (Daytona Beach, U.S.A.)	203.792
1928	M. Campbell in Napier Campbell (Daytona Beach, U.S.A.)	206.956
1928	Ray Keech in White-Triplex (Daytona Beach, U.S.A.)	207.552
1929	H. O. D. Segrave in Irving-Napier (Daytona Beach, U.S.A.)	231.446
1931	Sir Malcolm Campbell in Napier Campbell (Daytona Beach, U.S.A.)	246.09
1932	Sir Malcolm Campbell in Napier Campbell (Bonneville Salt Flats, U.S.A.)	253.97
1933	Sir Malcolm Campbell in Rolls-Royce-Campbell (Daytona Beach, U.S.A.)	272.46
1935	Sir Malcolm Campbell in Bluebird Special (Bonneville Salt Flats, U.S.A.)	276.82
1935	Sir Malcolm Campbell in Bluebird Special (Bonneville Salt Flats, U.S.A.)	301.13
1937	G. E. T. Eyston in Thunderbolt (Bonneville Salt Flats, U.S.A.)	312.0
1938	G. E. T. Eyston in Thunderbolt (Bonneville Salt Flats, U.S.A.)	345.5
1938	John Cobb in Railton (Bonneville Salt Flats, U.S.A.)	350.2
1938	G. E. T. Eyston in Thunderbolt (Bonneville Salt Flats, U.S.A.)	357.5
1939	John Cobb in Railton (Bonneville Salt Flats, U.S.A.)	369.7
1947	John Cobb in Railton (Bonneville Salt Flats, U.S.A.)	393.8
1964	Donald Campbell in Bluebird II (Lake Eyre, Australia)	403.1
1964	Art Arfons in Green Monster (Bonneville Salt Flats, U.S.A.)	434.18
1964	Craig Breedlove in Spirit of America (Bonneville Salt Flats, U.S.A.)	555.483
1965	Art Arfons in Green Monster (Bonneville Salt Flats, U.S.A.)	576.553
1965	Craig Breedlove in Spirit of America (Bonneville Salt Flats, U.S.A.)	600.841

The elegant Ferrari 330 G.T.C. Below is a 1924 Opel 4/12 PS "Laubfrosch". Germany's first mass-produced car.

CHAPTER THREE
POWER AT THE CROSSROADS

By 1879, three years after the famous exhibition at Philadelphia, George Baldwin Selden had deposited in the United States a historic patent for a "horseless carriage" driven by an internal combustion engine. This was destined to influence the development of the American motor industry for many years, right up to 1905 when Henry Ford had the courage to infringe it. The patent had no immediate results because, though Selden sensed the tremendous possibilities of the i.c. engine and the motor car, he was not particularly interested in their production.

Petrol tram

Towards the end of the century a number of interesting studies and actual cars began to make their appearance, all of American origin without any direct link with European industry, which continued to be relatively in advance.

Among these was that of Elwood Haynes who, having exhibited his engine at Philadelphia and gained some publicity in doing so, built in 1888 a petrol engined vehicle equipped with a wick type carburettor of the kind fitted to the engine exhibited at the show. In

the same year Connolly built a petrol engined tram and gave public demonstrations in New York and Elizabeth, New Jersey.

Vehicles driven by i.c. engines were also built or designed about that time by E. Pennington, John W. Lambert, F. A. Huntingdon and W. T. Harris. Pennington later pursued a chequered career in Britain, but already he was claiming that one of his creations had covered a mile in 58 seconds.

R. E. Olds, one of the American pioneers, driving his 1897 Oldsmobile. The illustration is from a woodcut of the time.

The remarkable power of Pennington's machine was due in part to his use of a system of double ignition, but this also caused the rapid death of the machine due to overheating. This explains the absence of the much talked of car from the race, which took place the following November in 1895. None of these experimental cars went into commercial production. Nor did a better fate await the technically interesting experiments of Henry Nadig, a mechanic of German extraction who, with his two sons Charles and Lawrence, built in Pennsylvania a crude vehicle powered by an engine inspired by Daimler's. His car was nearly destroyed by fire when the engine exploded, an accident due to the crude wick carburettor.

A similar vehicle was built in Milwaukee by another mechanic of German extraction, Gottfried Schloemer. In 1890 he appeared in the streets in his car which, in spite of having only two gears with no reverse, reached the respectable speed of 12 m.p.h. Charles H. Black, of Indianapolis, built a cyclecar in 1891, and J. I. Case in 1892 founded a company for the production of a tractor for commercial use.

To these should be added the name of Charles B. King, who was the first to take the rudimentary "horseless carriage" industry to Detroit, future world capital of motor production.

Probably the most interesting American car of the time was the famous petrol-engined car that was built at Springfield in 1893 by the brothers Frank and Charles Duryea. It was driven by a single-cylinder i.c. engine and was the first American car with electric ignition and spray carburation, both of which were designed by Frank.

One year later the Duryeas, who like many other pioneers came to the motor car after experience with the bicycle industry, produced a second model which among other things won the first American motor race, the Chicago-Evanston sponsored by the "Chicago Times Herald". This second car was propelled by a four-stroke engine in contrast to the first one, which was a two stroke. At the same time the Duryea brothers set up the first American motor company, the Duryea Wagon Company, but this was the cause of disputes between them and in 1898 Frank left the company, which went into liquidation after having built only eighteen cars.

The other interest attached to the name Duryea arises from the public controversy in 1912 between Charles and Elwood Haynes. This arose from a meeting in 1906 of the Smithsonian Institute officially according to Haynes the position of first pioneer of the petrol engine in America. Duryea reacted six years later only when Haynes began to make use of the title. On the basis of documents submitted by Duryea, the Institute had to recognise his claims.

Ford comes on the scene

In 1896 Henry Ford made his first appearance on the American motoring horizon, driving his first twin cylinder experimental quadricycle which developed four horsepower.

The other types of self-propelled vehicles, those not driven by i.c. engines, had by no means disappeared completely from the scene. Parallel to this first important period in the development of i.c. engined cars, a lesser story — that of steam and electric cars — unfolded on both sides of the Atlantic.

So far as the former are concerned, there was a design in 1883 for a steam lorry by an Italian pioneer, Pecori, but the outcome is uncertain. In 1887 the French mechanic, Léon Serpollet, of Culoz built a revolutionary

J. Frank Duryea driving the car with which he took part in the Chicago-Evanston race. Beside him is Arthur W. White, race judge. The photo was taken on 28th November, 1895, during the race.

boiler, giving instant steam; and in a tricycle equipped with this engine he and a friend made a memorable journey two years later between Paris and Lyons in ten days (a Serpollet "steamer" was to do 75 m.p.h. at Nice in 1902, setting up an absolute speed record).

In 1891 Pecori designed another steam car, the last in Italy before the i.c. engine established its unquestioned supremacy.

In the meantime in France the younger Amédée Bollée, having succeeded his father in the management of the steam vehicle factory which bore his name, built a whole series of vehicles of interesting performance.

These included the "Mancelle" built in 1878 and capable of 26 m.p.h. with 16 people on board, and the "Marie Anne", the giant of motoring at the time (100 H.P. engine, a weight of 28 tons, and capable of carrying 100 tons). One "Marie Anne" covered over 450 miles in 74 hours at an average of 6 m.p.h. The "Nouvelle" followed, a small six-seater bus which was a steam forerunner of the modern station wagon — it weighed three tons and could reach 30 m.p.h. Then came the "Avant Courier", a 40-seater bus which was a great success due to its solid build and reliability. In 1881 it was the turn of the "Rapide" which could exceed 37 m.p.h. Both models were built in some numbers.

World record

At this point even the famous Bollée factory had to recognise the progress made by the i.c. engine, and 1895 the production capacity was converted to meet the new demands. The following year a brother of the younger Amédée, Léon, built the first light vehicle with a tubular chassis mounted on three wheels, of which the front two steered and the rear one drove. It had a horizontal i.c. engine, air cooled and mounted on the rear wheel. This unusual vehicle, which developed 3 H.P. at 750 r.p.m. made its first appearance in the Paris-Marseilles race and in 1898 took the world 100 kilometres speed record at Étampes.

Around the same time, the car-making activities of Peugeot, an old-established steel-works with origins

Stanley steam car built in 1899 by the Locomobile Company of America. This car was also seen in Europe. It was driven by a vertical two-cylinder engine with boiler powered by petrol. Transmission was by single central chain to a crown wheel co-axial with the rear axle.

Henry Ford in his first car, built in 1896. A few years later he was to create a modern motor industry in the U.S. and to revolutionise industrial production. The car's warning bell was the forerunner of the klaxon horn.

in the eighteenth century, became an independent concern.

After an inevitable period of re-organisation Peugeot began motor car production at the beginning of 1890. The most important French motor manufacturers in the early years of motoring were Panhard-Levassor, Peugeot, and De Dion-Bouton, a company created in 1881 by an agreement between the Marquis Albert De Dion, the mechanic Georges Bouton and the latter's brother-in-law, Trépardoux.

The 'opulent mechanic'

In 1895, De Dion-Bouton began to produce — while continuing to build the successful light steam tricycle capable of almost 40 m.p.h. — a version of the same vehicle with a single-cylinder engine of 210 cc. producing 1¼ H.P. The crude carburettor consisted of a re-

ceptacle holding petrol through which air was bubbled before passing down a long tube into the cylinder. By 1899 22,000 of these tricycles had been built.

It was in the same year that the circle of early French manufacturers was completed with the birth of the first Renault.

The first Renault was created largely at the hands of Louis Renault himself, the outstanding example in the motoring field of the "wealthy mechanic". He was not a wealthy dilettante, limited to commissioning a specialist, but was entirely capable of designing and building a vehicle himself.

The car, built to a particularly advanced design, with much use of aluminium and roller bearings, had a gearbox which in top gear eliminated all intermediaries between crankshaft and drive-shaft and was virtually the first car with direct drive. Renault, a solid and reliable administrator of his affairs as one might expect from the son of a prudent Parisian button manufacturer, at once patented his invention. He quickly saw that the success of this car among his circle of friends merited series production.

Thus on 30 March, 1899, the Société Renault Frères was born with a capital of 60,000 francs on the family holding at Billancourt, where the twenty-two-year-old Louis had devoted two years to becoming a mechanic. Louis was joined by his brother Marcel who was already familiar with industrial operations. In "Number One", of which they were about to build 25, the small 1¾ H.P. engine was used. Later a water-cooled 3½ De Dion was used in the second Renault then being designed, which was to be the first completely enclosed car.

Silent and reliable

Italy in this period was still in the stage of experiments at small craftsman level. In 1896 the Turin mechanic, Giovanni Martina, built an i.c. engined car to a design by Giuseppe Steffanini, commissioned by Michele Lanza. It was indirectly from this car that the first Italian motor factory arose. The car was bought by a Milan industrialist, Commandatore Isotta, who also engaged Steffanini, thus creating in 1897 what was later to become one of the most famous European names — Isotta Fraschini.

Another type of mechanical transport with other than i.c. engines reached in the 1880's its peak of success in France and America, without any indication of the rapidity with which they were shortly to disappear. These were electrically propelled vehicles.

One characteristic that is immediately evident is the large number of names that figure in the list of manufactures in this chapter of the story of the car.

This is understandable when it is realised that the electric car presented far fewer problems than did those powered by steam or i.c. engines, and so its construction was relatively easy on a craftsman basis.

Nor is it difficult to imagine why so many enthusiasts were taken by the idea of building such a vehicle.

1892 Scotte steam bus. Eight seats, two cylinders, burning wood or coal. Speed — **7**$\frac{1}{2}$ m.p.h (Motor Museum, Rochetaillée)

The d.c. motor was already well developed, as were lead acid batteries, and thus all basic elements of an electric car were available. The intelligent exploitation of these elements permitted some of these vehicles, built between 1881 and the end of the century, to give outstanding performances in terms of speed.

The electric car's worst weakness, however, was its limited range between battery charges. It was this that was to lead to its virtual extinction around 1910.

Jenatzy's fantastic 'Jamais Contente'

In France the first to construct vehicles of this type on any appreciable scale, was Jeantaud, a carriage builder gifted with considerable ingenuity (among other things owed to him are fundamental studies on steering geometry, still accepted by engineers of today). He made his first model in 1881 and later, availing himself of the improvements recently made to batteries by his fellow countrymen, Faure and Planté took part in the Paris-Bordeaux race. So did two other builders of electric vehicles, the Englishman Park, of Brighton, and the Frenchman Pouchain. The years 1885-1890 saw many experiments with electric vehicles and a few years later cars of this type were recording some exceptional performances. In England the Gladiator-Pingault, an electric motorcycle, covered the flying kilometre in one minute 46 seconds and the five miles in eight minutes 56 seconds. A few months later, at the "Velodrome de la Seine" in Paris, Edmond de Parrodil recorded 57.8 secs. for the flying kilometre, while the journalist Breyer in

The Renault "coupé" the first totally enclosed car in the world.

the same year covered 10 kilometres in nine minutes 54 seconds — nearly 40 miles per hour.

This was the electric vehicle's peak period. The more important manufacturers were Doré, Bouquet, Garon, Mildé, Richard and Homard. There was a final sensational record when in 1899 Camille Jenatzy covered the flying kilometre in 34 secs. at the fantastic speed of 105.904 k.p.h. (about 65 m.p.h.), in an incredible vehicle, the "Jamais Contente".

Madame and Marcel Renault in the first Renault.

In America the appearance of efficient electric cars dates from 1891, the year in which Doctor Orazio Lugo, of Italian origin, designed one on behalf of the Electric Road Carriage Company of Boston, the first company in the world founded to build electric vehicles for private use. About the same time another electric car appeared, built by William Morrison of Iowa, recording an interesting record by running for 13 hours at around 15 m.p.h.

The World Exhibition of Chicago, held in 1893, gave a considerable impetus to the design of electric vehicles in America. The organisers of the show — which presented a mass of technical innovations the like of which has probably never been equalled, from the telephone to electric light, from the typewriter to a commercial camera — offered prizes for practicable projects for land vehicles with any means of propulsion other than animal. It was due to this incentive that the Chicago Perambulator Company developed an electric tricycle which, like other similar vehicles, was called a "rolling chair", for carrying visitors round the Exhibition.

Another interesting vehicle was built in the same period by David M. Parry, of Indianapolis, who received orders for one thousand immediately after the first successful trials. The death of the principal customer prevented this deal being carried through and Parry in disgust turned to the i.c. car, being responsible in 1916

for the V-12 Pathfinder. In lists of American manufacturers of eletric vehicles were two more names, those of Keller and Degenhart, whose "rolling chair" was used for some time as means of transport between buildings in large companies.

With the cyclists

By 1894, the year of the Paris-Rouen race, it was clear that the era of motor racing had been born. The competitive spirit was awakening in the hearts of enthusiasts together with the strong nerves necessary to undertake a journey in the rickety vehicles of those days.

In the same year as the Paris-Rouen race, the Austrian Von Liebig undertook a remarkable journey for those days — over 585 miles — in a "Victoria Benz" with a 5 H.P. single-cylinder engine. The engine consumed 30 gallons of petrol and 340 gallons of cooling water!

A steam delivery van, built at the time when electric vehicles were popular for use within cities.

Three years earlier a Peugeot had covered a much greater distance, 1,280 miles, in 139 hours at an average speed of 9 m.p.h. but this had been done in short stages and for a curious reason — it was the first "suiveur" car in the history of cycle racing. Authorisation to accompany the riders in the Paris-Brest cycle race was requested by the Peugeot company which intended to use the occasion for the final development of their car.

The 1,280 miles were covered by adding to the 750 of the race itself the journeys to and from the factory. Having obtained permission, a 2 H.P. Peugeot with a Daimler engine was sent from the factory at Valentigney. After meeting 206 cyclists at the start line in Paris, the Peugeot moved off with them and in stages successfully covered the whole course.

It was this unusual exploit which suggested to the "Petit Journal", which had promoted the Paris-Brest cycle race, the idea of the Paris-Rouen race for "horseless carriages".

A Baker electric brougham built in 1912 and re-equipped in 1960 with solar batteries (in the roof), supplied by the International Rectifier Corporation.

THE AMBITIOUS MARQUIS

Albert De Dion seen in 1932 driving his 1898 "vis-à-vis".

Panhard and Levassor were both engineers. Between another pair of names famous in the early days of the motor car, Albert De Dion and Georges Bouton however, there were enormous differences not only professionally but also in social background and even physique. Tall and stout, the Marquis De Dion was the son of an ancient Belgian noble family, the house of De Dion-Le Val, although he was born in 1856 at Carquefou near Nantes in France. His partner Bouton was a wiry little man of humble Parisian origin, a very able mechanic and naturally a motor enthusiast. It is not difficult to imagine the atmosphere in which their long and happy association came to be formed.

Model-maker

The imposing Marquis alternated his social duties and frequent visits to the workshop in which the first "horseless carriage" enthusiasts bustled around their cars. As for Bouton, he was at home in that workshop and his interests led him not so much to the somewhat crude petrol vehicles but to the much more highly developed "steamer" — the steam carriage with its decades of development, but whose slow but inexorable decline was beginning even then.

Georges Bouton had in a certain sense grown up in a more graceful tradition. His real profession was making models — toys for rich children — which he built in his shop together with his brother-in-law Trépardoux. It was probably this unusual ability to execute precision work in miniature which led to his future success. The Marquis De Dion was a frequent visitor to motor car workshops, and, with the cars that he bought from time to time, followed religiously the uncertain technical progress of the period. He did not limit himself to solemn parades down the Champs Elysées. He craved to race with other enthusiasts, to crown with a major success his position as a leading figure in that sphere. While waiting for one of the many suggestions for car racing which were discussed around 1880 to become reality, he decided to prepare for it by building for himself the vehicle which had been in his mind for some time — a steam tricycle with rapid steaming boiler, very light and therefore relatively fast. It was the first time that anyone had thought of building a vehicle exclusively for racing. Before this, and for many years afterwards, races were run with cars that were generally available for use on the roads.

Restless

The Marquis' ideas were good but did not progress beyond the theoretical stage. He needed a capable builder, capable enough to build something that no one had built before, and build it in such a way that it might go on working. That man proved to be Georges Bouton.

The industrial partnership between the two men dates from 1881, and the tricycle was quickly, and well, built. But the restless Marquis had to wait until 20 April 1887, before he could finally take part in a race. On that day in fact, the first car race in history took place, the Neuilly-Versailles-Neuilly, a distance of 20 miles, organised by the journalist Fossier. De Dion and his tricycle hurled themselves into the race and completed the course in 1 hour and 14 minutes — not so fast in a vehicle that could do almost 40 m.p.h. One detail should be added — he was the only competitor!

Alone again

It was the fate of De Dion never to taste the fruits of genuine victory even though this was probably his principal aim in life. Four years after the Neuilly-Versailles, he took part in the second race in history on the racetrack at Longchamps. This time he had an opponent, who also had a steam tricycle, a Serpollet. But the latter broke down halfway through the race and De Dion had to travel the second half by himself again.

A few months later it was a 25 miles race on the track at Vincennes, and again the only entrant was : De Dion-Bouton tricycle. The Marquis, probably out of pique, did not drive himself, but sent as his driver a certain Lacaux. It was just as well; otherwise he would have tasted the bitterness of having the race stopped by a representative of the police concerned about danger to the public after one spectator had almost fallen under the wheels of the tricycle.

For the first real and important race, the Paris-Rouen of 1894, De Dion used a much more robust "steamer" than his tricycle, because of the distance involved. But the first prize was awarded by the jury to the second car to arrive, a Peugeot, because the Marquis' vehicle was held to be too expensive and too difficult to handle, and therefore not in accord with the race regulations.

Organisation

From that time onwards the Marquis was never seen again among the competitors in a motor race on French soil, although he took part in organisation. He ran the Paris-Bordeaux race in 1895 with Pierre Giffard and soon afterwards founded the Automobile Club de France with the journalist Paul Meyan.

Though he no longer took part his name continued to be carried in races by the machines which came out of the partnership with Bouton at Puteaux. De Dion always appeared among the leading places in race results, whether carried by steam cars, the last of which appeared in the Paris-Marseilles in 1897, or by a series of i.c. engined vehicles, developed from the crude but successful tricycle of 1895.

The following year a second great motor race was run, the Paris-Bordeaux-Paris, suggested by the enthusiastic Marquis De Dion and Pierre Giffard. This was a very different race from that of the previous year. The regulations were much more severe and the race was a clear cut victory for the i.c. engine. It marked the virtual disappearance of the steam car, notwithstanding the excellent performance of the Bollée steam bus, the "Nouvelle", so large as to have even a toilet on board. In total there were 70,000 gold francs for this race in prizes.

As usual, most of the entries failed to turn up at the start and the list of the 21 who actually took part exhibits the variety of technical solutions that still persisted. In the race were Jeantaud's electric car, six steam vehicles (including "La Nouvelle"), twelve i.c. engined cars and two motor-cycles.

One of these two-wheelers was a remarkable device built by Félix Millet. The engine had a five-cylinder radial engine in the rear wheel, the movement of the conrods being transmitted to a crankshaft co-axial with the wheel hub. Another vehicle to arouse the curiosity of the spectators was the "Eclair", driven by Edouard Michelin, one of the brothers, who some years before had begun to manufacture pneumatic cycle tyres and who were now trying to introduce similar products into the motor car field. The "Eclair" was a Peugeot-Daimler modified to give 4 H.P. but its particular distinction lay in the four pneumatic tyres that for the first time lined the rims. The immediate outcome was not encouraging: 50 punctures, due in part obviously to the terrible state of the roads and to the excessive fragility of the covers used.

All the same it cannot be said that the results were entirely negative for in successive races there was an ever increasing number of cars fitted with pneumatic tyres.

1886 Benz single cylinder tricycle. Top speed — 10 m.p.h.

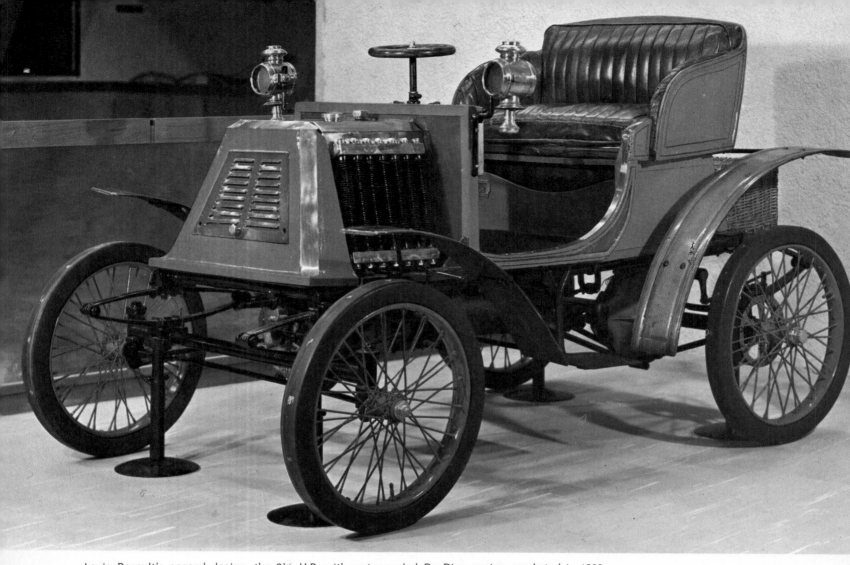

Louis Renault's second design, the 3½ H.P. with water-cooled De Dion engine, marketed in 1900.

The passion for veteran cars knows no frontiers. This fascinating, if expensive, hobby is found all over the world. The photo shows a 1908 Lion Peugeot. Below an 1895 Benz hotel bus.

The race was won, in effect, by Emile Levassor, who drove alone in one of his own cars. Having reached Bordeaux in 24 hours he at once began the return journey, meeting his competitors coming the other way. He arrived in Paris 48 hours and 47 minutes after he left, having averaged 24.6 k.p.h. (over 15 m.p.h.). But as the rules required that the winner should be in a four seater, the official victory went to the second car home, a Peugeot-Daimler driven by Koechlin.

Flooded Roads

In the year following this enthusiastic racing season, 1896, a third great French race, the Paris-Marseilles-Paris, was organised by the first French motoring weekly, the "France Automobile". For the first time the competition was divided into stages, ten to be precise. During the pauses the machines were put into *parcs fermés* supervised by the police. There was the usual last-minute reduction in the number of entries — 52 being reduced to 31 on the day of the race, 24 September. There were 23 cars, 3 Léon Bollée voiturettes, and 5 De Dion-Bouton tricycles.

This time even the weather was ranged against the heroic competitors. A series of violent storms burst over the course, felling trees and flooding the roads. Only 13 vehicles arrived in Marseilles, and the drivers had undergone every kind of adventure, one even finding himself near naked in the middle of one of the stages.

The wind had howled into a tear in his trousers, causing the consequent, involuntary, striptease.

There were, however, more serious accidents. Léon Bollée ran off the road (he was in one of the first cars built in his factory after the conversion from steamers to i.c. engines) and hit a tree blown down by the storm. Bollée was injured but fortunately not seriously, and succeeded in continuing the race. Later on, between Montélimar and Orange, Levassor's Panhard skidded and turned over in a ditch. Levassor was injured but his co-driver, D'Ostingue, continued after leaving Levassor in the care of the spectators. The injuries the great industrialist and sportsman had received turned out to be more serious than at first seemed. He never recovered and died the following year aged 53.

The race was won by Mayade in a Panhard-Levassor which completed the course in 67 hours and 43 minutes at an average speed of 25 k.p.h. (over 15 m.p.h.). Two other Panhard-Levassors were in the first four places. A sensational fact was that a De Dion tricycle arrived only 3 hours and 19 minutes after the winner, a result which was attributed to the fact that it was fitted with pneumatics. This was due to a new idea of the Michelin brothers who, far from being discouraged by the disastrous results of the Paris-Bordeaux race, had drawn the logical conclusions and had adequately reinforced their tyres. They then bought two hundred Bollée voiturettes and one hundred De Dion tricycles, putting

Tradition died hard. The driver of this 1906 Vauxhall had to sit high in the rear just as in a horse cab.

1897 Hugot. Rear single-cylinder 3½ H.P. engine. The brake was applied by a small wheel underneath the steering wheel. The body was in wickerwork.

THE ACETYLENE DAYS

The first "horseless carriage" had simple oil lamps when they had any at all. The yellowish flame rising from the wick, immersed in a small container of oil or petrol, provided just about enough light for the driver to avoid the larger holes. "Real" carriages, those with horses, travelled much faster but this light, conveniently beamed by a parabolic mirror and optical front glass, was good enough even for them. Motorists in those heroic times did not too often commit themselves to night travel, not only because it was ill-advised on the road surface but also because a meeting in the dark with any enemies of their noisy mechanical monsters might well have had unpleasant consequences.

At the turn of the century acetylene lighting began to be used on motor cars in view of the higher speeds that called for a more vivid and penetrating light. This was in spite of a certain resistance to their use due to a variety of well known limitations — the danger of explosion, the necessity of frequent inspection of the carbide-water reaction, the short life of the fuel supply. For about fifteen years acetylene lighting was the basic system in use on motor cars.

Efficient system

Contrary to popular belief, such systems attained a high level of efficiency, not only as regards the gas generator and the characteristics of the nozzle from which the vivid greenish flame issued, but also in the lamp itself. The latest models, produced just before their final disappearance 50 years ago, looked similar to those in use on modern cars.

The problem of dimming had been resolved by means of a hemispherical concave mirror which could be manually rotated through 180° until the flame itself was completely obscured. In this position, used for cruising in company with other vehicles or in the city, the headlamp sent out only a part of its light, reflected from the parabolic mirror behind. When, however, the dimming mirror was rotated until it was immediately behind the flame, it intensified the light.

This small mirror system, designed by Zeiss, was used for electric headlamps when they were first adopted in spite of the many deficiences of the batteries of the time. Later it was found more practical to adopt a second, less powerful bulb outside the focus of the parabola.

Double filament

The use of double filament (full and dim) bulbs dates from the second decade of this century. But as these only weakened the beam (due to the lower power of the second filament) and did not dip it, they had little success until fairly recent times. Improved manufacturing techniques have now permitted the construction of a lamp incorporating a small mirror designed to throw the light beam of the second filament upwards.

This was a big step forward. Not only was it possible to obtain a light thrown downwards (due to double reflection from the small mirror and the parabola) from the second filament, but it was also possible to eliminate the "hole" in the parabolic surface where the second lamp used to fit, thus improving the "full" beam.

This progress was for a while cancelled out by the need

to incorporate in the headlamp an auxiliary bulb — the side or parking light — as required by law in many countries. The transposition of this light to a separate housing occurred only after the Second World War when headlamps were built into wings or on the front of the car. The separate mounting of the headlamps had been a legacy from the time when they were not supplied with the coachwork but were chosen by the owner according to his preference.

With the parabolic mirror returning to its unbroken form in this way, and the bulbs themselves being im-

proved by the use of inert gases which reduced "aging", headlamps showed no major progress for about a decade. Towards the end of the fifties however, an international conference accepted the so-called "European unified asymmetrical headlamp" with the lens modified to lengthen the right-hand beam. This improves visibility for vehicles approaching one another, an important safety feature.

Soon after, because of new legislation, coupled lamps began to be used. These consisted of the normal full/dip headlamps with the full beam coupled in circuit with

a separate single filament long-range driving light. This development provided lighting suitable for the high level of cruising speeds which had become normal.

Another technical revolution now in progress is the increasing use of iodine vapour lamps. The advantages of this type of lighting system lie in the improvement in the quantity and quality of light produced for equal consumption, and in the absence of deterioration of the light with time ("aging" due to blackening of the bulb and consumption of the filament).

Iodine lamps require absolutely clean handling and create certain problems due to the high temperatures at which they work. Nevertheless they are now fitted as standard to certain cars and the number is rapidly increasing. Until recently their use was limited to cars with double headlamps because it had not been possible to produce a dipping type iodine lamp, but the necessary bulbs are now available.

A last-minute inspection of René de Knyff's Panhard-Levassor before the Paris-Amsterdam race run from 7 to 13 July, 1898.

them on sale after equipping them with their tyres. Another interesting point in the results of the Paris-Marseilles-Paris was the presence in the first ten places of two Delahayes. These were machines fitted with 6 H.P. engines, built by Emile Delahaye, an enthusiast and expert who had recently entered the ranks of manufacturers. He had applied an important novelty to his cars — the forced circulation of cooling water. The De Dion tricycles which took part in the race also had something new, a system of electric ignition similar to those in use today.

As an appendix to the story of these great races it can be added that the following year, 1897, was to see one of the last victories of a steam carriage, that of De Dion on the Nice circuit which included the novelty of a small hill climb. In that year competitive activity started in Italy, with the Arona-Stresa-Arona race organised by the motor club recently founded in Milan. This was a modest race of only 22 miles but it was the first step.

France was still the leading country of the world for motor vehicles but in other countries of Europe enthusiasts were beginning to lay the foundations of an industry that would make up the years lost.

1896 Peugeot coupé. (Motor Museum, Rochetaillée).

HORSEPOWER MEASUREMENT

Like people we meet often and with whom we have become familiar, even though in reality we know little about them, three motoring cyphers have come into use, although not everyone understands exactly what they mean. These cyphers are SAE, DIN and CUNA and one of these is usually found immediately after the word "horsepower" when we read information on the power characteristics of an engine.

This does not imply that different "sizes" of H.P. exist — the formula has been standardised by international convention — but that any given engine may be placed on the dynamometer, the device used for measuring horsepower, in varying degress of completeness. The engine therefore gives differing net output figures. The cyphers SAE, DIN and CUNA therefore refer to the condition of the engine when its power is measured. These three conventions used by motor manufacturers for measuring horsepower have been established respectively by the Society of Automotive Engineers (SAE) in America, by the Deutsche Industrie-normen (DIN) in Germany and, in Italy, by the Commissione per l'Unificazione automobilistica (CUNA). The differences are given below.

SAE

The engine is placed on the dynamometer after being stripped of its fan, water pump, dynamo, silencer and air filter. It is evident that an engine cannot function in normal use in this condition.

DIN

The engine is placed on the dynamometer in the same condition in which it is fitted in a vehicle. This method gives results much closer to reality but even this does not correspond exactly to the power of an engine installed in a vehicle because, as in the other systems used, such factors as climate, pressure and humidity of the atmosphere, the type of lubricants used etc. are controlled under the test conditions in a way that is not possible with normal use in a vehicle.

CUNA

This is a compromise between SAE and DIN. Only the silencer and air cleaner are removed for testing i.e. only those accessories not strictly necessary for the functioning of the engine. Clearly even without the silencer the engine will run perfectly well. Indeed it will work better as the silencer absorbs power.

LANGUAGE OF THE COACHBUILDER

In the story of the motor car there has never been a precise terminology to describe different kinds of bodywork, or a way of differentiating among the kinds of vehicle for transporting drivers and passengers. On the contrary, there has always been some confusion in terms particular words being employed at the same time to describe different kinds of cars and body style.

Furthermore, the same word has often meant different things to, say, an Englishman, a Frenchman, an American or an Italian. Confusion remains. today. It is possible, nevertheless, to detail a simple vocabulary for the period 1895 to 1915, to identify the various types of vehicle in use in that period. In alphabetical order, the terms are:

BERLINA - Rarely used before the first World War. In general it meant a closed luxury car, often with a small window which permitted the occupants to see but barely to be seen.

CAB - A term taken directly from horse-drawn carriage vocabulary and used to define a vehicle in which two passengers were enclosed while the driver was situated some distance away, usually in front and unprotected. But there were also electric cabs with the driver seated high up at the rear.

CABRIOLET - A word used towards the end of the period to describe a car with collapsible hood, with two or four seats.

COUPE - Originally a vehicle "cut" by a glass division, fixed or moveable, behind the front seats. The driving position was only partially protected by the roof whilst the totally enclosed rear was very luxurious.

COUPE -CABRIOLET OR DOUBLE-CABRIOLET - A long vehicle the front part of which was designed as a coupé, whilst the rear part had the collapsible hood of a cabriolet. There were often two supplementary seats.

COUPE -CHAUFFEUR - A coupé with the driving position completely covered by a fixed roof, which was an extension of the rear roof.

COUPE DE VILLE - A coupé with the driving position completely open.

COUPE -LIMOUSINE - A vehicle with a totally enclosed rear and with the front part closed on the sides only.

DOUBLE BERLINA - A lengthened berlina with the driving position enclosed but separated from the rear part of the vehicle.

DOUBLE LANDAULET - A lengthened landaulet with two permanent seats plus two occasionals in the rear, and a driving position in front.

DOUBLE PHAETON - A phaeton with two double seats, including that of the driver.

DOUBLE TONNEAU - A lengthened tonneau in which the front seats were completely separate from the rear.

LANDAU - A cabriolet limousine in which only the roof behind the rear windows was collapsible.

LANDAULET OR LANDAULETTE - A small landeau with only two seats in the closed collapsible roof portion.

LIMOUSINE - A lengthened coupé with double lateral windows in the rear part.

LIMOUSINE-CHAUFFEUR - A limousine with the rear roof extended forward to cover the driving position.

PHAETON - A term again taken from the days of the horse-drawn carriage. In the early days of motoring it described a light car with large spoked wheels, with one double seat and generally a hood.

RUNABOUT - An open sporting type of vehicle, generally with only two seats and simple bodywork.

SKIFF OR CAB-SKIFF - An open sports car with streamlined, light bodywork.

TONNEAU - An open vehicle with a bench seat in front and a semi-circular seat behind. A part of the seat was built into the rear door.

"GLASS" SALOON - A large closed vehicle, generally similar to a double berlina but with very large windows.

SALOON - A vehicle with the driving seat inside the enclosed car with no separation from the rear seats.

TORPEDO - A long sports vehicle with hood, which was attached to the windscreen.

VICTORIA - Another term derived from the era of horses. The Victoria was long and luxurious with a separate driving position and a large rear seat, and was equipped with hoods and side-screens.

VOITURETTE - Used to describe an early touring car with two seats only and no hood.

WAGON-SALOON - A particularly luxurious saloon used in America for civic and other official purposes.

Two cars for the sporting woman. There are over sixty years between the two photographs.

CHAPTER FOUR
FASHION GOES TO THE HEAD

The last decade of the 19th century not only saw the running of the first motor races, with exciting and sometimes tragic consequences, but also marked the foundation of a large number of companies both in Europe and in America, amongst which were several of the names that were to become important in the future.

In France, a great number of new manufacturers joined the names already well-known such as Panhard-Levassor, De Dion-Bouton, Peugeot, Renault, Delahaye and Bollée. In 1895-1896 Berliet, De Dietrich and Mors began production and the 1898 list of manufacturers worthy of mention included Chenard-Walker in Asnières, Éclipse, Minerva, Société Française d'Autos Electriques, Hurtu, Rheda, the Société Française d'Automo-

bile, Touraine, Créanche, Aigle, Richard (which later became Unic) Marot Gardon et Company, Energie, David-Bourgeois, Gobron-Brillié, Vedrine-Breugniot, the Société Ancienne d'Automobiles et Traction de Paris, Sphinx, Nationale, Dumond-Saralegui of Levallois and Gaillardet in Puteaux.

Pioneers amalgamate

Others, however, are worth more than this passing mention. In 1896 Alexandre Darracq founded at Suresnes the company which bore his name and was to figure prominently in the early years of the new century. In 1904, for instance, a 100 H.P. Darracq driven by Baras took the world's flying kilometre record and it was Darracq's branch in Milan which was to be indirectly the origin of Alfa Romeo in 1909.

In 1898 Emile Delahaye, the ingenious manufacturer of "sporty" vehicles in his small workshop in Tours, amalgamated with Desmarais and Morane, hydraulic machine manufacturers in Paris. He transferred his factory to the French capital, where production was recommenced on a larger scale. The moving spirit of this change was a young engineer, Charles Weiffenbach, who had benefited from experience with Léon Bolle voiturettes. The workmanship of the Delahaye models was of high quality, and the company quickly became famous.

In the same year another interesting new model was introduced — the Decauville 3½ H.P. built by the Société des Voitures Automobiles Decauville, which was founded to exploit the patents of two Bordeaux engineers, Cornilleau and Guedon. The engine, a vertical twin with separate cylinders, was rear mounted.

It had a capacity of 494 c.c. and produced 3.75 H.P. at 1,200 r.p.m.! The car had independent front wheel suspension, and none at all at the rear.

Four reverse speeds

Ignition was by means of a battery, two coils and two plugs; there were two forward gears and no reverse; and the engine was air-cooled. The Decauville has become famous in the story of the motor car for its lightness — it weighed under 4½ cwt.

In the meantime improved models began to issue from

In the early days of motoring, women drivers were rare — and taking a car ride to the country was a hobby of only the rich, as this photograph shows.

the workshops of established French companies, which were showing an adventurous spirit of innovation.

This was true of the "B 1" Panhard-Levassor, a more heavily built car than its predecessors; among many improvements common to vehicles of the time it had one characteristic of its own. By using a separate lever it was possible to reverse all four forward gears.

Renault in the same period built the first car with an enclosed driving position — a justly famous model though one which may have a ludicrous appearance to modern eyes. On a very short wheel base was fitted the high coachwork necessary to allow the fashionably dressed men and women of the time to enter comfortably with their imposing headgear. Surprisingly, the idea of totally enclosed coachwork was not followed for a long time by other makes, even though the car was in effect the forerunner of the modern saloon.

France at this time was the undoubted world leader in the field of motoring. The new mechanical means of transport had passed from being a curiosity, accepted or not according to taste, to being a fascinating possession. It provided the opportunity for adventure — besides

A less publicised one had been held in 1894 by "Figaro". In 1898 the first Continental motor show was held in the square in front of Les Invalides from 15 June to 3 July, almost at the same time as a similar show in Boston in the United States. It represented an act of considerable courage by which the Automobile Club de France challenged public opinion. In the previous year a few models had been shown in a corner of the Palace de l'Industrie — but in a show mainly devoted to bicycles.

Change of heart

It cannot be said that authority viewed the occasion with enthusiasm. The President of the French Republic himself, Félix Faure, as he hurriedly took his leave of the organisers, did not hesitate to say "How ugly these machines are, and how they smell!".

When the second edition of the show took place the following year, however, public interest had grown enormously. It was at this show that the tradition was born — it was to be maintained to the present day — of

A 1900 De Dion-Bouton.

This Amédée Bollée car of 1900 won the 1963 Paris-Turin rally.

A 1902 Georges Richard.

ostentation and eccentricity — for both sexes. In 1897 the first ladies' "world motor racing championship" was organised by a newspaper, "L'Echo de Paris", on a short road circuit at Longchamps. The name of the winning lady driver who attracted the attention of the men and not a little secret admiration from her own sex, is unknown. But it was perhaps the first tentative chapter in the still developing love story of woman and the motor car. In the Paris reports of the same year, a competition for new styles of coachwork was announced.

The Fiat-Abarth 2,000 Sports Prototype 1969 with Pininfarina body. The line of the front part meets the windscreen with a continuous line, which improves the air penetration and adherence to the ground. The two small doors are obligatory under the "Group Six" regulations.

THE STATURE OF THE STYLIST

The car stylist is both committed and involved. He has not only to be a brilliant artist but an engineer, an economist, a mathematician, a publicist and, quite possibly, a more than ordinarily competent speaker. If he works for a mass-producer, he is also the head of a team. He is not to be confused with the designer nor his team, although he may be within the department's structure. Above all, the stylist is, as he always was, an artist. It is in artistry that style differs basically from design, although each contains some elements of the other.

Only Functional

Every consumer instinctively understands style; function is unlikely ever to become the sole selling factor. Everyone, with one sense or another, reacts to what looks good or bad even if he does not know why.
Nature provides the highest standards... a cocoa bean, a palm frond, a seagull, a salmon. Artists have always been influenced by such things.
The earliest motor cars were unlovely because they were purely functional. But the stylist wasted no time in

getting to work, hence the surprising number of early beetle-shaped or cigar-shaped bodies or attempts at such pure design.

The more restrained stylists confined themselves to such aspects as the curved dash, baroque mudguards and fanciful bonnets and sides.

Fashions go in cycles, and this applies as much to automobile styling as to anything else. The alternations of soft and hard, round and square, squat and upright, fat and slim, simple and complex, take place throughout the ages.

There is a constant stream of progress and each successive creation, even if it is a revival, brings some innovation, some effective feature, which will add to the sum total of style.

Significant changes in style and design are, for the most part, well marked. Progress from contraption to horseless carriage was historic. Although the motor car remained a form of carriage for many years, the pattern was broken by the early roadsters, the boat bodies, the torpedoes and the out-and-out sports cars.

The stylist, as such, had not emerged and if anyone dealt with aesthetic considerations it was the draughtsman or the designer, who were often inspired by purely functional racing machines when allowed to ignore the carriage.

Trend-setters

For years the designers and the emergent stylists were inhibited by the composite method of construction, which followed the traditions of carriage building. They did their best, however, and there were trend-setting machines in "sticks and tinplate". Certainly the long, low line came in quite soon after the First World War, and the "perpendicular" styles were already being challenged by some moderately curvaceous creations. The use of aluminium helped to relieve the inhibitions of the stylist as well as those of the craftsman builder. It was eminently workable, and lent itself to cold forming of various kinds, whilst it could be beautifully polished or engine-turned if required.

Fabric bodies enjoyed a brief popularity. These were freaks and drove stylists to despair, but the challenge was met courageously by the Riley, MG and Morris stylists, among others. Such marques marketed semi-streamlined designs, possibly more for the sake of novelty than in the interests of aerodynamics, although the latter consideration has always influenced the conscientious stylist.

Before the introduction of large steel pressings fascinated designers and stylists, there were one or two bold attempts to exhibit new virtuosity in composite construction. Notable among these were the Burney and the North-Lucas, but beauty of line was not an outstanding feature of these designs.

While styling teams got into their stride which were often practical as well as beautiful for saloons and sports cars, the diminishing numbers of coachbuilders and of makers of high-quality cars found new ways of creating exquisite designs in traditional materials. They were stimulated by the importance at the time of the classic sports car races, particularly Le Mans.

Pace accelerated

The pace of progress in styling and design, as with most activities, has been greatly accelerated since the Second World War and the stature of both designer and styling artist is greater than ever before.

Sir William Lyons and his Jaguar design and styling teams brought beauty as well as high-grade engineering within reach of the masses. The great Italian stylists, led by Pininfarina, have shown that they can usually be a step ahead and can create and not merely derive.

Alec Issigonis, for BMC, threw aside the accepted designs and ideas for cheap small cars and had the courage and artistry to make the "box with wheels at the corners" not simply effective, but desirable. The result was an entire generation of boxes all over Europe, with Renault, Simca, Fiat and others adopting the "European shape" with optimum box dimensions — a viable selling feature.

Volkswagen did not conform, but the beetle has always been a fantastic accident of economics and certainly never a stylist's brainchild.

The interior view of the 1969 Fiat-Abarth 2,000 Sports Prototype.

Phase of Revival

Today an unpredictable development has again involved the stylist, if it were not indeed initiated by him. This is the astonishing dialectic between the estate car and the saloon, with the so-called GT car on the sidelines. Some stylists are concerned with making an estate car as smart, neat and compact as a saloon. Others strive after a saloon which is sportif, *yet as accommodating and practical as an estate car. Whatever emerges has usually been far removed from the boxy European car shape.*

With the sleek, curvaceous GT shape influencing every-day saloons, it is clear that stylists are once more in a revivalist phase.

What lies ahead from the stylist? A baroque period, a competition for lower centres of gravity, maxi bonnets and mini boots, the wedge shape of racing or the spindly angularity of the dragsters? Whatever happens, the car stylists, who are the aristocrats of draughts-manship, will need ultimately to appeal to the final arbiter, the customer.

Above the Simca 1,000 Coupé with Bertone body. Below the Quattroruote-Secura built by OSI of Turin in 1965.

Two of the prize-winning designs in the 1894 competition run by the Paris newspaper "Figaro".

a profusion of flowers and lights, and even an orchestra to entertain the visitors.

French industry was now expanding rapidly. There was a waiting time of two months for a Darracq, six for a Delahaye or a Peugeot, eight for a Mors and twenty for a Panhard-Levassor. Even then the customer received only the chassis and had to make his own arrangements for the bodywork with a specialist.

The police, faced with some thousands of cars on the dusty roads of the region of the Seine, met for the first time problems which other countries were to have to deal with shortly afterwards. As early as 1892 the Paris Prefecture had established a speed limit of 12 k.p.h. (under 8 m.p.h.) within the walls of the city.

By the beginning of the century the i.c. engine was revolutionising the carriage of goods. This is a 1898 Daimler motor lorry.

Now a succession of other problems arose. What was to be the Rule of the Road? How was precedence to be given at crossroads? How were vehicle and driver to be identified?

The last of these problems was solved by giving each car a registered number incorporating the number of the Départment as already used by the Ministry for Mines, to which body was given the responsibility for vehicle registration. This system is still in use in France today. Then there was the problem of the position of the steering wheel, which was beginning to replace the tiller — was it to be placed to right or left? It was not to be easily solved and was under discussion for several years to come.

Often decisions were contradictory, especially as there continued to be uncertainty on whether to drive on the right or the left. It was not until 1908 that, perhaps due to the influence of America where it had already been decided to drive on the right, it was generally decided to mount the steering wheel on the left. Even then there were many exceptions as any early British motorist on the Continent found.

The walking man

The explosion of popular interest was to be reproduced in other European countries within a few years. In Britain before the turn of the century the venture of a firm such as Wolseley into car manufacture was exceptional, when it is remembered that the country still suffered under *the* notorious "Red Flag Act", though the red flag itself was a fiction. The truth was, however, little better, since cars on the road had to be preceded by a man on foot — undoubtedly not the best of encouragement for starting a car factory. Although the law was rescinded in 1896, the motorist was still severely restricted by a limit of 12 m.p.h. which was to be raised to 20 m.p.h. in 1904 and remain at that speed until 1930. The English branch of Daimler was founded in Coventry, with the intention of building for the British market cars identical to those of the German parent company. Some official recognition of the motor car was given when the Prince of Wales, the future Edward VII, visited the Coventry workshop. The Prince accepted a short drive in a "Cannstatt" driven by F. R. Simms, who had invented an improved version of the hot-tube ignition fitted in all Daimlers of the time. In fact, the English company was to remain faithful to this system for many years even after high tension systems were available and were being fitted by competitors.

The engine of the first English Daimlers was a 1,500 c.c. Vee-twin with four gears. Later a 3-litre four-cylinder was fitted. A characteristic common to all Daimlers for many years was unequal diameter of the wheels; the front ones were smaller. The company was to produce some of the most luxurious vehicles ever to be built in the British Isles.

Also in 1896, an agreement was made between Selwyn Francis Edge and Montague Stanley Napier. From this was to arise the company bearing the latter's name and

A 1932 Riley in a race for post-vintage cars.

which was to become famous both for its outstanding cars and aero-engines. Edge was a racing cyclist who became a motoring enthusiast. Napier, a friend of his youth, went into partnership with Edge to study French racing cars and to build similar ones in England.

Pneumatic tyres

Edge and Napier bought the Panhard-Levassor which René de Knyff had brought into second place in the Paris-Marseilles race, having borrowed the 30,000 gold francs purchase price. After various modifications, including the fitting of Dunlop pneumatic tyres in place of the original solid tyres, replacing the tiller by a steering wheel and fitting an English engine, a new Napier 9 H.P. as born in 1900.

Later that year a four-cylinder 16 H.P. was built, the first of a long series of fine cars which, right down to 1924, were to delight motorists on both sides of the Channel with their outstanding technical qualities.

Edge himself, having become in the meantime the United Kingdom concessionaire for De Dion-Bouton, was to figure in 1907 in fierce dispute with the Marquis when Edge created the company of De Dion-Bouton Limited.

A solemn example of the working in Britain of the "Red Flag Act", under which all vehicles had to be preceded by a man walking ahead. The car in the illustration is an 1895 Knight two-seater. The man, as can be seen, is not carrying a red flag.

A 1912 Chenard Walcker.

A 1902 De Dion-Bouton imported into England by S. F. Edge.

The same historic year of 1896 saw also the birth of Humber in Coventry by the conversion of an existing bicycle factory into one for building motor cars. The first Humbers were an immediate public success. The Four Cylinder, designed in the opening years of the new century by a young French engineer, Louis Coatalen received so many orders that assembly lines were set up in the streets outside the factory.

In 1898 Riley built a prototype car, thereafter making motorcycles and tricars until 1906, when their first production four wheeler was marketed. Its 10 H.P. successor was noted for its unusual round radiator, and this vee-twin was produced until the outbreak of the First World War.

BRAKING BY TREE TRUNK

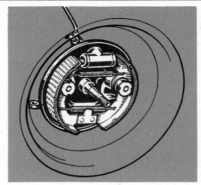

Drum brake.

Disc brake.

The story of motor car brakes has ironical elements for a motorist of the 1960s who was driving before The Second World War. In the 1930s some manufacturers were still building cars without front wheel brakes. The relative slowness of designers to accept the idea that it was necessary to provide an efficient braking system is even more disconcerting when it is realised that, right from the first decade of the century, motor cars were capable of such speeds that instant braking was a necessity if an emergency arose.

The casual attitude towards braking in the early days is illustrated by the first car crossing of the St. Gotthard Pass, by the French engineer Arrou in a 3½ H.P. De Dion-Bouton in 1901. The account of the trip records that "the leather-lined brakes were burned out after only a few minutes of the descent" and that, having reduced speed to almost zero to avoid going over the mountain side at every bend, it was necessary "to fasten a tree trunk to the car with a steel cable, which was then dragged behind".

Dual system

The brakes of these hurtling vehicles consisted then of shoes acting on the wheel-rims, a logical consequence of the ancestry of the horse-drawn carriage. A series of tests in New York in 1902, which was considered impressive for the time, showed that from the braking point of view the car was considerably safer than the carriage. The car could stop in a quarter of the distance required by a carriage with four horses.

Of course, this would now be considered far from a safe braking distance.

In the following years, partly because of the legal requirements operated in some countries, there was general adoption of a dual braking system, one acting on the rear wheels and the other on the transmission.

The first of these continued for some time to depend on external shoes lined with leather or camel skin, but this system was soon replaced by internal shoes and drums. The transmission brake acted on the differential when transmission was by chain or on the transmission shaft itself when these were introduced.

Although the general introduction of four-wheel brakes was slow, the first studies came quite soon. Early ex-

periments took place between 1905 and 1910 and some strange solutions were envisaged, such as the control of brakes through movement of the stub axle (Renouf) or a system which used compressed air and necessitated the carrying of an air bottle (Cavello).

The complexity of these ideas came partly from the need for braking to be independent of the position of the front wheels and partly from the need to avoid dangerous reactions by the braking on the steering itself. Isotta Fraschini introduced four-wheel brakes in 1909, and they were fitted as standard to most of the Italian company's products by 1914. The credit for a successful system controlled by one action is due to the manager of Argyll, Henry Perrott, a Scots car manufacturer. In 1913 his brakes were first fitted to racing cars, above all due to the interest of the racing driver Boillot. Slowly, during the 1920s, they were adopted by more and more companies, and extended to production cars. Hydraulic actuation gradually came into general use, though the first users met difficulty in guaranteeing their reliable and safe functioning, because of the danger of fracture of the often exposed pipes or because the liquids then used corroded the seals or froze at low temperatures. In the meantime the friction materials themselves were being improved, first by using cast-iron shoes and later asbestos lining compounds. The design of shoes was also improving to give braking effect in proportion to the speed of rotation of the hubs, while in some cases the adoption of alloys for the body of the drums assisted heat dissipation.

Drum and disc

Recent years have seen the gradual substitution of the drum by the disc, pioneered by the British concerns Girling and Dunlop. This system — which offers intense braking especially at high speeds, resists "fade" and is unaffected by water and mud — is now used on all four wheels for high-speed cars and on many family cars' front wheels. Pads can also be substituted easily.

The types of brake-servo mechanisms which reduce the effort required from the driver — in most general use today are those that use the depression (vacuum) in the engine inlet manifold.

Celebrated motoring pioneer St. John C. Nixon receives an appropriate salute in 1959 when starting out to repeat the "1,000-mile trial" run round Britain in the 1899 Wolseley used in the first trial in 1900. Below an 1899 Darracq.

Much later Riley was absorbed by Morris Motors; then, like Wolseley, it became part of the British Motor Corporation and subsequently of Leyland Motors. About this time, Panhard-Levassor cars began to be imported into England. The fact is of particular interest because the man concerned was the Hon. Charles Stuart Rolls, youngest son of Lord Llangattock, who was to become famous in motor car history as the co-founder of Rolls-Royce. This young man lived for motoring and even in 1898 his "stable" consisted of a Bollée tricycle, and the ex-de Knyff Panhard-Levassor bought from Edge.

Making of a name

In Italy, where the early enthusiasts had worked in a country insensible to the lure of the motor car, a motor industry was now at last emerging, By 1898, the year in which a small group of Piedmont pioneers started what was to become the biggest Italian manufacturer, Fiat, and is now the largest in Europe, there were already a number of small workshops devoted to the production of cars. These included those of Miari and Giusti, of Padua, builders of Bernardi's car, Prinetti and Stucchi, who assembled De Dion-Bouton tricycles under licence, and the Milan bicycle factory of Edoardo Bianchi, who built a prototype cyclecar (series production of i.c. engined vehicles began some years later). The limited success of these companies was probably due then to the Italian passion for foreign goods rather than to any intrinsic defects. A strong personalty such as the former cavalry officer, Giovanni Agnelli, was

necessary before a home-produced car could overcome this tendency of the Italians.

The agreement out of which Fiat was born was between Agnelli, Count Emanuele Cacherano di Bricherasio, Count Roberto Biscaretti di Ruffia and the banker Gustave Deslex. The first prototype was constructed for the partners in 1899 by Giovanni Ceirano, a young motoring enthusiast from Turin who, with his brothers, had built up a flourishing cycle business. As soon as the 5 H.P. prototype had been approved, the company that was to build a model was soon formed, "Fabbrica Italiana Auto-

mobili Torino" (the Italian Motor Car Company, Turin), the initials giving the brand name F.I.A.T.

The first car of this company was similar to the prototype and had a twin-cylinder, 600 c.c. engine. The car, called the "3½ H.P.", had its engine mounted horizontally in the rear, with water cooling. The inlet valves were automatic, petrol being fed by gravity to the constant-level carburettor; ignition was by battery and coil. There were three gears. Transmission was by chain and differential and there was a leather clutch. The car had two hand brakes, one acting on the rear axle, the other on the rear wheels.

At the same time that Fiat was beginning its activities, a bicycle and sewing machine company, Orio & March-and in Piacenza, also started production of motor cars. It was destined to be well-known for a few years both inside and outside Italy, but was to disappear in 1909. In the meantime Prinetti & Stucchi, who had also moved to cars from sewing machines, added to their assembly

An 1895 Peugeot "vis-à-vis", with a horizontal twin-cylinder engine of 1,056 c.c. and three forward speeds plus reverse. Output was 8 H.P. and top speed 20 m.p.h.

An 1892 Peugeot "vis-à-vis" with a twin-cylinder engine.

A photograph and a drawing of the 1899 Fiat "3½ H.P.".

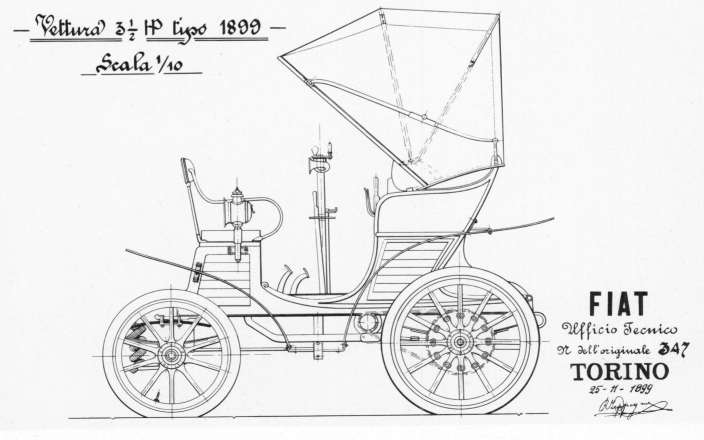

Vettura 3½ HP tipo 1899

Scala 1/10

FIAT
Ufficio Tecnico
N. dell'originale 347
TORINO
25-11-1899

of De Dion-Bouton tricycles the production of a new car designed by a certain Ettore Bugatti. It had a half-litre two-cylinder engine mountend forward, with two speeds.

Bee-hive radiator

In Germany Daimler radically modified its design in 1897, getting nearer and nearer to the motor car as known today. Among other features, the engine was mounted forward, the four wheels were given the same diameter, pneumatic tyres were fitted and the wheel replaced the tiller. The bee-hive radiator was adopted instead of the finned-tube type, and for the first time there was a starting handle.

In 1898 another motor company appeared, Adam Opel, converting to car production after many years of general engineering. The first car, a small 4 H.P., was followed by an Opel-Darracq in which a German engine was fitted to a French chassis.

In Belgium Goldschmidt founded the Compagnie Belge de Construction Automobiles, which took as its trade mark the symbol of a pipe. The Pipe was, for some twenty years, to be among the best cars in Europe. At the same time a number of other companies were formed — Dasse; Métallurgique; Henri Pieper; Lemaire & Paillot; Vincke; De Cosmo and Minerva.

In Austria manufacture was begun in the same year, 1898, of an unusual car by and old-established coach-builder, Jacob Lohner. The vehicle had a petrol engine but electric transmission and its designer was to figure prominently in motor car history. His name was Ferdinand Porsche.

On large scale

At this time, across the Atlantic there was impressive activity in the United States. The economic conditions which were being created were to take America to the forefront of world motor car production, at least so far as quantity was concerned. Almost from the beginning, manufacture was to be by large scale production methods that Europe was to know only many years later. At the end of the century America was discovering the importance of the motor car, not only as a vehicle but also as an industrial activity.

Its enthusiastic businessmen threw large sums of money into the industry of manufacturing cars with the near-certainty, rather than the hope, of success.

This part in the story of the motor car is that of men of enormous willpower who were able, above all due to the favourable economic climate, to achieve spectacularly swift success. In these ranks of courageous, ambitious men, the outstanding figure is that of Henry Ford.

A 1911 Isotta Fraschini Model B 28/35 H.P. Engine — front mounted 4 cylinder in two pairs. 130 × 150 mm. bore and stroke, 7,964 c.c. Ignition by high tension magneto. Output 30 H.P. at 1,000 r.p.m. Leather cone clutch, 4 speeds and reverse. Final drive by chains. Weight — 2,464 lbs.

PETROL INJECTION GAINS GROUND

Charging an internal combustion engine by the direct injection of petrol into the cylinders (direct injection) or into the inlet manifold (indirect injection) are not new ideas. Experiments to this end were begun in 1935 and 1936, above all by Daimler-Benz who were interested in applying the system to an aero-engine to permit it to go on working indefinitely even upside down, as in aerobatics.

This was not the only advantage of petrol injection as the engineers of the time knew perfectly well. These included better charging of the cylinders, and therefore more power or more economy; better cooling by injecting the fuel at the hottest points; elimination of flat spots in the power curve and better performance at low engine speeds.

The principal difficulties met by Daimler-Benz lay in the injectors. Each of these very fine jets has to spray, in a fraction of a second, a precise quantity of petrol at a pressure from 300 to 550 lb per square inch. Above all they work at high speed and must be efficiently lubricated without the oil interfering with the fuel.

Furthermore, they must continue to work efficiently for a long time.

These technical problems have long since been solved, but remain relatively costly to overcome and for this reason mainly, the carburettor is still widely used. Injection, however, is gradually gaining ground, being used by a certain number of companies such as Triumph, Lancia, Chevrolet, Jaguar, Maserati and Ferrari, apart from all constructors of racing cars where economic factors are less important.

The choice between direct and indirect systems is above all an economic one. In racing cars the former is almost always chosen because, other things being equal, it gives a higher specific output. For touring cars, however, the indirect system is usual, even though its advantages over the carburettor are less pronounced. This is because, apart from the fact that it is cheaper, the pump is smaller and much less noisy and because it can be used with engines designed for carburettors, which is not possible with direct systems. In this way it is possible to supply indirect injection as an extra or alternative to normal carburation.

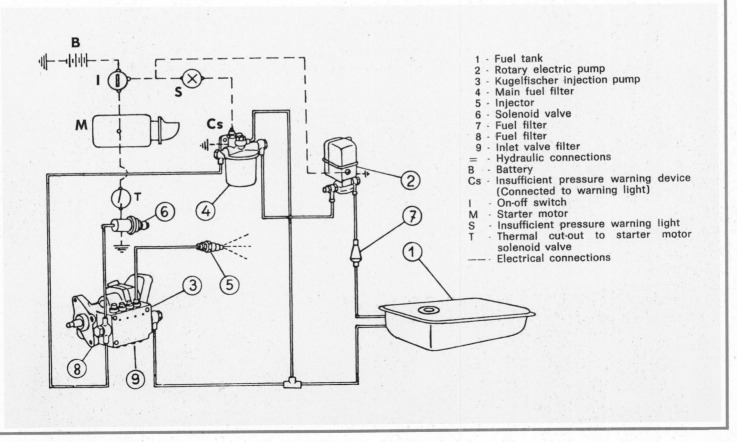

1 - Fuel tank
2 - Rotary electric pump
3 - Kugelfischer injection pump
4 - Main fuel filter
5 - Injector
6 - Solenoid valve
7 - Fuel filter
8 - Fuel filter
9 - Inlet valve filter
= - Hydraulic connections
B - Battery
Cs - Insufficient pressure warning device (Connected to warning light)
I - On-off switch
M - Starter motor
S - Insufficient pressure warning light
T - Thermal cut-out to starter motor solenoid valve
--- Electrical connections

Two publicity photographs of different eras. The one below was intended to underline the performance of the 1909 Buick.

CHAPTER FIVE
THE BIRTH OF A MARKET

It is 1895, the year of Duryea's victory in the Chicago-Evanston race. The influence of this race, so modest in itself, was powerful in its effects. The vast publicity it received from newspapers drew the attention of the American public to the new self-propelled vehicle and also stimulated a major industrial process.

The attitude of heroic pioneering — or dubious bravado, according to one's point of view — surrounding the early European manufacturers is difficult to find.

Nevertheless, at the same time that the future captains of the American motor industry were considering their first steps in the new business, other "old fashioned" figures were still in the limelight. They were motivated by passions similar to those of their colleagues in the old world.

Frank Duryea, fresh from his victory in the race, applied himself on three fronts. First was his business, destined to reach a total of only 13 production models

A car with an engine designed by Henry Leland, for the Detroit Automobile Company, from which idea was born the Cadillac Automobile Company, taking its name from the French explorer Antoine de la Mothe Cadillac, founder of Detroit.

of the famous tricycle, the first series production in American motoring history. Second was his role of roving ambassador for his company: in 1896 he crossed the Atlantic and founded with Henry Sturmey, Editor of The Autocar, the Duryea Motor Company in England, an enterprise which had no success and was finally wound up in 1908. His third activity was racing.

Horse lovers' war cry

Duryea took part in the New York-Irvington race organised by the editor of "Cosmopolitan", following the example of his journalist colleague of the "Chicago Times Herald" who had promoted the Chicago-Evanston. Thirty four machines were entered but only six started. An accident involving one of the four Duryea vehicles entered caused the arrest of the driver, and another driver was excluded for having knocked down a spectator.

The course of the race included a short hill with an appalling road surface where the competitors had to get out and push. From the public on that occasion was first heard the cry "Get a horse" which was to be heard on many similar occasions. It was to be the war cry of the enemies of the motor car for some years.

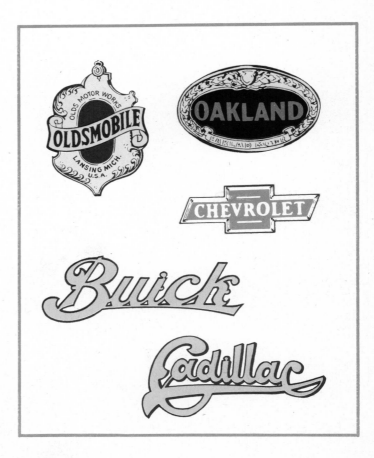

In September of the same year the first motor race on a track in America was run at Narrangansett horse racing course near Providence, Rhode Island; seven cars took part, five Duryeas and two electric cars.

The rules were unique — five circuits of a mile each, to be run as separate races. In the event, due to darkness which settled early on the track, it was possible to run only three races, with the inevitable protests from the back-markers who had counted on the last two races to improve their position. All three races were won by an electric Riker Electric Stanhope at an average of 27 m.p.h.

On the other side of the Atlantic there was an epic event in England, following the repeal of the Locomotives on Highways Act. The London-Brighton Run was staged on 14 November, 1896, and was appropriately called the "Emancipation Run". Duryea did not hesitate to go to England to take part — he had also commercial reasons for going — and publicly announced that he would beat the Bollée i.c. cars, considered to be the major threat, by at least an hour.

On this occasion, too, the outcome was confused. Due to the thousands of spectators who lined the route between London and the seaside town, it was not even possible to establish an order of arrival. The compet-itors had been forced to stop many times to avoid spectators. Duryea objected, claiming he should have been awarded the victory. His claim was not recognised, but he received gratifying publicity from the Press for his car, which aroused much interest in Europe.

Cars at the circus

The indefatigable Duryea quickly returned to America to appear with his now famous car in Barnum and Bailey's Big Top, between the Indian elephant act and the ape-man from Borneo. It was a resounding success, even though the rickety vehicle limited itself to a few circuits of the ring. The Franklin brothers, owners of a rival circus, quickly approached Charles King in Detroit, to obtain another horseless carriage with which they formed another equally successful act.

The same historic year, 1896, saw the introduction of the first i.c.-engined car in the U.S. and also the first American industrialist in the modern sense of the word — Ransom Eli Olds, a young man from Ohio who had established himself at Lansing in Michigan. After working on stationary petrol engines, he had had some experience with steam vehicles, building first a

A typical road of the period.

A NAME
OF ITS OWN

The name "Curved Dash" given to the early Oldsmobile was obviously derived from the existence of a handsome scroll-shaped front bulkhead of the car. The continued use of the name was probably due, however, to the fact that no one regarded it as a real car, because of the extreme simplicity of its appearance and its mechanical parts, coupled with its exceptional lightness. The car, in fact, was never given an official title by Ransom Eli Olds.

The christening of this famous car with its own name was to be repeated with the famous Ford "T" which, apart from its official designation, was known affectionately everywhere as "Lizzie".

The similarity with America's most famous car does not end here. The "Curved Dash" had all the attributes to achieve aesthetically what the model "T" Ford was to do later in terms of commercial success. It had also the necessary simplicity of construction which enabled it to

be sold at the then unheard of price of only $650. But Old's exciting industrial adventure with the "Curved Dash" was to be limited to a five-year boom, at the end of which production ceased, with output having reached the then incredible figure of 5,000 a year.

The mechanical components in this car were reduced to the minimum. There was a single horizontal cylinder engine mounted at the rear, trembler coil ignition, epicyclic gear change, chain drive, a rudimentary differential, leaf springing and light spoked wheels with pneumatic tyres. Steering was by tiller. Behind the two seats was a box which contained all the mechanical parts.

The "Curved Dash" could barely exceed 20 m.p.h. but because of its lightness (800 lb.) it was able to climb gradients impossible for other vehicles of the time. Its abilities in this aspect can be noted in the annual Commemorative Run from London to Brighton, when several can usually be seen among the entrants.

A 1903 Mercedes with a "Tonneau" body with access to the rear seats. In the background is a Thornycroft of the same year.

tricycle and then a four-wheeler. Olds was 30 years old when, in 1897, he went along the streets of Lansing in his first single-cylinder i.c.-engined car. A year later he built a more advanced vehicle and, feeling already capable of competing with Duryea's cars, the only ones so far produced in series, he went in search of financial aid.

Capital from his friends in Lansing was soon found to be insufficient for large scale production. At this point Olds received a visit from an acquaintance from Detroit, Samuel L. Smith, a scrap merchant, who said he was prepared to put up the capital to start a company provided it was situated in Detroit. It was due to this casual circumstance that the first U.S. motor company was established in Detroit, then a virtually unknown town a few miles from the Canadian border.

Birth of Oldsmobile

The beginnings of the new company, which took the name of Oldsmobile, were anything but promising. Eight thousand dollars were spent on prototypes, some electric, before some models were finally built. Some of these were light and some heavy, and it was the latter which were placed on a reluctant market at a price of $1,250 At the end of 1901 the factory caught fire due to the carelessness of a workman, who went to near a forge with a can of petrol, and in a few hours the entire plant was destroyed. Due to the courage and initiative of a young tester, J. J. Brady, the prototype of a new light vehicle that Olds had just completed was saved. It was this design in the months to come — thanks to Olds' tenacity and the support of his partners the factory was rebuilt — that was to be the basis of Oldsmobile's first great commercial succes.

The car, which soon acquired the famous name "Curved Dash" among American motorists due to the elegant contours of its front, was put on sale at $650, an act of commercial faith. The outcome was profitable; before the end of the year, 433 were on the roads in America. For 1902 Olds planned a production of 2,500, demonstrating both the enormous immediate potential of the

The Louis XIV interior of a 1927 Rolls-Royce Phantom, a masterpiece of elegance reminiscent of the horse-drawn era

If it were not for the plates showing the years, it would be difficult to tell which car is the earlier. Early body design was relatively slow and unadventurous. The 1905 car is a Peugeot with two seats for passengers and the driver behind. The single-cylinder 7 H.P. engine was capable of nearly 20 m.p.h. Below is an 1892 Peugeot four-seater "Victoria" with a twin-cylinder engine. With three speeds plus reverse, it could reach nearly 20 m.p.h.

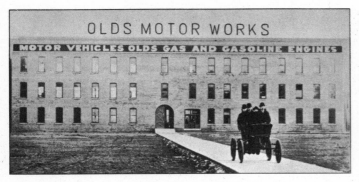

America's first motor factory, built in 1899.

American market and the initiative of its industrialists who were prepared to invest heavily in such a new product. In 1903 four thousand "Curved Dash" models were built, and in 1904 five thousand.

The next year saw the separation of Olds and his partner, Samuel Smith. More and more acute disagreements between them caused Olds to leave the company and start another, the Reo Motor Company, financed by his old friends in Lansing.

The Oldsmobile company continued its life until 1907, when it was absorbed by that of another great figure in American car history, William Crapo Durant.

By the service entrance

A curious episode forms part of the history of Oldsmobile. It concerns one of the journeys from coast to coast, along stretches of rough country, which in the early years of this century attracted the attention of the Press all over the world. The episode was in 1902 when, for publicity purposes, a young tester, Roy D. Chapin, undertook to make the long journey from Detroit to New York to arrive in time for the motor show in the city.

The journey took 7½ days in appalling conditions. The driver, partnered by John Maxwell, a future motor manufacturer, was forced to follow canal-side roads and many times risked being bogged in the mud.

When the "Curved Dash", which had suffered no damage during its adventures on the trip, finally reached Fifth Avenue in New York one of its wheels hit the kerb — and fractured. After making an emergency repair, Chapin succeeded in travelling the few hundred yards to the entrance of the Waldorf Astoria. He forgot, however, that he was masked in mud and that his clothes were filthy; the doorman refused him entry to the hotel. Thus Chapin (who was to become Secretary for Commerce under Herbert Hoover) reached the objective of his heroic adventure via the service entrance.

The great journeys which characterised motoring history of the time almost everywhere had begun several years earlier in America, with Alexander Winton's undertakings.

Winton, an ex-mechanic from Cleveland who built cars of his own design, succeeded in covering the 800 miles from his native city to New York in ten days, though the roads of America in 1897 were even less adequate than those of Europe. Two years later Winton repeated his exploit, covering the same route in exactly half the time.

From coast to coast

After Chapin's feat in 1902, the American public looked forward to other tests of endurance, which were well publicised by the newspapers. Doctor H. N. Jackson, of Bennington in Vermont, drove a Winton, accompanied by a mechanic, from San Francisco to New York between 23 May and 26 July, 1903. A month later the exploit was repeated by Tom Fetch in a single-cylinder Packard, "Old Pacific". He did the journey in 53 days, ten less than his predecessor. A few days later yet a third team, L. L. Whitman and E. T. Hammond, made the third crossing of the continent on the same route, this time in an Oldsmobile.

It is natural at this point to refer to the great European trials, in particular the most famous and adventurous motor car competition ever held, the legendary Pekin-Paris race, and an account of the race is given later.

In 1897 the imminent industrial boom was probably best exhibited by the activities of the Studebaker brothers in Michigan. Their activities were quickly to reach large scale production. The brothers were already the largest coachbuilders in the world and they visualized series production of several hundred vehicles at a time. It may be noted in passing that many of the existing

The famous "Curved Dash", illustrated in a brochure of the time, gave rise to a popular song "In My Merry Oldsmobile".

An Audibert et Lavirotte with horizontal twin cylinder 16 H.P. engine.

companies which converted to motor car production at that time did so from a field very different from that of Studebaker. In fact, many were manufacturers of bicycles, for which there was a huge market in America. The first Studebaker car, an electric one, was made in 1902. Also in 1897 other manufacturers — most of them destined to have little success, however — were building experimental cars in America. Amongst them were Louis S. Clarke and William Morgan, who founded the Pittsburgh Motor Vehicle Company (later renamed the Autocar Company), and Gilbert Loomis, a mechanic from Westfield in Massachusetts. In addition to building his own single-cylinder car, the latter passes into history as reputedly the first holder of a motor insurance policy. The premium was $7.50 and the maximum cover $1000, the contract being based on those for horse-drawn carriages.

Another company, the Pope Manufacturing Co. of Hartford, Connecticut, continued to produce electric "phaetons", the term used for many years in America to indicate large open four-wheelers and derived directly from the use of horse-drawn coaches. These vehicles were

A 1905 Rolls-Royce, with familiarly elegant gauges and detailed finish. This car was found on an Australian farm and restored.

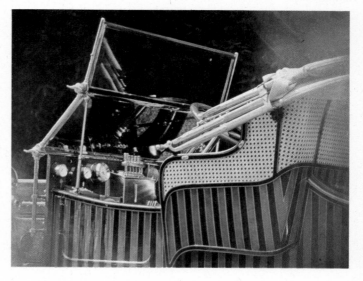

full-size craft to improve efficiency. They "contained" the air cushion more effectively than the air curtain, and permitted appreciable obstacle-clearance without fear of damage to the hard structure.

The hovercraft industry has come to achieve a high level of sophistication in the short period between 1956 and the present. Hovercraft of a number of different designs and capabilities are in use in many different parts of the world, ranging from the Canadian Arctic to the Persian Gulf.

One hovercraft operator on the South Coast has carried well over a million fare-paying passengers across the Solent since 1965.

So far all hovercraft yet manufactured have been designed for maritime applications, though most of them have a worthwhile amphibious capability. Whether there will ever be suitable vehicles for exclusively overland operation depends, to a large extent, on whether there is a pressing need for them in that role.

Hovercraft on roads?

If so, the present problems, such as skirt wear and the ingestion of dust and sand, would quickly be overcome. Perhaps one possibility at present being explored by a potential purchaser may point the way ahead. An Australian is studying the purchase of a number of hovercraft to connect locations in the outback; he is confident that a fleet of fast hovercraft would be much less costly than the construction of many hundreds of miles of roads.

As regards the use of hovercraft on congested urban roads, little is being done at the moment. A true hovercraft (that is, one completely clear of the ground) would not be sufficiently easy to steer to permit its use on crowded roads, but a wheeled vehicle with a cushion of air to take most of the weight has many attractive features.

The next ten years of hovercraft development are likely to be as spectacular as the first decade of this century proved to be in the case of the "revolutionary" motor car.

An outstanding pilot, Prince Bernhard of the Netherlands, at the controls of a Vickers VA-2 hovercraft.

A gymkhana organized at the first National Automobile Show in New York.

The last of the four shows in 1900 was also the most important. It carried the seal of authority as it was organised by the American Automobile Club. At this Automobile Show in Madison Square Gardens, New York, 34 makes exhibited, 19 having petrol engines, seven being steam powered, and six electric, whilst there were two with mixed propulsion — i.c. engine and electricity.

Going up the ramp

Ironically, the biggest attraction was outside the show, due to the initiative of John Brisbane Walker, editor of the magazine "Cosmopolitan" and manufacturer of motor cars. Not being able to obtain space inside the show, he hired the hanging garden itself and built a ramp, up which he ran Mobile steamers 20 times a day from ground to roof.

As a result of the show's success, the Automobile Club decided to prolong a part of it and in a special pavilion they exhibited a dozen so-called "veteran" cars, including the 1890 Nadig and the 1893 Duryea. Even in the youthful days of motoring, age had its attractions!

The first Vauxhall, in 1903.

BUILDING IN SAFETY

General concern throughout the world with road and vehicle safety is comparatively recent. In the absence of the ability to improve significantly the safety of the highways themselves, because of economic difficulties, most of the burden of reducing road dangers rests on automotive manufacturers and users.

Whether the roads system is good or bad, an obligatory and minimal requirement for vehicles is that they should steer and they should be able to stop in an emergency. These have been the basic qualifications for roadworthiness since the days of the horseless carriage and, legally, they are the same today in most European countries. The motorist, it must be added, has to have lighting equipment that works reasonably well.

Compared with the large, fast and relatively clumsy American cars, European cars have generally been inherently safer over the years to meet the challenge of more complex road and traffic conditions.

It says much for the sense of responsibility of the European motor industry that the safety factors engineered into the modern car go far beyond the legal requirements. It is from America that there now comes a wave of social and industrial preoccupation in matters of vehicle safety.

Head-on Impact

The number of possible sources of injury due to driving motor cars is perhaps bewildering. An analysis of the subject inevitably focuses on the more obvious and dramatic aspects, and then takes in the countless other factors in decreasing order of urgency.

In a recent report, for instance, the Road Research Laboratory suggested that the most important type of accident for which protection was required was the head-on collision and that the way to improve passenger protection lay through the use of better seat belts designed as integral parts of the seats, matched by appropriate crushing characteristics in the front part of the car.

It is estimated that by these methods it may be possible to guard largely against serious injury in head-on impacts at 50 m.p.h. Protection obtainable by elaborate re-design of the whole vehicle, but without using seat belts or their equivalent, is inevitably much inferior. In effect, the recommendations relate primarily to improvements to safety belts, and to changing the shape of the passenger compartment as well as increasing its strength.

The interior view of the famous 1963 Pininfarina's Sigma with the sliding door open.

A prototype of a safety seat on which research and development tests were carried out before production of the final design.

At a world conference on road safety in Brussels last year, suggestions were advanced for replacing webbing restraints by insolvolumetric systems (i.e. by means of a pneumatic bag, plastically deformable padding applied during impact, large area netting restraints, etc.).

Defects of seat belts might be offset by fitting a polyurethane energy absorber at the anchorage. It uses a shock sheath in which the passenger is bound by textile restraint and whereby, during a crash, the seat moves forward and is slowed down by an energy-absorbing device. In the latter system, decelerations are two or three times less than with seat belts, and the risk of whip-lashing disappears.

At the conference the project for the New York safety car was presented. The aim of this undertaking is to design and fabricate a prototype car embodying all feasible safety devices that are practical for limited mass production. The car will have a forward 260 H.P. engine, and gross vehicle weight of 5,100 lb. and combined front and rear wheel traction. It will give the driver an all-round visual field, partly through a periscope system. The safety car will withstand the loads associated with a 70 m.p.h. uncomplicated roll-over.

Divergence in design

There are still wide contradictions, both in theory and practice, where design for safety is concerned. Whilst many designers will admit of no argument against the practice of having a strong main central body section with deformable front and rear sections, others continue to use thin panelling in main locations. Some advocate the use of glass fibre and new types of alloy, for central as well as the end sections; one high-performance car even has a body with a plywood basic structure.

It was the famous Italian designer Pininfarina, with the famous Sigma safety car, who was largely responsible for popularising the graduated-resistance theory for body construction. The bonus to safe collapsibility came with his contention that "if a collision were severe enough to rip the engine from its mountings and drive it towards the passengers, it would be deflected and directed downwards beneath the car, where it could not cause injury".

This car has many other important safety features. Not the least important is the diffused lighting behind the grille to stress the outline of the car to other road users. The entire interior of the car is well padded; an outstanding feature is the use of sliding doors, well proven on commercial vehicles. Screens and glasses are ejectable, the latter in case the doors should jam after deformation. As an exercise in body design the Pininfarina car is not notable for mechanical safety features, but the steering gear, column and wheel were given special attention.

Minimising Risk

Primary and secondary safety are highlighted in BMC's 1800 model. The former aspect is defined as safety incorporated in the design, in order to minimise risk

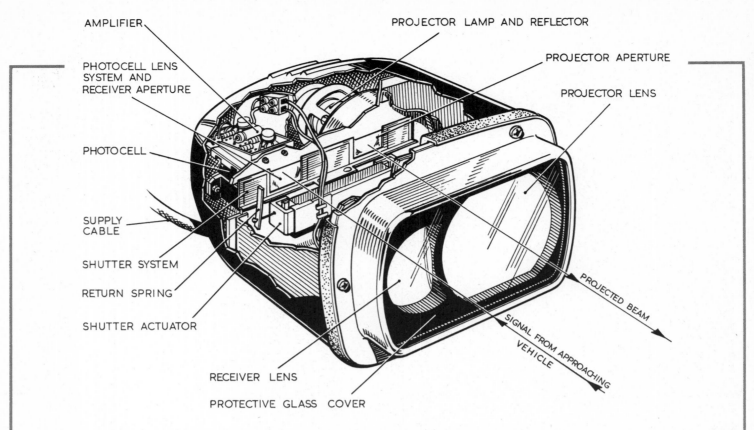

AMPLIFIER

PHOTOCELL LENS
SYSTEM AND
RECEIVER APERTURE

PHOTOCELL

SUPPLY
CABLE

SHUTTER SYSTEM

RETURN SPRING

SHUTTER ACTUATOR

PROJECTOR LAMP AND REFLECTOR

PROJECTOR APERTURE

PROJECTOR LENS

PROJECTED BEAM

SIGNAL FROM APPROACHING
VEHICLE

RECEIVER LENS

PROTECTIVE GLASS COVER

A cut-away view of a Lucas "Autosensa", which automatically dips the beam when the headlight from a vehicle coming in the opposite direction strikes the receiver alongside the beam projector.

of collision involvement; and the latter as safety incorporated to protect the occupants after collision.

The primary safety aspects are a front engine, contributing to directional stability under all conditions, especially gusty weather; front-wheel drive for optimum road-holding; independent suspension on the Hydrolastic principle, contributing to good driver control; and braking system with servo-unit and incorporating an anti-lock valve for rear brakes giving optimum compensation.

The secondary safety features comprise an all-steel body with exceptionally high torsional stiffness and robust construction; immensely strong cross-tube in front of the passenger compartment which, together with the transversely-mounted front engine, gives high crash-protection to occupants; rack and pinion steering located to give maximum protection in a crash; fuel tank concealed below the rear boot floor, giving it maximum protection in a crash; and seat belt anchorages built in as standard equipment.

Simulation Tests

In both America and Europe, General Motors and its associated companies have been particularly active in researching and programming for safety. It is as long ago as 1924 that the GM proving ground was opened at Milford; in 1933 the first barrier impact tests were started and the scientific study of crash injuries began. Ten years ago the automatic vehicle guidance system was tested and in 1962 the first impact sled built for simulated crash tests. In these tests, GM study systems for holding in passengers, the door latches and hinges and seat retention.

Passenger kinematics — how passengers move under impact conditions — are also under examination. These trials are now to be augmented by Vauxhall Motors, which is to install a sled in a new safety test laboratory. It will be the first to go into operation in Europe and similar to those in use in America. The research rig will supplement outdoor barrier-type impact facilities and safety test equipment currently used by Vauxhalls.

New safety on the race-track: the 1969 Ferrari-Pininfarina-Automobil Revue "Sigma Grand Prix".

A 1903 Oldsmobile "Pirate". Below the first Chevrolet, built in 1912. Louis Chevrolet, famous as a racing driver in the early years of the century, was persuaded by W.C. Durant to design a new engine. From this partnership were born the Chevrolet car and company.

The joys of the open car and the open road — but not only the weather must be fine. While the modern couple can relax, a testing time faced early manufacturer Adolphe Clement and passengers (below) about to leave home for a drive in the country. Masks are functional: only the mechanic has his face unprotected against the dust.

CHAPTER SIX
MUD AND DUST BELOW ZERO

At the dawn of the century, when the first car factories were being built in Europe and the U.S., considerable technical progress had been made after the first twenty years. So far as the engines were concerned, two cylinders were most frequently used. Many solutions, differing widely one from another, were to be found with each manufacturer trying to avoid each other's patents.

Thus there were side-by-side twins such as the Gobron and Décauville, and horizontally opposed "flat twins", but many manufacturers built single-cylinder engines. De Dion was a convinced adherent of this simpler form, as was the youthful Packard in America, who obstinately refused advice to build a twin (it was Packard who was to put into series production fifteen years later a 12-cylinder engine!).

In 1900 four-cylinder engines were just passing from the experimental phase to that of production. French engineers were prominent in this respect. Forest was experimenting with multi-cylinder engines for marine use, including an in-line six. Mors, noted for his racing cars, built the first practical Vee-4 in 1897, and Tent-ing, an ex-Peugeot driver, was building big four-cylinder engines.

Without exception, these engines adopted automatic inlet valves but positively actuated exhaust valves. Ignition was generally by hot-tube though electrical systems were gaining popularity. The magneto was invented simultaneously in this period by Frederick Simms in England and Robert Bosh in Germany, opening a new chapter in motoring. Also at this time the Frenchman Claudel invented the so-called "submerged" carburettor, in which the jet was situated below the level of the petrol in the float chamber.

Wheel differences

The year 1900 marked a turning point: henceforth coachbuilders no longer looked back to the horse-drawn era, but started to study the motor car as an entity. Thus some of the vehicles built at that time had wheels of equal diameter, while the rest had wheels with substantial differences between front and rear. Pneumatic tyres had already almost completely replaced solid ones, but most wheels were still similar to those of carriages, with thick wooden spokes. Nevertheless, light spoked wheels were appearing on many smaller cars.

By this time the engine was nearly always at the front, hidden by the finned-tube radiator. Already there was the choice, which still exists today, of air or water cooling. The steering wheel had been adopted instead

Passengers in a De Dion-Bouton receive an old-world greeting.

A 1902 Gillet Forest overtaking a stationary 1899 Haynes-Apperson, appropriately beflagged, on a London to Brighton Run.

An 1895 5 seater Peugeot V-2. The 1,645 c.c. engine developed 12 H.P. There were four speeds plus reverse and a leather cone clutch. Top speed about 20 m.p.h.

of the tiller by almost all manufacturers. There was, however, the widest variety in coachwork, every builder having his own ideas. Some did not supply a body at all, limiting themselves to producing only the mechanical chassis.

Starting handles were fitted on most cars. A fracture of the wrist was to constitute one of the occupational hazards of motoring for another quarter of a century, due to backfiring of the engine at the moment of ignition.

Furs, goggles and gauntlets

The cars of 1900 were nearly all open — the Renault enclosed driving position had remained unique, an eccentricity viewed with amusement — and this meant that the driver was exposed to all weathers. This was the reason for the bearskins, still impressive in today's yellowed photographs, and explains their function: it was the only way to keep warm. This was in spring or autumn (in the depths of winter it was better to give up the idea altogether, in view of the condition of the roads).

A 1903 Mercedes "Simplex" tourer with 4 cylinder 28/32 H.P. engine giving a top speed of nearly 40 m.p.h.

The masks, the mufflers, the goggles were all strictly practical accessories often hiding the entire face under the flat, peaked cap worn to fight another terrible enemy, dust.

In the first motoring magazines is found straightforward technical advice ("it is essential to drain the radiator water after each journey, and during pauses it should be kept warm by starting up the engine briefly every twenty minutes or so"), beside invaluable remedies for burns from the exhaust pipe, a process for waterproofing driving clothes, a prescription for "driver's eyesalve" (1 lb cocoa leaf brewed, 1 oz. cherry laurel water, ½ oz. sodium borate), a method to prevent steaming of goggles (smear the insides with glycerine) and instructions for cleaning dusty furs at the end of a journey. Fashion advised semi-opaque veiling for lady motorists, with a tiny transparent opening over the eyes.

While fashion played its part, especially for the ladies, the more serious affairs of racing held the masculine interest. It was not always an occasion for celebration. In 1898, during the Périguex-Bergerac-Périguex race, the Marquis de Montegnac lost control of his car as he waved to another competitor, Montarid, who was overtaking him. The other car collided with his and the marquis was killed instantly. Some months later Mayade, winner of the Paris-Marseilles two years earlier, was also killed.

In Italy in 1898 Luigi Storero won the Torino-Asti-Alessandria-Torino race, which might be considered the first real motor race in Italy, after the relatively unimportant Arona-Stresa of the previous year. In fact a Torino-Asti-Torino race had been held three years before, but it was so slow that the five competitors were overtaken by a group of cyclists.

From Seine to the North Sea

The most important competition of 1898 was the Paris-Amsterdam-Paris, organised by the Automobile Club de France with detailed regulations. It comprised both

A 1904 Roy drives in with suitably accoutred occupants.

Benz "Victoria" in the 1895 Paris-Bordeaux.

The sellers of useful car accessories were quick off the mark.

Cars are losing the "motorised carriage" look and becoming more functional. Above — a 1904 FIAT "16/24 H.P." and below a 1901 FIAT "8 H.P." in which the radiator was still a finned tube. Note the gear change, brake levers and the huge single headlamp.

1892 Peugeot with 1,645 c.c. twin cylinder engine, leather cone clutch and chain drive. Below a Daimler proudly bears its age.

what is now called a rally and an out-and-out race. It was held in three stages between the 7 and 9 July over a total of 820 miles. There were 26 and 29 entrants for the "tourist competition" and the race respectively. The first competition proceeded smoothly, but the second ran into great difficulties with the police, whose first requirement was that every competitor should have a certificate of origin. Because hardly any driver had one, they ordered the race to be postponed. The drivers were so determined to proceed, however, that a detachment of hussars and a troop of artillery were sent to Champigny, where the start was to take place, and barred the road with an impressive show of armed force!

The drivers therefore discreetly moved to Villiers-sur-Marne, a town in the Département of Seine-et-Oise and therefore outside the jurisdiction of the police representative M. Bochet, who had imposed the ban. From there they expected to set out at once for Château d'Ardennes, the finish of the first stage.

Fashion and function are offered as attractions to cold weather motorists in this advertisement for an all-purpose muffler.

Certain idiosyncrasies were born early. In 1903 Lord Russell waited all night to get the first numberplate, A1.

They raced, they bounced and often they turned over. There were no road patrols in those days!

A 1906 Edwardian Ford gets police direction in Rome.

In fact, when they arrived at Villiers they found that the drums of petrol to be used for the first stage were still at Champigny. So Amédée Bollée set off on a dangerous raid, going back to Champigny and securing the drums from under the noses of the guards. At last, the drivers set off.

One competitor, Richard, had 14 punctures between Paris and the first village, Epernay; another, Koechlin, finished in a canal near Maastricht and had to return to Paris in a schoolboy's suit, all he could find to replace his own sodden clothes.

There was a major complication on the return journey. When the 26 surviving machines reached Verdun the competitors were required to turn on to the road for Corbeil and Versailles. It was a subtle move by M. Bochet, who was already preparing for his revenge when the speeding cars finally entered his area of authority. But once again he had reckoned without the resource of the drivers. They simply refused to continue, and

A F.I.A.T. 130 H.P. - F2 - prototype prepared for the 1907 French Grand Prix.

RACING-MOTORING'S TESTBED

It is all very spectacular, colourful and thrilling, with awe-inspiring noises and the drama of the fight for the lead, but what use is motor racing to the ordinary motorist and the ordinary motor car?

The simplest answer is that racing is the forcing house of car design, the great accelerator of design development which, by the varying stresses it imposes on a vehicle, brings out the virtues and the faults more quickly. It may be argued that these could be discovered equally well on manufacturers' road test programmes, but these simply prove the design in hand; racing brings out the best design, not just for speed, but for reliability, road-holding, good handling and safety. If it does not have these, a car cannot win.

Trial and error

In the beginning, car designing was very much a groping in the dark; there was no yardstick to work by, nothing to say the engine should be at the back or the front or amidships, that the transmission should be belt, chain or shaft. These things had to be found out, often painfully and expensively.

The first motor races, exciting manifestations of a new travel medium though they were, were also admirable in forcing design towards greater efficiency. To survive the early town-to-town races, cars had to be tough, and breakages soon taught the manufacturers to strengthen their engines, brakes, axles, wheels and other components.

Then, as competition between makes intensified, racing taught them to get more power from their engines, the twin-cylinder engines became fours, valve gear was improved, and crankshaft speeds went up. Tiller steering rapidly yielded place to the steering wheel, spoon-type cart brakes gave way to more efficient ones, and tyre design advanced by sheer compulsion.

All the best makes raced in the early days — Panhard, Peugeot, Benz, Mercedes, Fiat, Renault and others; even Rolls-Royce, had their fling, and won races. Each of these manufacturers learned invaluable lessons which they applied to their production touring cars.

The greatest value of racing to the designer is the speed with which it brings defects to light. The private owner of a private car uses it carefully to avoid trouble and wear; design faults can take months to manifest themselves under such gentle usage, but in racing there is no mollycoddling. The pressure is on, the driver is out to beat the opposition, and every part of his car is under maximum stress. A faulty clutch, defective brakes, weak castings, poor tyres... such things soon come to light in the crucible of racing.

Components improved

No doubt steady development without racing would eventually have established automobile design principles much as they are today, but racing accelerated the process. Having proved the principle more quickly, racing since the pioneer days has played a vital part in the development and improvement of various components. The tenet that "the racing car of today is the touring car of tomorrow", coined in the 20s, may seem hard to substantiate when comparing the two today, but it is the principles beneath the svelte lines of a racing car which reappear in refined form in subsequent road cars that uphold it.

They have done so now for many years. Engine design benefited enormously from racing in the first two decades of the century, the twin overhead camshaft layout which speeds the modern Jaguar, Lotus Elan, Alfa Romeo and other high-performance cars was pioneered by Peugeot for racing in 1912. Four wheel brakes, a sine qua non to safety on modern roads, were tried on touring cars in 1909-10 and failed, were retried and made to work on racing cars, then re-introduced to touring cars, successfully this time.

All-round suspension

Hydraulic brakes, today taken for granted, were first proved through racing, when the American Duesenbergs came to Europe in 1921 and won the French Grand Prix — to the horror of the French. Shock absorbers, those unseen servants which damp the unpleasant bounce of suspension springs, came directly from racing early in the century. All-round independent suspension was proved to the world on the German

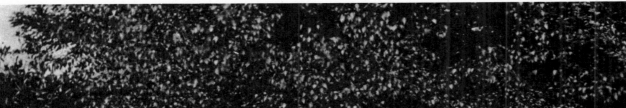

A 1908 Austin 100 H.P., with six cylinders, about ten litres, forerunner of the Grand Prix model.

A cut-away view of a 1969 Ferrari-Pininfarina-Automobil Revue "Sigma Grand Prix".

Mercedes-Benz and Auto Union Grand Prix cars of 1934-39.

The superiority of disc brakes, now widely used, was established by Jaguar's overwhelming 1953 victory at Le Mans. Fuel injection helped Mercedes-Benz to world championships in 1954 and 1955, brought Vanwall and Britain several valorous Grand Prix wins in 1957-58, and today appears in Mercedes, Triumph, Peugeot and other saloon cars.

Wheels, tyres, brake linings, steering, valve gears, torsion bars, light alloys, streamlining, fuels and lubricants, glass fibre bodywork... development of all these was advanced immeasurably by motor racing; because it constitutes the quickest, most ruthless and searching testbed of all for the motor industry.

One British concern which fully appreciates this is Ford of Dagenham, who compete extensively in saloon car racing, sports car racing, and Formula 1, 2 and 3 single-seater racing. Another is British Leyland, who in 1969 are running a team of Mini-Coopers in saloon car events, and have more ambitious plans for the future.

In the U.S.A. Ford, Plymouth and Dodge are among the most active makes in competition. Further afield, the Japanese value the experience of racing in the saloon and sports categories, too. In all these instances one may be sure that publicity is not the sole benefit of success; the manufacturers learn quicker how to make better cars.

Aerofoil innovation

Today the great innovation in racing is the aerofoil or "wing", a controversial attachment which some wish to see banned as an unpractical "blind alley" development taking design into a dimension beyond practical motoring bounds.

Others ardently support it for the benefits it imparts to performance. The wing puts downward pressure on the wheels, making the car hold the road better and corner more effectively at high speeds. If it can do this for racing cars, say its supporters, it could do so for fast road cars by embodying an aerofoil in the roof or straddling the tail.

Should this prove effective, then motor racing will have contributed one more useful factor to road safety. Should it prove wanting, then motor racing will have proved that too. There lies the hidden value of the sport.

Tazio Nuvolari after the start in the 1936 "300 Miles" at Westbury, U.S.A.

A 1901 Progress finishes triumphant in the London-Brighton Run.

City to city trials were common in Great Britain in the early years. The photograph shows officials and members of the Automobile Club of Great Britain and Ireland (now the R.A.C.) in their cars before a heavy vehicle trial in June, 1901.

the Automobile Club agreed to finish the race at Mont-géron, outside the jurisdiction of the Paris Préfecture and M. Bochet. The cars then drove slowly to Versailles, being careful to give the police not the slightest excuse for interference.

Interest in the Paris-Amsterdam-Paris was not limited to the results, but also indicated the social attitudes of the time. Racing drivers in particular, and motorists in general, found a section of the public nursed a fierce antipathy towards them. This was not entirely without cause, perhaps, in view of the manoeuvres by some drivers in the presence of a public who were not yet accustomed to their vehicles and who therefore considered themselves exposed to considerable danger.

The police often gave official backing to such a reaction. But the obstacles placed by authority only served to develop the spirit of motoring supporters.

First 'Round France' race

The year 1898 closed with a minor hill-climb at Gaillon in France which is memorable for one fact. It was won by Ettore Bugatti at the wheel of a car built by himself in the workshops of Prinetti and Stucchi. The same name appeared in first place in the tricycle class of the Verona-Mantova-Brescia-Verona race the following years, while the car category was won by another famous driver — Giovanni Agnelli, founder of Fiat — in a Phénix.

The next year passes into history as the year of the first motor tour of France. The Automobile Club of that country had decided to organise a much tougher race than those of the past in view of the growing robustness of cars then being manufactured. They organised, there-fore, a race to be run in seven stages over three quarters of France for a distance of 1,375 miles, including hill sections.

Two major "stables" took part in the race — Panhard-Levassor with eight 12 and 16 H.P. cars, and Bollée with four 20 H.P. models having independent front suspension. This time there were no incidents, though many competitors, including Jenatzy who was to set up the world's speed record in that year, had a fantastic number of breakdowns but still finished the race.

Mountain stages

The principal problem for all competitors was that of punctures due to the poor roads in the mountain stages. The result was a triumph for Panhard-Levassor, led by René de Knyff, who won in his 16 H.P. at an average speed of over 30 m.p.h. A Bollée finished fifth, behind three more Panhards, a Panhard was sixth, and a Mors seventh.

A success similar to Panhard's was achieved by the Renault 1 ¾ H.P. in two other races, the Paris-Ostend and the Paris-Rambouillet-Paris.

In all these cases the results of the races were reflected immediately in increased sales, a confirmation of the commercial as well as the technical importance of racing.

Three Edwardians in the Monte Carlo "Tour de la Principauté" in 1966. From top to bottom — a 1909 Rolland-Pilain, a 1908 Clément and a 1910 Lion Peugeot.

Above — a 1917 Ford "T" coupé. Below — a 1926 model. Built nine years apart, the two cars are almost identical.

The year 1900 marked the first Gordon Bennett Cup race. This famous race was run to regulations which seem quite usual today, but which were a major innovation at the time. For the first time vehicles were classified by their characteristics. These races were held over a number of years and are associated with the first period of "maturity" of the motor car.

James Gordon Bennett was the wealthy son of the owner of the "New York Herald" and lived in Paris, managing the European edition of that paper. A challenge thrown out by the American manufacturer Alexander Wenton to Fernand Charron gave Gordon Bennett the idea for his trophy.

Gordon Bennett decided that the only way to resolve the matter was to organise a race between the two countries' manufacturers. A condition which was to give rise to much criticism was that requiring cars to be built entirely in their country of origin.

The Gordon Bennett Cup was formally instituted a short time later by its promoter. He invited the seven existing national clubs — those of France, Germany, Great Britain, Belgium, Austria-Hungary, Switzerland, and Italy to nominate official teams. The regulations required that no team should consist of more than three cars.

The race was first held in France over a course of just over 340 miles; it was to be held each year in future in the country which had won the cup the year before (a formula similar to that of today's Davis Cup in tennis). A difficulty was that few nations could enter teams because of the requirement that cars should be built entirely in the countries they represented. This restriction included accessories and even tyres.

The Automobile Club de France decided on a course on the route Paris-Chartres-Orléans-Nevers-Moulins-Roanne-Lyon, and appointed as its representatives De Knyff, Charron and Garardot. Winton himself represented America. Germany decided on two Benz and a Canello-Durkopp and Belgium a team of Bolides. On this occasion for the first time national colours were given — blue for France, yellow for Belgium, white for Germany and red for America (red was later to be used also by Italy).

As usual, a much smaller number appeared at the start line — the three French contestants, the Belgian Jenatzy in a Bolide and Winton in one of his own cars.

The race began with an unexpected complication — the unauthorised participation of a private entry, Levegh, who proposed to beat them all. In fact, he won the first stage to Orléans by half an hour but then no more was seen of him. Breakdowns made the course difficult for all competitors. Jenatzy was late and Winton went out of the race at Orléans, so there remained only the three Frenchmen, of whom Charron had a broken half-shaft, Girardot had steering trouble and De Knyff's gearchange would not work. Each of them was aware of the others' situation and each tried hard to stay in the race and be the one to win the cup for France.

Round the trees

As if mechanical troubles did not present enough problems, there soon came more from another source. Dogs seemed to be maddened by the noise of the cars and frequently threw themselves under the wheels, often killing themselves but also causing damage to the cars. Charron had already killed at least five when, leaving the village of Arbresle, an enormous St. Bernard jumped on his Panhard and damaged the steering. At over 60 m.p.h., the car jumped a ditch, circled two trees and rushed down the road in the opposite direction. Fournier, Charron's mechanic, succeeded once again in getting the car back in the race. They finally reached Lyon, after having averaged about 39 m.p.h., beating Girardot by an hour and 27 minutes, after he also had been delayed by steering troubles. Thus finished the first race for the Gordon Bennett Cup, with the exciting and eventful victory of the French representatives.

The first Alfa built after the break with Darracq — the 24 H.P. built from 1910 to 1915. It had a 4,084 c.c. 4 cylinder engine which produced 42 H.P. at 2,200 r.p.m.

THE FIRST MERCEDES

The name of the 1901 Mercedes, which many enthusiasts regard as one of the first "modern" motor cars, was chosen not by the man who built it but by the one who was about to sell it. It involved the dropping of the famous name of Daimler, which to that date had been applied to all the products of the factory at Cannstatt.

Publicity

To the ears of the man concerned, Emile Jellinek, an Austrian banker, the name sounded too Germanic and ugly. So the new car designed by Wilhelm Maybach was called Mercedes, the name of Jellinek's daughter.

Jellinek was the Daimler representative for the Côte d'Azur, and the new car owed much to him as he had requested its design. The Nice week with its local motor race was a few months ahead, and Jellinek wanted to strengthen his position as a car salesman. He was keen to obtain useful publicity from the race.

To win, however, it was necessary to have something more powerful than the 24 h.p. Phenix then in production at Cannstatt, and the 35 H.P. Mercedes was the result. Jellinek contracted to buy 36 of the new model — a huge figure for the time — and to undertake distribution in France, Belgium, Austria-Hungary and the U. S.

Maybach, who had been for some time the important figure at Cannstatt though often overshadowed even now by the aging Daimler, who died in 1900, met the challenge with a car full of new ideas. It was to be the inspiration for cars for many years to come.

For the first time the chassis was of pressed steel. The engine was mounted in front under a true bonnet, in front of which was one of the first honeycomb radiators which had begun to replace the fragile finned tubes. It was a four-cylinder in-line of nearly six-litre capacity; all the valves were mechanically operated and ignition was by magneto. The gearchange was the selective gate type. The 35 B.H.P. developed was enough to give it a good chance in the Nice-Salon-Nice race and in other races yet to come.

The first models were already in production and the problem of a name raised by Jellinek, was still unsolved.

Famed beauty

"Mercedes" was an acceptable solution. Fräulein Jellinek herself was a beauty famous all over the Côte d'Azur, though it seemed cronic that Gottlieb Daimler's name should be dropped when he was mortally ill. Daimler, however, died soon after, and any possible embarrassment was avoided.

The Nice race, won by Werner, was a triumph for the Mercedes, which was much admired. So was the flesh and blood "Mercedes" who had a warm ovation from the grandstand. For many years Maybach's "white jewel" (nearly all of the models were in this colour) was synonymous with prestige among wealthy Europeans.

8547 CH 75

Circuits as well as cars have improved over the years. Above is a Formula III Lotus-Ford on a modern track. Below an Opel racing model rounds a bend in the 1914 French Grand Prix.

CHAPTER SEVEN

CAPITAL-TO-CAPITAL RACES

In 1901 most of the important races were again in France; and if the routes were international, these races were also organised there. The first of the latter was the Grand Prix de Pau, which was held in the middle of February.

Opinion at that time was divided among manufacturers as to the ideal racing car from the point of view of weight. Race regulations varied; one race classified cars into as many as four groups according to weight.

The results of the Grand Prix de Pau demonstrated a success for the protagonists of the voiturette, or light car. The heaviest category was won by Maurice Farman in a 24 H.P. Panhard, while that for medium cars was won by his brother Henri in a 12 H.P. Darracq. Louis Renault won the light car class in one of his own voiturettes. (The racing exploits of Louis and his brother Marcel were to be impressive in days when it was not unusual for an industrialst to drive his own products in races.) The following month the Nice-Salon-Nice race was run, in which Emile Jellinek entered the new 35 H.P. Daimler named after his daughter Mercedes, and won with Werner at the wheel.

The second Gordon Bennett Cup race followed. It will be remembered that the regulations permitted three cars from each nation and required that these should be entirely built in the country they represented. This latter regulation was bitterly resented by those manufacturers it excluded.

For the second Gordon Bennett it was not possible to change the regulations, but it was possible to lessen their effect by running it in conjunction with a second edition of the Paris-Bordeaux to which the disputed rule did not apply.

The 1901 Paris-Bordeaux: Renault team: Louis Renault, Marcel Renault, Oury and Grus.

Thus, though there were a considerable number of participants, only a small proportion were competing for the Gordon Bennett Cup; the distance to be covered was 525 kilometres (328 miles). Some of the drivers achieved miracles of improvisation. Baras reached the finish with his engine tied to the chassis with electrical wire.

The race was won by Fournier, who had figured in the first Gordon Bennett as Charron's mechanic. His Mors averaged more than 50 m.p.h. The technical progress made over the previous six years may be gauged from

the fact that the 1895 Paris-Bordeaux race was won by Levassor in his Panhard at only 15 m.p.h.

Behind the Mors were five 40 H.P. Panhards. The touring category was won by another Panhard, a 12 H.P. driven by Giraud, ahead of three Darracqs. The light car category was won, as usual, by Renault; Louis and Marcel, Oury and Grus took the first four places in that order.

A short while afterwards the Paris-Toulose-Paris race was run, in three exhausting stages, over a total of 710 miles, mostly on poor roads. In the light car category only Renaults finished the race. One of the two

The 1903 Paris-Madrid. Marcel Renault and Vauthier entering the fatal curve at Couhé-Vérac at 80 m.p.h.

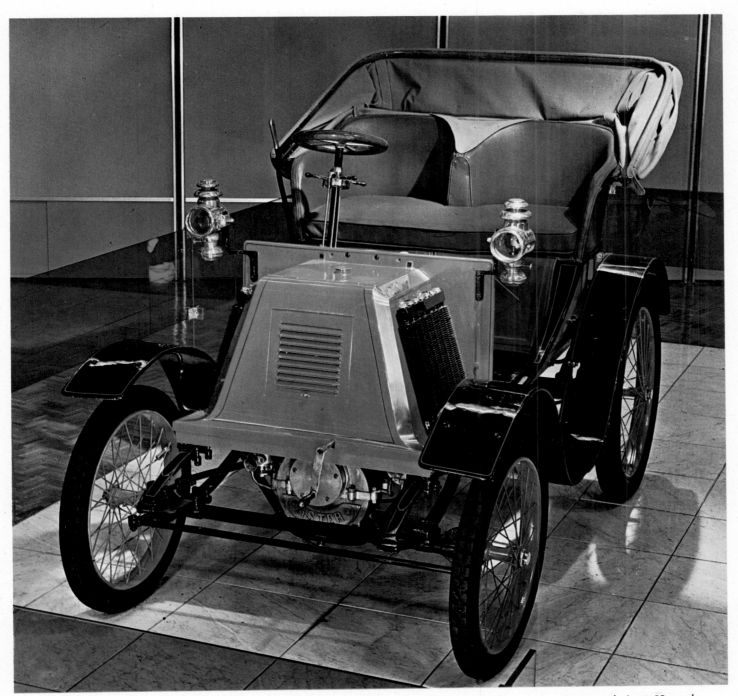

A 1901 Renault voiturette "type D" Single cylinder 450 c.c. engine with three speeds plus reverse. Top speed about 28 m.p.h.

famous brothers, Louis, was injured but managed to keep his badly damaged car running; though he was the last competitor to reach Paris he did so without assistance. He repeated the exploit the following year, in the legendary Paris-Vienna race.

The peak of the 1901 racing season, however, was the race from Paris to Berlin, the first of the big inter-capital races which were characteristic of the first years of the century. The last of these races was the 1903 Paris-Madrid. Accidents had taken too great a toll.

The Paris-Berlin was run over 750 miles in three stages, Paris-Aix-la-Chapelle of 285 miles, Aix-la-Chapelle-Hanover of 280 miles and Hanover-Berlin of 185 miles — a more severe test for men and machines than any race so far run. The rules were also strict. No competitor could spend more than 15 minutes on his car at the end of each stage; in this time he had to do all the repair work, greasing, tyre changing and other jobs. After the 15 minutes, the cars were locked in the *parc fermé* until the start the next morning.

There were 110 competitors in the Paris-Berlin race, divided into 40 heavy cars (weighing over one ton) 51 touring cars (from 880 lb to one ton), nine light cars and 10 motorcycles. The most important European manufacturers were represented, including Mors, Panhard and Renault from France, Mercedes from Germany and Napier from England.

Details of the race are scarce, though it is recorded that when Pinson in his 40 H.P. Panhard suddenly found the road blocked by a tram in the village of Metternich, he deliberately ran into the vehicle to avoid the crowd of spectators. The tram was knocked off the rails; the

107

Two typical racing cars of their period. Above is a 1905 Panhard and below a 1913/1914 four-cylinder Opel, with four valves per cylinder and 12-litre capacity.

had the official title of "Circuit du Nord", it was known everywhere and remembered as the "Concours du Ministre" — the "Minister's Competition". It was open to any type of i.c.-engined vehicle, provided in ran on alcohol. This stipulation was made by the Third Republic's Minister for Agriculture, Jean Dupuy.

Confronted with a glut of beetroots that year, he was anxious to turn this to the nation's advantage by encouraging motorists to use home-produced fuel.

The minister and his permanent secretary sounded out the mayors of the towns through which it would pass. They were afraid of opposition from local public opinion, which was apt to think motor vehicles as dangerous. When all fears had been allayed, the race went ahead. It was in two stages, from Champigny to Saint-Germain and then to Arras.

car was hardly damaged. At Rheims Brasier hit and killed a child with his Mors.

The lack of background information was not surprising. The Press showed little interest before the race, which was described as madness by most journalists. French enthusiasm increased dramatically as Fournier won all three stages. His Mors averaged 70.5 k.p.h. (about 44 m.p.h.); immediately behind him was the usual group of Panhards, this time seven in the first ten places. Again the touring category was won by Giraud in a 12 H.P. Panhard, which was also eighth in general classification. The results gave little satisfaction in Germany as the first Mercedes to arrive, driven by Werner who had won the Nice-Salon-Nice race, came in seventeenth.

An unusual event was staged in 1902. Though this race

Welcomed

The race was almost a disaster because of persistent downpours, which led to some spectacular skids: further the new alcohol caused engines to run erratically. The only exception in performance was Rigolly's Gobron-Brillié, which was modified specifically to use alcohol.

The race was won by Henry Farman, who had won the Grand Prix du Pau the previous years. Once again all the Renaults which were entered finished at the head of their category. "Alcohol races" were later held in other European countries, including Italy, where Lancia and Storero finished first and second at an average of nearly 70 m.p.h.

At rest behind glass in the Renault museum in Paris. This sleek car performed with honour in the Paris-Vienna race of 1902.

The Paris-Vienna race of 1902 was hailed as the "race of races" by the Press, which was much more interested than in the previous year's Paris-Berlin.

The public was excited by the prospect. When 137 competitors gathered at the start line in the afternoon of 24 June, a tremendous crowd of 10,000 saw them off. Spectators arrived by special trains, carriages and bicycles.

Increase in power

This time the race was over 1060 miles through Burgundy, Switzerland, Tyrol and the Arlberg on roads where motor cars had never previously ventured.

It was by no means easy for the organisers, headed by the Automobile Club de France, to obtain official agreement. Authority considered the cars dangerous, not least because of the spectacular increase in power of the engines specially designed for the race. The Swiss government gave permission for the competitors to cross its territory but not to race, so the Belfort-Bregenz stage was simply a parade.

All the big manufacturers were represented, and those who had hopes of winning had made special efforts in view of the difficulties of the race. Panhard, fresh from success in the "Concours du Ministre" and their experience with alcohol, put their faith in a 70 H.P. using that fuel. The engine was a four-cylinder of no less than

13,700 c.c. Mercedes, which led the German contingents, had a "Simplex" model of 40 H.P. Mors had a 60 H.P. racing car.

As usual, the Renault brothers concentrated on the light car category and were present with a new 16 H.P. four-cylinder with which they had been experimenting for

Oury in the 1902 Paris-Vienna.

Veterans on show: above, a 1906 Mercedes which took part in the Paris-Geneva-Turin Rally. Left, from top to bottom, a 1908 Fiat, a 1909 Rolland-Pilain tourer and a 1913 De Dion-Bouton.

months. It developed 30 to 35 H.P. at the relatively high engine speed of 2,000 r.p.m. The car weighed about 1,300 lbs. The regulations provided for three categories, vehicles over 650 kg (about 1,430 lb), for cars between 400 and 600 kg (from 880 to 1,320 lb) and another for cars under 400 kg — tricycles and motorcycles.

From 3.30 a.m. the competitors began to leave at one-minute intervals, beginning with the big cars. The first to start was Girardot in a C.G.V. He was followed by Edge in his Napier, René de Knyff in a 60 H.P. Panhard fuelled by alcohol and the Renault brothers.

Over the mountain

The beginning of the race was promising, even as a spectacle. Fournier and his Mors succeeded in overtaking a special train taking motoring enthusiasts to the finish of the first stage at Belfort. All the same, Fournier had to pay a high price for over-stressing his car — he had covered the first 50 miles at an average of 70 m.p.h. — and at Chaumont, 150 miles from the start, he fell out with a broken gear-change. Girardot also dropped out. The first stage was won by Knyff, who averaged over 60 m.p.h. for the 260 miles, followed by Farman and Jarrott, also in Panhards.

But the situation changed completely following the relatively gentle drive from Belfort to Bregenz. The drivers then had to face the terrible mule tracks of the Arlberg on the third stage, finishing at Salzburg. These were very different conditions from the long straights of the first stage. The great strain on the cars was matched by the

CAR
AS LIGHT
AS A
FEATHER

One of the cars which had a major influence on styling was the Panhard-Levassor "Skiff", built in 1911 by Henri Labourdette, a well-known French coachbuilder. Up to then, in spite of one or two tries only partially successful, no-one had definitely broken away from the early styling of the century. It was René de Knyff, who was a daring and successful racing driver and subsequently became manager of Panhard-Levassor, who put Labourdette on the right lines.

De Knyff wanted a 20 H.P. sleeve-valve engined car for his own use, but not the usual heavy body with consequently lower performance. He asked Labourdette for a car to be "light as a feather" and preferably of new streamlined appearance. He suggested that aeroplane techniques might be used in the construction, that field having already passed beyond the canvas and plywood stage.

Thus Labourdette, impressed, too, by the commercial importance of his client, set to work to produce something new — not only from the technical point of view but also from that of appearance.

Labourdette produced something which was a cross between a canoe and an aeroplane, with no doors and covered in a light triple sheathing. In styling, the "Skiff" was equally revolutionary, with a long smooth bonnet flowing into the low inclined windscreen and with a low hood.

This was the forerunner of the long series of sports cars which still persists today. The spoked wheels contributed to an unusual and attractive appearance and are echoed on the G.T. cars of today.

The "Skiff" had a tremendous effect on the motoring world, so much so that Labourdette had orders to build many variants, all of which took the name of "cab-skiff". It is hardly necessary to say that with this method of construction they were very expensive, but for those who could afford them it was money well spent — not least for the suggestion that with a machine like this the owner was superior to ordinary motorists of the time.

A 1909 four-cylinder Rolland-Pilain which came in second in the Mont Ventoux hill climb.

demands on the nerves of the drivers, who had to climb long stony tracks flanked by sheer drops, round thousands of bends.

While climbing the pass, which rises to a height of 5950 feet, one of the drivers, Max, made a mistake on a bend and hit a bollard. The car rolled over the edge and fell 100 feet down the mountainside, but fortunately Max and his mechanic had been thrown clear on to the road. Max climbed down the mountainside to examine the car and, seeing that nothing could be done, began to climb up again.

A short while later another competitor, Baras, passed just as Max as reaching the road. At the end of the stage Baras reported that Max and his car had fallen 100 feet over a cliff and Max had then walked up on his own two feet!

Another competitor finding his car would not go up a hill, turned it round and, using the reverse gear, went up backwards. To reach the top he had to leave behind anything moveable in the car, including drums of petrol and oil, tools and spare parts and even pieces of bodywork. When he had taken the car to the top, he had to walk back and carry up the most essential pieces.

A 1904 Renault followed by a Cadillac of the same year.

Edge and his Napier ended up in a ditch but he managed to man-handle the vehicle out and continue to Innsbruck. By reaching Innsbruck he won the third Gordon Bennett Cup, which was run concurrently with the Paris-Vienna race as far as Innsbruck. His competitors were the Frenchmann Girardot and de Knyff for, respectively, America and France; de Knyff, though he succeeded in crossing the Arlberg, broke his differential 20 miles short of Innsbruck.

At this point a series of misfortunes began to afflict Louis Renault, whose car had performed well over the pass and beyond. At Innsbruck Renault accidentally hit the car of another competitor, Baron de Caters. This lost him and his mechanic much time while thney repaired the differential by using wire, string and hemp; he added sawdust to the differential oil to thicken it and to reduce leaks.

At last Renault and Grus set off for Salzburg, but in the

The 1902 Fiat "24 H.P." Lancia won the Sassi-Superga hill climb in such a car, beating Mercedes. The 6,370 c.c. four cylinder engine had low tension magneto ignition, leather cone clutch, chain transmission and gave a top speed of about 60 m.p.h.

The 1907 120 H.P. Itala.

dark they ran into a level-crossing barrier. Yet again they set off after having repaired the car as best they could with the help of a local smith. The most unlikely materials used this time included a chair for making improvised wheel spokes. After they got moving again they found the radiator was leaking, and Grus had to sit on the bonnet, as the car went along, continually pouring water into the radiator.

'Special technique'

The Salzburg stage was won by Baron De Forest's Mercedes and the next day the Renault brothers set off on the last stage to Vienna. The course of the race was at once influenced by Marcel Renault's remarkable driving. He left in seventh position and, risking all, he took the bends at high speed. Slowly Renault caught up on Farman until he drew level. For a long time the two cars raced along side by side until at last Renault, with what he called his "special technique" on bends, succeeded in overtaking the Panhard some 33 miles from the finish.

Still at full speed, Marcel Renault reached the trotting track at the Prater in Vienna, the finishing line, two hours sooner than forecast. It was mid-day and not even the judges were waiting for him; they were at lunch. People near the line at first refused to believe he was one of the competitors in the race — and Renault's command of the German language was almost non-

existent. At last every doubt was cleared and the spectators, though they had hoped for a Mercedes victory, sportingly carried him off in triumph.

The performance of the little Renault, small in comparison with the giants in the race, was interesting from the technical point of view. The average speed — almost 40 m.p.h. — was high. Above all the Paris-Vienna race demonstrated that sheer power was not everything. A little time after the Paris-Vienna race there was another outstanding car achievement, almost incredibly by a steam car. Serpollet, inventor of the famous flash steam boiler, took his aerodynamic "Oeuf de Pâques" (Easter Egg) on the Promenades des Anglais at Nice, and raised the flying kilometre record to 120.761 k.p.h. (about 75 m.p.h.). His unofficial mile record was about one m.p.h. higher. The record was to be taken back by an i.c.-engined car shortly afterwards, still in this memorable year, 1902, when Fournier in a Mors achieved 123.28 k.p.h., this figure being beaten afterwards by Angiel's 124.14 k.p.h. at Dordan.

In France these were triumphs of speed, but in England there was still a speed limit of 20 m.p.h. and, indeed, until a few months earlier it had been 12 m.p.h. This caused some embarrassment to the organisers of the fourth Gordon Bennett Cup race. As the third event in the series had been won by Edge, it was England's turn to organise the fourth.

The impact of races elsewhere was strictly national. So far as Italy was concerned, one race of some interest arose out of a challenge by the Duke of Abruzzi to Garibaldi Coltelletti, the Panhard representative in Italy, concerning the merits of their respective cars, a 24 H.P. F.I.A.T. and a similarly rated Panhard. Giovanni Agnelli had the foresight to add Felice Nazzaro as an unofficial competitor. The race, run between Turin and Bologna, had two winners. Coltelletti won the stake of 5,000 Lire when he arrived in triumph at Bologna, the Duke having literally fallen by the wayside at Alessandria when he hit the parapet of a bridge. Nazzaro, nevertheless, covered the course in his 12 H.P. in four minutes less than Coltelletti, at an average speed of 22 m.p.h.

Round the world

In the meantime the passion for long-distance trials had crossed the Atlantic from the U.S. In 1902 a Dr. Lehwess left London at the end of April in a kind of bus, built by Panhard-Levassor, the "Passe Partout", to drive round the world. A little more than six weeks later the "Passe Partout" reached Paris — evidently speed was not their principal concern — and then took another four months to reach Warsaw. They called at St Peters-

The proud owner climbs aboard his 1905 three-cylinder Rolls-Royce, which he found abandoned in a shed and restored.

The Italian racing driver Cagno in the 100 H.P. Fiat in which he won the Mont Ventoux hill climb.

THE DETERMINED INNOVATOR HENRY FORD

Henry Ford, perhaps the most important figure of all in the story of the motor car, would have become a farmer if his parents had had their way. He was born in 1863 of a father who was an immigrant from Ireland and a mother of Dutch origin. From a very early age however, he had little interest in his father's plans for him, being fascinated by all things mechanical, particularly clocks, spending all his time taking them to pieces and putting them together again.

Years of experiment

He was young when he left his native town of Greenfield in Michigan and went to Detroit, a much more attractive place to Ford's mind. His first job was with Flower Brothers, manufacturers of machine tools. Then he went to a marine engine company, the Dry Dock Engine Company, and finally to a small firm which installed Westinghouse steam engines. All these companies represented useful experience for him and formed the basis of his mechanical knowledge.

When his father died he was left 40 acres of land, but this was not enough to draw him back to his home town.

A little later, in 1888, Henry married Clara Bryant and took a small isolated house where he set up a workshop. It was from this time that he began ten years of experimenting and building prototypes in his spare time. In the meantime the Detroit Edison Company had offered him a reasonably well paid job — 135 dollars a month — firstly in charge of fire precautions and then as an engineer. Then came the moment when his first "quadricycle" was ready and the town council, in spite of some opposition, had given him permission to use it on the public roads. He saw the great Edison himself who advised him to follow his inclinations, and so Henry resigned to devote all of his time to the motor car.

Powerful friends

Thus began a hard, wearing period of experiment and unsuccessful tests which caused him disillusionment and the loss of a lot of money. With a partner, Tom Cooper, an ex-racing cyclist, he built a few racing cars. One of these won the challenge against Winton and served as a springboard for further activity, thanks to the publicity received.

A little while later, scraping up everything he possessed, Henry formed the Detroit Automobile Company with 5,000 dollars. The beginning was hard and the help of some powerful friends, such as the mayor of Detroit himself, proved to be of little use. The company got into serious difficulty even though Ford himself drew only 100 dollars a month. It was necessary to sell the company to Leland and Faulconer in 1900: this firm was later to become Cadillac.

But at last the worst was behind him. On the wave of popularity generated by his Grosse Pointe victory against Winton, Ford was able to found the Ford Motor Company, once again risking everything he had, using as capital 28,000 dollars provided by 12 fortunate subscribers — fortunate because, to give an example, Senator Couzens' investment of 2,500 dollars increased to 30 million!

Lowest possible price

The reasons for this immediate success were many, including the victories of Ford's racing car "999", and the technical characteristics of his cars, but above all it was due to the startling ideas of Henry Ford himself whose conception of the automobile was as transportation of the masses. To this end he consistently cut costs, standardised wherever possible, and marketed his wares at bargain prices.

His actions speak loudest, for instance the theory in which he first laid down a modern law of economic production, or the seven months of inactivity he imposed on the company in 1927 after the finish of the model "T" and before the introduction of the new model. There was his "Peace ship" which he sent to Europe in 1915 to try to stop the war; his unsuccessful attempts to enter politics, first in 1918 as Democratic candidate for the Senate and then for the Presidency in 1924; and the huge industry he set up when already old, to ensure his company an important position in the tyre business. His only son, Edsel, to whom the old Henry Ford had given control of a good part of his huge industrial empire, died young, but before he himself died, Henry was able to pass his job to his grandson who bore the same name. Henry Ford died at the age of 84 in 1947, leaving behind him a substantial number of books in which he had expressed his social and economic ideas, often original and always enlivened by understanding.

The cabin in the oak tree where Ford worked.

Henry Ford in one of his first cars. Edsel Ford is behind in the 25,000,000th.

burg and reached Nijni-Novgorod where they stopped, their vehicle being unable to travel further.

In 1901 an American, Charles Glidden, began a fantastic journey of over 50,000 miles in one of the first Napiers. Having crossed Europe, Glidden went into Scandinavia as far as the Arctic Circle, and in the years that followed he went round the world twice.

A 1902 Renault shows its paces.

A view of the Ford factory at Dearbon in 1914 — an early assembly line. Below the Oldsmobile machine shop in 1901.

1901 saw a race that was to have a more lasting effect on the history of the motor car. It was held on October 10 on a track at Grosse Pointe, near Michigan, arising out of a challenge between manufacturers.

One was Alexander Winton and the other was Henry Ford, who had recently left his job with the Edison Illuminating Company to devote himself entirely to building motor cars in partnership with a racing cyclist, Tom Cooper. This was Ford's second adventure into motoring, after his famous light car had noisily attracted the attention of his fellow-citizens some years before.

The great challenge

Ford was not a racing driver but he had recognised the tremendous publicity value of racing and decided that he too must make use of it. He therefore sent a formal challenge to Winton, suggesting a 10-mile race. This challenge had a more positive outcome than the one which, two years before, Winton himself had sent to all American manufacturers, challenging them to a race between Chicago and New York. In the end, this challenge came to nothing because each competitor insisted on the race being held in his own area.

This time things were different. The Grosse Pointe race, well publicised by the local Press, drew a large crowd of spectators. The prize at stake was a glass of punch, but in effect the stake was much higher. At Ford's instigation, a third competitor took part in the race, William N. Murray, millionaire owner of one of the fastest cars in Pittsburgh. He withdrew, however, at the last moment owing to an oil leak.

Winton took the lead in the race at once, and gained an advantage of half a mile. At the end of the seventh lap, his engine began to smoke and the car gradually slowed to a halt. Ford could then just coast to victory. His time was good, his car covering the course in 13 minutes 23 seconds at an average of 45 m.p.h. In their enthusiasm for the young and as yet unknown winner, the public forgot Winton's brilliant performance in setting up a new one-mile record of one minute six seconds. Ford's industrial fortune sprang indirectly from this race.

RUDOLF DIESEL - TRAGIC GENIUS

Tragedy on the classic scale marked the life of Rudolf Diesel, whose invention has had such an effect on transport. His childhood and youth were difficult. At the time of Rudolf's birth in 1858 his father, who was of German origin but living in Paris, was extremely poor. Twelve years later he moved with his family to London when the Franco-Prussian war made life impossible for them in the French capital.

Rudolf himself was solitary and taciturn but quickly showed his interest in mechanical things, spending long hours wrestling with theoretical problems.

After the family returned to France, Rudolf attended the Conservatoire des Arts et Métiers and began to study what was to become one of his specialities, refrigeration. A little later, when he was just 20 years old, he published his first paper on the internal combustion engine.

In subsequent years he was to pursue in parallel his studies in these two fields, the former under the guidance of Professor Linde in Berlin, to which he had moved, and the latter on his own account.

In the field of the i.c. engine he turned his back on the direction others were taking — most studies of the time were concerned with gas engines — and devoted his time to an engine powered by ammonia gas, a project on which he wasted much time and money.

At last, however, he got on the right lines and began a series of experiments to perfect an engine in which the mixture of air and fuel was exploded not by a spark or other outside means, but by the extreme heat produced by very high compression.

The first engine of this type — it was patented in 1892 — used coal dust blown into the combustion chamber. It was extremely temperamental, but the first step had been taken, though his adversaries duly claimed that a compression ignition engine was impossible.

Backers enthusiastic

Later experiments with other hydrocarbons, particularly diesel oil (as it is now known) and petrol, were much more successful. As a result the powerful Krupps-Essen and MAN group got in touch with Diesel and entered into an arrangement with him. The consequence was the birth of the first true "diesel" engine, in the sense we know it today, in 1893.

Many technical problems had been overcome, but many remained. Diesel's backers were prepared to continue however, encouraged mainly by the low fuel consumption of the new engine, which proved to be about half that of the petrol engines of the time.

Fortune began to smile on Rudolf Diesel as his engines became more and more widely used for heavy industrial purposes and for marine and stationary uses. He crossed the Atlantic to market his invention in the United States and quickly became wealthy.

With the money he began to speculate on the stock exchange, particularly in petrol shares, and he even tried to set himself up in competition with Rockefeller himself.

Disappears overboard

Then his marvellous intellect began to fail. This at first showed itself in excessive optimism and delusions of grandeur, which led him to be put under medical care. His business affairs were neglected and started to go badly; his mental state deteriorated.

He disappeared from the ship "Dresden" as he was crossing the Channel from Antwerp to Harwich on the night of 29-30 September, 1913. This inevitably gave rise to rumours of commercial espionage and even of the murder having been committed through competitors. It is more likely, however, that the great inventor, much envied and renowned though he was, could no longer live a life in which bitterness and disappointment finally destroyed him.

For many years most of the world has driven on the right with the steering wheel on the left. In Great Britain and in many countries of the Commonwealth, however, the reverse is true. Above is a Vauxhall Viva in Sydney, and below a Prince Henry Vauxhall of 1911.

CHAPTER EIGHT
THE GREAT NAMES EMERGE

After his victory of Grosse Pointe, Ford prepared a second machine, the "Arrow", in which he reached a speed of 97.37 m.p.h. — a record which was broken by a narrow margin two weeks later by William K. Vanderbilt, Jr. An Oldsmobile, the "Pirate", then raised it again; and finally in 1902 a Baker electric car, the "Torpedo", achieved 104 m.p.h.

Not long afterwards the powerful figure of Barney Oldfield impressed itself on American racing when he held a meeting at Yonkers, near New York, called "Mile-a-minute Racing", which attracted a large crowd for the time, 5,000. Oldfield set up a new mile record of 61 seconds.

Later the "999", a new Ford car, astounded the public

A 1906 Cadillac.

because it consisted only of essentials — chassis, engine, wheels and controls — and in this Oldfield covered the mile in 56.25 seconds at Columbus. Then, in the same vehicle, he returned the spectacular time of 55.8 seconds on a circular track at Yonkers.

The first races staged on the famous beach at Ormonde-Daytona in Florida, took place in 1902. The promoter was W. J. Morgan, an ex-sports writer who had specialised in cycling and motoring and had passed to organising races. He organised a number of "special carnivals", including various "beach runs" across the 20 miles from Daytona to Ormonde. The first run in 1902 did not

produce any exceptional results, and it was not until 1906 that spectacular records were set up, including the prodigious 127 m.p.h. of Marriott in his Stanley Steamer.

Cadillac is born

At the beginning of this century a new name was added to the list of American motor manufacturers, that of Cadillac. Its origins lay in the dramatic events at Oldsmobile. The fire in 1901 had set Olds on a desperate search for capital with which to re-equip and start production of the famous "Curved Dash". Among those who helped him was Henry Martin Leland, a 58-year-old industrialist, who since 1890 had owned, with his partner Faulconer, a machine tool factory which also built i.c. engines for boats.

Leland helped Olds in two ways: he gave him financial assistance and he provided him with parts for the new car. (Among others who helped Olds at this time were the Dodge brothers, who were to back Ford and later still to set up their own company, which was to be absorbed in later years by Walter P. Chrysler.)

Leland's relationship with Olds in 1901 created an interest in motor cars that led him to decide on a direct involvement. At that time the affairs of the Detroit Automobile Company, set up by Henry Ford, were faring badly and Ford had to give up his company and his workshop. It was Leland and Faulconer who bought it up and started production of a light car with a single-

A 1908 Cadillac, the year in which the company won the Dewar Trophy for the interchangeability of its components.

A 1903 White Steamer, with a 10 H.P. twin-cylinder engine.

taken to Brooklands and run for 500 miles. They emerged in perfect condition.

This proof of the interchangeability of Cadillac parts impressed technical experts, and the company was awarded the coveted Dewar Trophy for the most significant demonstration of motor car technical progress in the year. (In 1913 Cadillac won the Dewar Trophy for the second time, the only occasion it has ever happened, for their new system of electric starting.)

In Europe, too, the early years of the new century marked the creation of new companies. In Great Britain Sunbeam started to make cars. Their first production model was decidedly heterodox in that the four wheels were arranged in a rhomboid, i.e. one forward, two amidships, and one at the rear.

Working abroad

The idea was due to an engineer who had non-conformist ideas, Mabberley Smith. He persuaded the company to build this car even though they had been building bicycles since 1887. The engine of this strange vehicle had a water-cooled single-cylinder engine of 327 c.c. and developed $2^3/_4$ H.P. Ignition was by coil and contact breaker. The vehicle had two speeds; transmission was by chain and belt; and suspension was by full-elliptics for the front and rear wheels, while the centre axle was rigid. The French engineer, Louis Coatalen, joined Sunbeam in 1909 after working for Humber and then for Hillman. It is strange that these three then independent companies should be united 50 years later in one complex, the Rootes Group.

cylinder engine designed by an acquaintance, A. P. Brush. One year later the car was given its name — it was the first Cadillac, named after the French nobleman who was credited by legend at having founded Detroit.

The Cadillac Automobile Company changed its name in 1904 to the Cadillac Motor Car Company. From the start Leland's cars earned a reputation for precision engineering and a high standard of finish. Leland always insisted on this, as did Royce in England, and the prestige which their names still have is a continuing demonstration of the importance which the public has always given to quality.

Interchangeable

A proof of the value of quality was given by a series of tests to which three Cadillacs were subjected in 1908. The cars were shipped across the Atlantic and completely dismantled in Britain. All the parts were mixed and, under the supervision of the Royal Automobile Club, the cars were rebuilt under the supervision of judges. They chose at random so that each of the three cars was rebuilt with components and parts that could have originally been used on the others.

The mechanics could use only four types of tools for the assembly — screwdrivers, spanners, hammers and pincers. As soon as the cars were re-assembled they were

Jack Brabham at the wheel of a 1904 Sunbeam 12 H.P. in the 1960 London-Brighton Run.

Displayed like works of art — a room of the Renault museum in Paris.

Another name that is repeatedly found in the history of British motoring is that of Thomas Charles Pullinger, an English engineer who had spent many years in France working with Teste, Moret and Cie., a well-known motor manufacturer in Lyons. Pullinger also assisted in the birth of Humber and Sunbeam and was to design one of the most successful Scottish cars, the famed Arrol-Johnston.

Another interesting name in British motoring at the time is that of Clément-Talbot, founded by D. M. Weigel, representative of the French company Clément, and the Marquis of Shrewsbury, whose family name is Talbot. The ubiquitous Coatalen was to arrive there, too, though much later.

The first Sunbeamland, built in 1899.

In 1901 and 1902 no French car companies of lasting interest were formed, though there were to be many in the following years. In the former year the Paris Salon de l'Automobile finally found a worthy home in the Grand Palais, and attracted an impressive number of visitors — no fewer than 170,000.

Among the large manufacturers, Panhard launched the new 16 H.P., directly derived from the 24 H.P. which had won the first Gordon Bennett, and from its more powerful version, the 28 H.P. On the 16 H.P., the engine was again mounted in front but the car was a four-seater. The radiator was still a finned tube.

In 1902 Renault recruited M. Viet, a brother-in-law of Georges Bouton. Viet was the author of a technical revolution in the expanding Bilancourt factory. He was an excellent engineer and had designed a four-cylinder engine with many new features. He had first turned to the Marquis De Dion to produce it, but the latter was still wedded to the single-cylinder (he was soon to opt for multicylinderism in a big way, with a Vee-eight) and refused.

When Renault met Viet he was at once impressed by his abilities and added him to his team of designers. The engine of the 16 H.P. with which Marcel Renault won the Paris-Vienna was, in fact, the work of Viet. It was this victory which convinced Renault of the merits of the four-cylinder engine. At once he put one into production that was more suitable for general use; thus was born the "20 H.P.", which, though subjected to many improvements and changes, was to be the basis for Renault production until 1928.

In the meantime, in 1901, the first light cars built by Darracq at the famous Suresnes works were born. It was the "9½ H.P." which had a "coal scuttle" bonnet similar to the Renault. Underneath, the engine and its accessories were arranged in a sensible way to allow easy separation from the chassis.

Darracq was also preparing cars for record attempts, such as that in which Baras was to set up a world land speed record three years later at 105 m.p.h. on the track at Mongeron.

Bicycles to cars

In contrast to France, there were a number of new manufacturers who entered the field in Italy in the early years of the century. Many of them were to last only a short while, such as the Adami and the Bugatti-Gulinelli of 1900, the Devecchi-Strada, the Dobelli and the Florentia of 1903 and the Aquila Italiana of 1905. Other companies, however, were more important.

In 1901 the Società Fratelli Ceirano was formed in Turin. Giovanni Battista had come from Cuneo to Turin, where he spent his early years first selling and then making bicycles. In 1898 he formed a company, Ceirano G. B. & C., to produce a light car, the "Welleyes" designed by Faccioli. Lancia and Nazzaro also worked in the company as mechanics. A year later Ceirano G. B. & C., with all the prototype Welleyes so far built, was bought by Fiat. The prototype was to become the first Fiat. The restless Ceirano and his nephew created a number of other companies — the Società Fratelli Ceirano in 1901, the STAR (Giovanni, in 1904), the Itala (Matteo, 1904), the Junior (Giovanni, 1905), the SCAT in 1906 and, much later, Ceirano S. A. in 1919. The first of these companies lasted only a year but produced some models with a rear-mounted single-cylinder engine of 640 c.c.

At Fiat, in the meantime, only two years had passed since the first "3½ H.P." and only one since it had been replaced by the racing car with which it was hoped to gain useful publicity. Already a third car was ready; this was an "8 H.P." with a vertical twin engine that went into production in 1901. It was the first Fiat with the engine mounted in front.

This four-seat, four-door saloon "X" was designed and built by Pininfarina for Fiat in 1960. The four wheels were in rhomboid layout with the front one steering and the rear one driving. All-rubber suspension and 1,089 c.c. engine.

1911 Vauxhall.

1903-1904 Fiat 16-24 H.P. with four vertical cylinders in two pairs and 4,181 c.c. Multiplate clutch and chain drive. Top speed — 45 m.p.h.

1907 Dupressoir.

A 1908 Oakland. This car was famous in its day for its ability to climb hills.

It was this car which caused the break, in 1901, between Agnelli and his chief engineer, Faccioli. The former had returned from the Paris Salon, where he had been impressed by the honeycomb radiator which could replace the fragile finned-tube type used till then. Agnelli wanted to fit one of these new radiators on the "8 H.P." but Faccioli preferred to wait until it had been tested by other companies. Faccioli left.

The new chief engineer, Enrico, then designed a four-cylinder engine which was fitted to the next model, the 1902 "12 H.P.". This was a new car from back to front. It had a wooden chassis reinforced with metal, pneumatic tyres, automatic lubrication and an inclined steering column.

The three pedals were placed in what was to be the standard position for many years in Europe — clutch to the left of the steering column, brake immediately to the right of the column and the accelerator further

The vogue of the "torpedo". A 1908 Peugeot "116" with 4 cylinders, 16 H.P., 2,211 c.c. engine, four speeds plus reverse, a leather cone clutch.

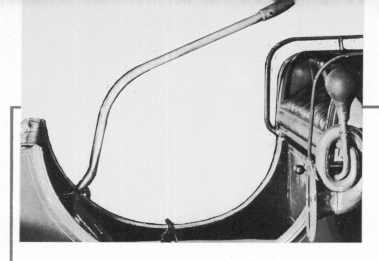

FROM TILLER
TO TWIST
OF THE WRIST

Early motor cars were not controlled by a steering wheel but by a different and much less convenient system. It is surprising, however, that a system so natural and effective as the steering wheel took so long to be adopted. The reason, however, is not altogether inexplicable. It should not be forgotten that in the first 15 years of their life motor vehicles were called "horseless carriages", not as a colourful metaphor but because they really were considered only as a slight deviation from the horse-drawn carriage, as may be seen by the coachwork adopted. When manufacturers of the new motor car had to design

a method of steering — because steering devices did not exist on the horse-drawn carriages — they stayed as close to the cart shafts as they could.

This explains the origin of the "queue de vache", "cow's tail", or tiller — a bar of metal or wood, usually suitably curved in two directions, which, through a simple linkage, varied the angle of the front axle to the centre line of the chassis.

It was obviously a system practical only for low speeds, as it was impossible to have precise control of steering due to "whip" in the bar.

The tiller continued to have its supporters even after it had been rejected by most manufacturers; then at the end of the 19th century a considerably less crude system was introduced. It was mechanically much more complicated, and generally known as the "two-handle" system.

Vertical handle

It consisted of a vertical steering column connected at the bottom to steering linkages similar to those in use today, so that instead of the whole axle pivoting, only the wheels turned on kingpins.

The upper end of the steering column was rigidly attached to a horizontal bar some 20 to 30 inches long, with a vertical handle at each end held in the hands. This system was a vast improvement on the tiller, but could not cope with sharp angles.

It was but a short step to the steering wheel, which was itself used at first with a vertical column. It was quickly adopted almost everywhere, partly because its convenience was apparent to everyone and partly because it was not protected by patents.

At first these wheels were smaller than those in use today. With the introduction of inclined columns, wheels grew considerably larger, reaching enormous sizes on sports cars in the first decade of the century.

There was, however, a practical reason for the large wheel. The poor road surfaces of the time transmitted heavy shocks through the steering linkages to the steering wheel (research to eliminate these was to come much later). The only remedy was to minimise this tiring effect by increasing the diameter of the wheel.

Early wheels usually had five spokes but these were soon reduced first to four, then to three. If the wheel rim was made of metal tube, it was usually thick, be-

cause of the technical difficulties in those days in making small-diameter tube. Some rims were made of wood. At first they were covered in leather, if covered at all: Celluloid being used later to cover metal rims and spokes.

Fitting on wheels

A familiar fitting on steering wheels for 40 years was the manual ignition advance/retard lever, usually mounted in the centre. This lever was used every time the load on the engine varied, such as going up a hill or when there were wide variations in engine speed. This is now done automatically.

The horn button at the centre of the wheel came much later, and for many years other acoustic warning devices were used. These included not only the well-known bulb horn but also much more complicated devices; one was actuated by exhaust gas and operated by a foot pedal. It has been fashionable to mount secondary controls on the steering-column since the early 1930s.

There has always been considerable variety in the design and number of the spokes. Recently two were in fashion, but a reversion to three has been noticed over the past few years.

There is, however, one famous steering wheel with only one spoke — that of the Citroën DS family. Even this, though, had a worthy, but little-known, ancestor in the type found on pre-1914 Humbers.

Safety rules

Developments today are not so much with regard to the wheel itself but on the steering column and shaft. This is especially true in the U.S., where severe government safety regulations have led to the use of a shaft consisting of two tubes of different diameter connected by a plastic link which will break in the event of a head-on collision. The two tubes telescope, one inside the other.

The steering wheel as a device may now be verging on obsolescence. Particularly in America, much research is being done on alternative methods of steering to eliminate the potential danger of the wheel in a crash, to permit steering by one hand only at low speeds and to improve steering control.

Of the many systems tried so far, the most satisfactory appears to be the so-called "wrist-twist". This consists of two small wheels five to six inches in diameter mounted at the ends of a T-shaped steering column. A fixed ring gives rest for the thumbs while the fingers grip the two wheels in indentations.

The two wheels are inter-connected so that steering may be done by only one hand; a servo device is used to reduce effort required.

From tiller to a twist of the wrist... in the meantime the present-day driver continues happily with the wheel.

1903 De Dion Populaire (Turin Motor Museum).

1907 six-cylinder Standard. The company was formed in 1903 and the first car was a 6 H.P.

to the right. Bodywork was of the type already known as "tonneau". The 12 H.P. model sold well in 1903 in France, England and America as well as in Italy.

Two more models followed the "12 H.P." within a few months, similar except for their engines. There was a 4,181 c.c. which, from its "square" 110×110 mm. engine, produced 16 H.P. at 1,000 r.p.m. to give 44 m.p.h., and a 24 H.P. which at first had a hotted-up version of the same engine.

Production figures

Production statistics for 1903 are illuminating. Total world production of motor vehicles was 61,927, of which 30,204 were made in France, 11,235 in the U.S., 9,437 in Great Britain, 6,904 in Germany, 2,839 in Belgium and 1,308 in Italy. These figures show that the big French manufacturers were rapidly expanding, with 25, 30 or even 40 chassis being assembled at a time. Technical progress was world-wide. Hot tube ignition was moribund, and the magneto on the way in. Single cylinders were going out; two were normal and four were soon to be common. Engine speeds were up to 1,200 and even 1,500 r.p.m., which meant more comfort for motorists as the jolting was replaced by an acceptable rumble.

As far as bodywork was concerned, the closed car was

still to come. This may seem remarkable, but interest in motoring was largely due to the great races and all the cars taking part had been open. Thus the aspiration of those who could afford a car was to own a similar one. But not many years were to pass before common-sense prevailed, with the birth of many cars that could be closed or converted — the coupé, the limousine, the landaulet, the cabriolet, and the saloon.

In 1903, however, the universal desire was for a "torpedo" — dashing, open and low-built now that engineers had discovered the safety of a low centre of gravity.

Months of waiting

There were signs of things to come — in the Belgian Pipe with its overhead valves and magnetic clutch, in the overhead-camshaft Maudslay, in Fiat's compressed air starter, and in the Wilson-Pilcher with its rudimentary preselective gearbox.

But it was a long way from the modern situation where the customer goes to the Motor Show or to a dealer and chooses his car, either driving it away or waiting for delivery. In either case, he has little else to do but pay. In the early years of the century the first item bought was the chassis; and then began months of discussion, contemplation and patience. The coachbuilder probably was still working on a custom-built basis, each successive body being different and difficult to classify.

Most bodies were built by men who had come from the horse-drawn carriage trade and wanted to innovate where possible. They transferred in entirety the techniques and methods that were inappropriate for the new field. Thus their products were often masterpieces of finish and ornament, but were impractical and inefficient.

A beauty which has not aged. An elegant 1906 Rolls-Royce Silver Ghost attracts its young admirers.

1902-1903 Fiat 12 H.P. with four-cylinder 3,370 c.c. engine developing 14 H.P. Three speeds plus reverse and leather cone clutch. Top speed — 45 m.p.h.

From the "torpedo" to the "char-à-banc" A 1911 14 H.P. Renault showing the stepped seating.

An 1898 Opel 4 H.P. "Système Lutzmann" with single-cylinder water-cooled engine, chain drive, 2 speeds plus reverse, top speed 10 to 13 m.p.h. Cost, at today's prices: about £ 4,000.

THE HAND-BUILT CAR

Motor car production took its first major step forward when assembly methods were revolutionised half a century ago. Today a factory may turn out thousands of cars a day.

But the building of the modern craftsman-manufactured saloon of the grand touring class — using techniques much in the manner of the pioneer car-makers — is still an important factor in the industry.

To make one such car may take up to 16 weeks, though this does not mean that only one is produced in that period. Teams of men work on sections of numerous cars at a time, producing up to a score a week. Such is the low rate of production of the world's really great craftsman-built models.

There is a compromise in the form of the luxury mass-produced car, but even the rate of production of some 600 units for Jaguar and Daimler is high compared with production of cars such as the Aston-Martin.

Link with past

Though the latter is inevitably up-to-date as far as styling and specification are concerned, it has an obvious link with the past in its methods of construction and the people concerned in its production. Even in its latest form, it has the De Dion type of rear suspension, which is almost as old as the automobile itself; its wire-spoked wheels were already going out of fashion in 1932! The upholstery is made by workers using much the same methods used in the days of horse carriages.

This historic continuity is seen in the workshops of the make at the Newport Pagnell factory, once the head-quarters of the famous Tickford bodybuilding concern. The use of the file, saw, hammer, gas welding torch and the tinsman's snips are complementary to that of the modern equipment for bonding metal and welding nylon. The steel rule, the T-square and the scriber are still in constant use.

In a modern quantity-produced car, little more than half the components are actually made by the principal manufacturer whose name the car bears. This is not so at Newport Pagnell, where at the Aston Martin factory there is a rule that one man should build up one complete engine and be solely responsible for it. Each man's personal characteristics are reflected in his work.

Engine builders grind in valves in much the same way as the practical owner-driver of the early 1900s overhauling his machine. The main bearing bore is finished to an accuracy of six ten-thousandths of an inch. Connecting

The Aston Martin DBS, styled at Newport Pagnell factory.

rods are carefully selected and weighed to make up a perfectly matched set of six, which stay together "for life" once this is done. Each set is initialled by the man who selects them. A complete detailed history of each engine is kept, right from initial assembly to the time it reaches the customer, encased in the splendour of the three stock models.

Co-operation on styling

It takes up to a fortnight to build an Aston Martin engine. It is the bodybuilding and the associated work such as trimming, wiring up and painting that takes up most of the time. The sleek bodies are panelled in an alloy of magnesium, manganese and aluminium over a steel superstructure — heavy-looking but in practice a relatively light chassis.

Styling has been a co-operative effort for some years with Carrozzeria Touring, the Italian coach-building firm, and the bodies have been built on the Superleggera principle. They involve a metal skin — a kind of alloy body stocking — which tightly hugs the light but rigid "bone structure" of steel tube and angle. The latest of the three models — the DBS — was styled at Newport Pagnell, but the construction principles are similar and there is a strong family resemblance in the other models. The body has more than 30 separate welded panels making up each shell; craftsmen butt-weld, beat and file the shining silvery alloy to produce the beautifully contoured body.

Leather seating

Firstly, the main panels such as the front wing, bonnet lid or rear quarter are stretch-formed on a concrete-filled former. Each is then hand-beaten on a wooden, steel or glass-fibre mould, according to its application. The beaten panels are welded edge-to-edge; this demands the highest degree of skill in gas welding and in the use of welding rods made from the parent alloy. In this way the shell will be made up in two main parts, the front end, finishing at the door pillars, and the rear end, complete with fast-back in the case of a saloon.

Every door of the car is a complex operation in itself. On a mass-produced motor car, the door is something made from two pressings of thin steel — an instant door, made in millions. But the door of the hand-built car is the work of craftsmen. The skilled metal-workers, tinsmiths and lockmakers produce a compact and complicated mechanism.

In the quality-car factory one of the busiest, and quietest, sections is the upholstery shop, where the humming and throbbing of the women's sewing machines lends almost a domestic atmosphere. The women work in calico and fine glove-soft leather. Five complete cowhides are used for the upholstery and trimming of one car, one for each of the front seats and three for the rear seating and trimming.

There is a concession to modernity in the shop, for the latest types of foamed plastics can sometimes take the place of latex, though the seat frames are made in the factory.

Reinforced glass fibre plastic is used for items such as the transmission tunnel.

Done by hand

Instead of "coach paint" the most advanced spray techniques are used; the only difference compared with methods 60 years ago are in the time, effort and application. All spraying and rubbing down are still done by hand. Between 20 and 22 coats of primer and colour are applied to each body, and the last coat of rich colour goes on only after road testing.

Each car is indeed an individual achievement of dedicated men. Each is a proof that craftsmanship will continue as long as awareness and appreciation of distinction in design persists in the current age, which increasingly regards the car merely as functional and expendable.

Only vaguely reminiscent of the assembly line of mass-produced models, a row of bodies await trimming in the Aston-Martin works.

Two cars purpose-built for their markets. A 1909 Rolls-Royce Silver Ghost in dream-like surroundings and, below, a Fiat 500 "Topolino" of 1936.

CHAPTER NINE
RACE WITHOUT A FINISH

The last and most dramatic of the great European capital-to-capital races was the Paris-Madrid of 1903. Only the first stage, Paris to Bordeaux, was run and this was memorable by a chain of tragedies. The reasons were varied. There was the enormous increase in the power which manufacturers had given their cars, arising from their experience in the earlier big races. Drivers were relatively inexperienced in controlling such monsters, which had inefficient brakes and precarious road-holding, and the authorities were inexperienced in organising and controlling such a race.

Finally, there was the lack of discipline on the part of the spectators, who were enthusiastic but extremely ignorant of the potential danger of these hurtling machines. Even the members of the army and police who lined the route were unable to discipline the public, precisely because no one was aware of the risks.

The Paris-Vienna of the previous year had provided a foretaste of the increase in power, and the major competitors who presented themselves for the Paris-Madrid race had vehicles capable of speeds which had been unthinkable only a few months earlier.

So far as the public was concerned, between Paris and Bordeaux there were several hundreds of thousands of spectators. Ten dead and an uncounted number of injured, was the terrible result of the one day's racing. The suspension of the race was inevitable.

It was not until 1927 that racing on the public roads was revived with the Italian Mille Miglia sports car event, and this, too, was to succumb in its turn for the same reason — the number of accidents to the public. The Paris-Madrid race was organised jointly by the Spanish and French automobile clubs. It was agreed that the race should be run in three stages — Versailles to Bordeaux, passing through Chartres, Tours, Poitiers and Angoulême; Bordeaux to Vitoria by way of Bayonne; and Vitoria to Madrid through Burgos and Valladolid.

Baron P. de Crawhez's Panhard-Levassor arrives in fifth place at Bordeaux in the Paris-Madrid race.

More than 300 cars entered and, even after the inevitable withdrawals, there was still 275 starters. Alongside many amateur drivers were several professional racing teams, such as that sent by De Dietrich with 12 of their new low cars. Mors had 14 cars entered, one of them driven by Fournier. Panhard had 15 and Renault four cars, two being driven by Louis and Marcel. There were also teams from De Dion, Mercedes, Wolseley and Ader, and there was one Fiat entered.

Cyclists' escort

A number of the regulations represented new ideas in motor racing. For example, as a safety measure it was ruled that time spent in crossing cities should not be counted in the race. On approaching a city, each competitor was stopped, his time of arrival registered, and he

J. B. Warden in a Mercedes 60 H.P. arrives at Bordeaux in sixth place.

was escorted by cyclists at a slow pace through the city, where his time of departure was then recorded. The cars had a sort of post-box into which "counters" were placed at each control point to register its departure. A sign of things to come was the presence in this race of lady competitors. Madame du Gast drove a new De Dietrich, Madame Lockert an Ader and Mademoiselle Jollivet a motor-cycle.

The vast gatherings of spectators turned the race into a national event. The Italian newspaper "Corriere della Sera" of 24 May reported, "Last night 100,000 Parisians were making their way to Versailles to see the start of the Paris-Madrid race. From the Bastille to the Madeleine all the cafes, restaurants and night clubs, brilliantly lit, had every table occupied by diners who had their cars, motor cycles and bicycles outside, waiting to take them to Versailles.

"The great boulevards of Paris presented an extraordinary sight. Every minute two, four or even six cars passed amidst clouds of dust and enthusiasm! There was a sort of pre-race competition among the competitors going to Versailles, where the race was to start at 3.30 a.m. It was almost impossible to move in the streets. Still people continue to come from every part. Order was maintained only by battalions of troops and gendarmes".

Waiting to start

At the "Pièce d'Eau de Suisse", the start of the race, the last preparations were being completed. In the ranks of the drivers waiting alongside their cars were many who had won fame in earlier races. There was Charles Jarrott, an Englishman whose 45 H.P. De Dietrich had a great novelty, an electric headlamp; he had been selected by lot as first away. Louis and Marcel Renault,

De Knyff, Lorraine-Barrow, Théry and Fournier were also there.

At last the signal was given and Jarrott set off; at two-minute intervals the rest followed. Louis Renault was sixth to leave and at once set out to overtake those ahead of him.

Cathedral close

Dust was the universal enemy; it blinded the drivers, blocked engines, covered goggles and hid curves. The only way to avoid it was to overtake everyone else, and Renault passed driver after driver until, in sight of Chartres Cathedral, he finally overtook Jarrott's car. Up to this point he had averaged 70 m.p.h.

Without slowing down, Renault increased his lead over Jarrott at an astounding rate. At Poitiers he was

The Hon. C. S. Rolls, co-founder of Rolls-Royce, with his 1901 Paris-Berlin type Mors racing Car.

Tragedy for the Renault — Fernand tells Louis that their brother Marcel, who crashed at Couhé-Vérac, is dying. The mechanic, who has heard nothing because of the noise of the engine, smiles unknowingly. Spectators point — and the race goes on.

20 minutes ahead, at Angoulême 23, and he ended the stage in Bordeaux 35 minutes in the lead, arriving there at an average of just over 60 m.p.h.

This drive enabled him to take second place in the general classification to Gabriel, in a 70 H.P. Mors, who had driven an even more remarkable race. He had left carrying the number 168 and arrived fourth at Bordeaux, at an average speed of over 65 m.p.h. Jarrott was third in the general classification and Warden fourth in a Mercedes.

Battleground

The race had been a battleground for the cars, not more than 100 finishing the stage. This was probably due to the fantastic pace set by Louis Renault as the cars were, in fact, much stronger than those that had taken part in the Paris-Vienna in the previous year.

Public opinion was to be more shocked by the reports in the Press throughout Europe of a more serious massacre — this time of people.

A foretaste of what was to happen was given at Ablis, where a spectator who had leaned too far forward was hit by one of the cars but not fatally injured.

A little while later, 20 miles south of Poitiers, Marcel Renault first passed Farman and then set out to pass Théry. The two cars ran side by side at high speed until they came to a right-angled bend at the entrance to the village of Couhé-Vérac. Théry, who was in the lead, saw it in time, slowed down and rounded the bend. Renault, blinded by Théry's dust, saw the danger too late and shot off the road into a deep ditch, turning over several times.

Théry, who probably had no idea what had happened, continued on his way and it was not until Farman came by a few minutes later that the accident was discovered. Marcel Renault was already unconscious and died the next day in the little hospital at Couhé-Vérac.

His brother, Louis, was told of the accident when he arrived at Bordeaux. When it was confirmed that his brother had died, he retired the whole Renault team as a sign of mourning.

Marcel's death was to have important consequences in the works at Bilancourt. Louis was full of remorse and he even thought of closing the Renault factory, but a third brother Fernand shut his own button factory to enter the company, and resolved the family crisis.

Level crossing

A short while after Marcel Renault's accident, in which his mechanic Vauthier was also seriously injured, Théry

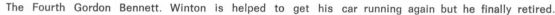

The Fourth Gordon Bennett. Winton is helped to get his car running again but he finally retired.

Veteran and vintage cars in the sunshine. Backs to the lake, from left to right, a 1929 Fiat 514, a 1923 Citroën 7.5 H.P. and a 1913 Le Zebre "A3".

A 1912 Le Zebre.

was hurt. While he was trying to overtake Porter in a Wolseley, he ran into a ditch; the petrol tank exploded, seriously burning both driver and mechanic. Then Porter himself was involved in a crash. Blinded by the dust of a vehicle in front, he did not see that a level-crossing barrier was descending at Bonneval. His machine hit the barrier and caught fire, and his mechanic was killed. Another driver, Tourand, swerving to miss a little girl, finished in the crowd. A woman and two soldiers were killed; Tourand himself was gravely injured, and so shocked that his brain was damaged for the rest of his life.

A similar tragedy marked the arrival of the drivers at Angoulême. A journalist there reported, "A young girl tried to cross the road just as a car came by. Private Dupuy of the 1st Company of the 107th Infantry Regiment rushed out to save her and was struck by car 23. The driver tried to avoid them but struck a tree, killing a spectator and a mechanic and seriously injuring another spectator. The mechanic of the car was also

The accent was on comfort. The stirring times of the pioneers were ending in 1907 when this Renault "type X" series B "Double touring saloon" was built. It had a 3,051 c.c. four-cylinder engine and a speed of 40 m.p.h.

1902 racing De Dion-Bouton with a two-cylinder engine. This car took part in the Paris-Madrid.

60 m.p.h. but though his car rolled over, he escaped without a scratch.

Stead, in a fierce duel, hit a car with his De Dietrich and, losing control, ran off the road. His car ended upside down with Stead trapped underneath. Madame du Gast arrived and gave first-aid, later continuing and coming in 77th; she had also stopped when Marcel Renault crashed. Just before the end of the stage Richard hit a horse and cart and seriously injured three people.

Faced with the horror of this wholesale killing the authorities made drastic decisions. The Prime Minister himself signed a decree which not only stopped the race but banned the competitors from returning to Paris under their own power. The cars were even forced to leave the city of Bordeaux at once, drawn by horses. At the railway station of Saint-Jean they were loaded on to railway trucks and sent back to Paris

killed. At the time of the accident the car was travelling at 80 m.p.h.".

Lorraine-Barrow's mechanic in a De Dietrich was pinned against a tree when the driver tried to avoid a dog. Lorraine-Barrow himself was seriously injured and died two weeks later. Like Poter, another driver, Gras, hit a closed level-crossing barrier and his car caught fire; fortunately both driver and mechanic were saved. A journalist, Rodolphe Darzens, skidded off the road at

Still steaming

Though this was a bitter and inglorious end to the intended Paris-Madrid race, it had indicated considerable development. The big cars could now average 60 m.p.h. and more. Even light cars — with 12 to 30 H.P. engines — could complete long journeys at high speeds. This fact was yet another blow at steam cars, whose depleted ranks still raced despite the increasing inadequacy of their vehicles. In this case the vanquished were Le Blon and Chanliaud. But steam cars were not quite finished, and three years later one such vehicle was to put up an astounding speed.

Finally, tyres — nearly all were Michelin — were impro-

Publicity for the Lanza in 1897.

The first Humber, built in 1900 at Coventry and designed by Alec Craig. This car had a single-spoked steering wheel

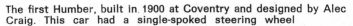

THE MIGHTY "FIGURE 8" ENGINE

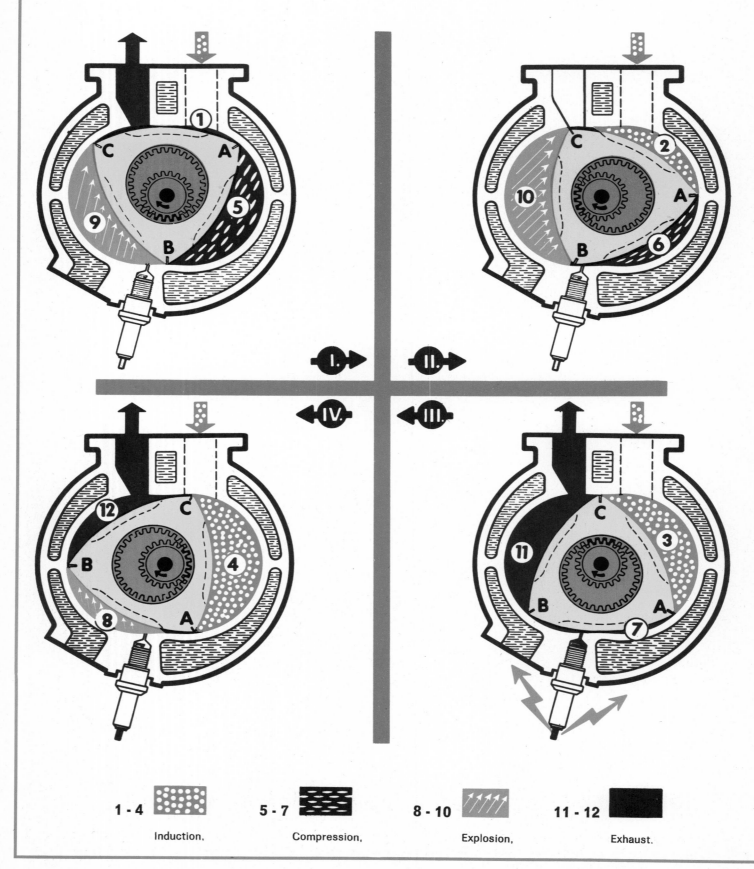

1 - 4	5 - 7	8 - 10	11 - 12
Induction,	Compression,	Explosion,	Exhaust.

From the early days of the invention of the petrol engine thousands have been built which were based on principles or cycles different from those of the classic two or four stroke cycle. Of these, one type has laboriously approached a satisfactory state of development after years of study and experiment — the rotary piston engine or, nowadays commonly, the "Wankel" engine. The first car to fit such an engine in series production was the NSU two seater sports car, and it created much interest in motoring circles for its smoothness, very small size, and for the amazing power developed by its half-litre capacity (though this is not comparable with the half-litre of a reciprocating piston engine, as we shall see).

The essential principles of the Wankel engine are not easy to describe and before doing so it will be useful to look at the engine's history. Its origins lie in 1951 when Felix Wankel, who was in charge of a technical research department in Lindau, made his first contacts with NSU engineers to study the problems of sealing irregular spaces. These studies resulted in the discovery that a more or less triangular rotor (but with convex sides) rotating in a chamber which had, roughly, a figure-eight shape (the descriptions are, of course, mathematically very inexact) could give rise to a true four stroke cycle.

Joint experiments

The first application of the principle was in the form of a compressor for the 50 c.c. NSU two stroke engine with which world records were taken at Utah in 1956. The rotary compressor enabled this small engine to develop 260 b.h.p. per litre. This gave the small car a speed of nearly 100 m.p.h.

In 1958 Wankel agreed with the American company Curtiss-Wright for joint experiments towards the building of a large engine based on his principles. Later, tests were begun with cars powered by various forms of Wankel engines of varying characteristics. Between then and 1963 the engine gradually took definitive form and was then fitted in the small NSU two seater, which was introduced at the Frankfurt Motor Show in the autumn of 1963. Since then a licence has been granted, among others, to Mazda in Japan, who have a twin rotor version in commercial sale.

Perhaps the best example, is the magnificent twin-rotor NSU RO 80, which went into series production in October, 1967; the righthand drive version was introduced on the British market at the end of 1968.

This, then, is how the engine works. In essentials it consists of a chamber whose internal shape approaches a figure of eight, as shown in the diagram. Inside this revolves the somewhat triangular rotor — the piston — which revolves eccentrically in relation to the crankshaft, or mainshaft of the engine. The shapes of these two elements are such that while the corners of the pistons are always equidistant from the walls of the chamber — and very close to them, thus forming a seal — they successively enlarge and reduce the space between the convex sides of the "triangle" — the rotor — and the chamber walls.

The NSU sports with Wankel engine.

Thus, if a mixture is injected into one of the chambers as it is increasing in size, it will be compressed on the subsequent decrease in volume as the rotor, or "piston" rotates. In this way the classical cycle of the four strokes of induction, compression, firing and exhaust is produced, and, furthermore, the three faces of the rotor are at three different phases of the cycle at the same time.

Multipied by three

In the diagram the face CA of the rotor can be seen in positions 1 to 4 gradually passing through successive stages of the first phase, that of induction, of drawing in the explosive air-petrol mixture into the chamber.

Now go back to diagram I and look at side AB. This is now beginning the next phase to that which AC has reached in diagram IV, that of compression. This phase may be followed through positions 5 to 7.

As soon as this point is reached the single sparking plug fires, and the expanding gases may be seen in position 8 providing the power to drive the rotor.

In position 9 and 10, side BC can be seen passing through the phase of explosion and expansion. Then in positions 11 and 12 it sweeps the burnt mixture out of the exhaust port for the exhaust stroke of the cycle.

As we have said, three phases of the cycle are being passed through respectively by the three sides of the rotor, displaced 120° one from the other, and this explains why a "500 c.c." Wankel engine can easily develop 50 b.h.p. The 500 c.c. referred to is that volume between the chamber and one side of the rotor and, as we have seen, this is multiplied by three by the three sides of the rotor.

For and against

The advantages of the Wankel engine over the normal reciprocating piston type are many. In first place is the absence of vibration due to the fact that there is only a rotary movement, and this in turn means less wear and longer life. The consumption of the Wankel engine is rather less than that of the conventional. It can be made significantly smaller and the number of components is fewer, and the engine is therefore inherently less complicated.

The drawbacks include a rather inelastic power curve and problems of maintaining a seal between the corners of the rotor and the faces of the chamber, the latter causing difficulty in the maintenance of production tolerances as well as of design.

What is certain is that today there are cars on commercial sale which perform satisfactorily. Whether the complex of design, performance, production and commercial advantages and disadvantages will come down in favour of the "rotary piston" engine is something that we shall see within the next few years.

Goux in a Lion-Peugeot at the Grand Prix des Voiturettes at Dieppe in 1908.

1906 Corre seen in Monaco.

1904 Gordon Bennett Cup. Girling at the wheel of a Wolseley 7.2 H.P.

A 1904 Marchand "12/16 H.P.". This was one of the more successful cars produced by this firm. It had a 5,429 c.c. four-cylinder engine producing 12 H.P. at 1,000 r.p.m. Four speeds plus reverse and chain transmission. Below a 1908 Grand Prix Itala on a present-day track.

ved and were now able to stand up to the mechanical and heat stresses of a major road race.

Shortly after the disastrous Paris-Madrid race, the fourth Gordon Bennett Cup race was run. This valuable trophy had been won the year before by S. F. Edge in his Napier, as one of the stages of the Paris-Vienna race.

Over to Ireland

In accordance with the regulations, the race now had to be held in England. There was, however, the insurmountable obstacle of the rigid laws imposing a maximum speed of 20 m.p.h., which was to remain in force until 1930. The organisers of the race found an acceptable solution. They decided to hold the race in Ireland, where it was relatively easy to suspend the traffic regulations by means of a local decree.

Just before the race the situation changed dramatically when fire in the Mercedes factory at Cannstatt destroyed five of the six specially prepared 80 H.P. cars. Jellinek — who had become manager for Mercedes — decided to enter the race just the same, using some 60 H.P. touring cars which were awaiting delivery to customers.

Hasty modifications were made and the cars were sent straight to Ireland.

At the same time, a large French contingent set sail for Dublin and Ballyshannon — the start of the race — in a specially chartered ship, the Ferdinand de Lesseps. The race was disastrous for the Americans. Neither Winton nor Owen in Wintons, nor Mooers in his own Peerless was placed. Of the three Napiers nominated to represent England only one, driven by Edge, finished the race and that was disqualified, because Edge was assisted by a spectator at some stage.

The Red Devil

Thus the race became a duel between the French and German teams, and was won by one of the 60 H.P. Mercedes entered by Jellinek — this car was driven by the Belgian, Jenatzy, who had set up a world record in 1899 in his electric car, the "Jamais Contente". Jenatzy was to remain prominent in racing and to

Wrapped up for the Paris-Madrid race — a car in the touring category sets off with good wishes.

A 1906 Peugeot "torpedo" 81B with 2,208 c.c. four-cylinder engine, four speeds plus reverse and chain drive (Peugeot Museum).

A 1906 1,100 c.c. single-cylinder OTAV photographed in Italy in 1957.

acquire the title of "Red Devil" From one point of view, the victory of the German touring car was probably even more impressive than if a racing car had won.

Behind Jenatzy, who averaged almost 50 m.p.h., came three French cars, De Knyff's and Farman's 80 H.P. Panhards and Gabriel's 60 H.P. Mors.

Rolls and Royce

The year 1903 saw the birth of the first Rolls-Royce engine. Then, as today, this famous name stood for engineering perfection. The two founders were able to impose and maintain standards of absolute integrity

and skill. It should be said at once that the official date of the birth of the Rolls-Royce is not 1903, but 1904.

But it was in 1903 that Henry Royce, in his factory in Cook Street, Manchester built his first engine characterised by the same high standards which were to mark the products of the company not yet born.

Royce in 1903 was 40 years old. He was at that time a brilliant electrical engineer on whom fortune had smiled modestly. He was concerned with electric cranes but he had time to spare; he used this time to design and build an i.c. engine without the faults which his able and fastidious mind had found in a 10 H.P. two-cylinder Decauville which he had bought. He had quickly decided that modifications to the engine of

149

A sentimental journey for 80-year-old Ernie Wooler, who returned to England many years after emigrating to the U.S. He returned to the factory where he had been an apprentice, and was able to drive a 1905 Rolls-Royce which he had helped to build.

this car were not worth while, and that the only way to have a really good engine was to build it himself. In fact, Royce built three cars — one for himself, one for his partner, A. E. Claremont, and one for Henry Edmunds, a friend who had recently been made a director of Royce Ltd. Edmunds was enthusiastic about his car. The Honourable C. S. Rolls and his partner Claude Johnson were equally impressed and Rolls, who had been selling imported cars for some years, saw at once that Royce's design was the one to meet all the requirements of his customers.

Royce's first engine was a 10 H.P. 1,800 c.c. twin. It was quiet, reliable and clean — properties which were uncommon in cars of that period. When Rolls-Royce was formed in 1904 a variety of cars was produced, consisting of a 10 H.P. twin, a 15 H.P. three-cylinder, a 20 H.P. four-cylinder and a 30 H.P. six-cylinder. In 1905 Rolls entered two of the 20 H.P. cars in the Tourist Trophy, Percy Northey's taking second place; in 1906 he won at an average of 40.2 m.p.h.

Only one model

It was in 1906 that the next Rolls-Royce was produced. This was a remarkable vee-eight engined car, governed down to 20 m.p.h. and thus called the "Legalimit". It was as clean, quiet and as vibration-free as an electric car. For 1907 Rolls-Royce Ltd. decided to concentrate on only one model, which was to be the finest car in the world. Royce, who designed, built and personally tested all the previous cars, set to work.

The result was exhibited at the Olympia Motor Show at the end of 1906 — and so was exhibited one of the finest cars ever built. The 40/50 Rolls-Royce had a six-cylinder in-line engine with bore and stroke of 114×120 mm., and gave a capacity of 7,434 c.c. There was dual ignition (coil and magneto) and valves were at the side. The whole car was built with fantastic precision.

One of the early cars was referred to as a "silver ghost" because of its silent running — and the name at once stuck, the car being known ever since as the "40/50 Silver Ghost". In addition to being silent, the car was long-lived and free from breakdowns. It was kept in production for 19 years — a record surpassed only by the front-wheel drive Citroën.

Though the car was never intended for racing, it was decided to demonstrate its qualities in endurance tests and trials, and one "Silver Ghost" was entered for the Scottish Reliability Trials in 1907. It won a gold medal for its class, and then went on to complete 15,000 miles without the engine stopping. This it did, apart for a stop in error for one minute. The car was then stripped down and all replacements necessary were made to bring it back to its former condition. The cost came to less than £2 5s.

MR. CHARTER'S "WATER ENGINE"

To build a self-propelled vehicle powered by an engine using substances supplied by nature in abundance, air and water, has often been the dream of automotive designers. Unfortunately, water and air will not combine together to release useable energy.

All the same, a car fitted with a "water" engine was once built and ran on the roads of America about 1903.

Wishful Thinking

It was the Charter, a phaeton produced after years of experiment by James A. Charter.

It should be made clear that the expression "water engine" was given to the car by the public, probably out of wishful thinking. In fact, Mr Charter's feet were more firmly on the ground and he himself called it the "water-gasoline" engine.

It was, in any case, a strange vehicle. At that time, in spite of the considerable advances made since the days of the "horseless carriage", carburation was a long way from being perfect.

Bizarre and peculiar devices were designed to achieve the miracle of a perfect mixture of air and petrol vapour whatever the circumstances of the engine — at low and high speeds, climbing, descending, hot or cold, under load or not, wet or dry.

Even today, after tremendous advances have been made, the problems have not been completely solved.

James Charter decided he could improve carburation by obtaining the oxygen necessary for combustion from water, where oxygen certainly exists in abundance, rather than from air. He used a mixture of two parts of petrol to one part water.

The weakness of his engine lay in maintaining it at the correct temperature, which had to be high enough to cause the instant vaporisation of the mixture droplets drawn into the cylinder by the pistons, while not being so hot as to cause overheating and pre-ignition.

Under the seats

The system that Charter used to indicate overheating in the engine was also somewhat unusual. He placed the engine directly under the seats of the driver and passenger. In this way the sensitivity of the occupants themselves showed when it was necessary to stop the car and cool off the engine as soon as it became overheated.

Charter's car, it might be added, had only a short life.

American styling simplified over the years — the 1967 Oldsmobile "Cutlass" (above) and the 1958 Cadillac "Coupe de Ville" below.

CHAPTER TEN
"TIN LIZZIE" IS BORN

The creation of the Ford Motor Company was to play a vital role in the development of the motor car. It was the first to set up genuinely large-scale production; it also created a commercial and special concept hitherto unheard of. This concept presented the car as a vehicle designed for mass consumption and therefore designed with robustness and durability; at the same time, everything superfluous or irrational was eliminated. So was anything which would prevent the price being kept as low as possible. Ideas like this were revolutionary for their time.

Henry Ford — who was always firmly in command of his huge factory, notwithstanding the presence of major shareholders — also introduced a number of organisational and social reforms inspired by certain principles. In particular, he held that the greatest number of people should benefit from the use of a sound product at a low price, and that as many as possible should share in the material benefits created by its production.

In 1903 the tremendous social and technical differences between the Old and the New Worlds were illustrated by the beginnings of Rolls-Royce and the establishment

1905 Ford model "C" 2-4 seater. All the rear body is detachable along the sloping joint.

Steam-powered vehicles were still being produced before World War I. Here is a 1913 Stanley Steamer.

the Ford Motor Company. One was to become the byword for refinement and the other for robust, almost spartan, simplicity. The fortunes of both companies were based on technical honesty and on the absolute refusal of both founders to accept anything but the best solutions for their different purposes, without which neither company would have had lasting success. In later years Henry Ford was to drive a Rolls-Royce.

Publicity Value

When Ford was involved with his first racing cars he demonstrated the relationship between the end desired and the means to be used. This was to remain typical of all the acts of the great manufacturer.

Building racing cars was not an end in itself for Ford but after his disappointments and losses on his earlier cars, he knew the value of the publicity and popularity that came from winning races.

He had his first personal success against Winton and later successes with his second car, the "Arrow", and with the third, the "999", in the hands of the popular Barney Oldfield.

Ford in three years won a fame and popularity which in themselves meant little to him but which he judged sufficient to enable him for the third time to become a manufacturer of popular cars.

On 16 June, 1903, the Ford Motor Company was set up with a capital of 150,000 dollars. Henry Ford himself became vice-President, Head of Engineering and General Manager. Among the shareholders were John and Horace Dodge, ex-mechanics who had for some time had their own bicycle business using ball-bearings designed and patented by themselves. At the moment when Ford suggested they should take shares in his company they had a factory producing transmission components for Olds. Against all the advice of their friends, who considered the new enterprise much too risky, the Dodge brothers accepted Ford's offer of 10 per cent of his company in return for equipping the new factory with

1904 Ford model "B".

1907 Ford model "R".

The start of the 1909 transcontinental race. Below, the 1910 Ford model "T" had a separate rear seat called "the mother-in-law's seat".

machine tools and for the temporary manufacture of Ford engines in their own factory.

This decision enabled them to receive 25,000,000 dollars in 1919 in exchange for their initial investment of 20,000 dollars.

Strong competition

Among the founder-shareholders in the Ford Motor Company was Andrew Strelow, who contributed his metalworking factory in which Ford intended to set up his first assembly line; Alexander Y. Malcolmson, who supplied 7,000 dollars; Charles J. Woodall and James Couzens, both employees of Malcolmson; John S. Gray, a banker; two lawyers, John W. Anderson and Horace H. Rackham; an estate agent called Vernon Fry; and finally Charles H. Bennett, an inventor and manufacturer of air rifles.

The beginnings of the Ford Motor Company were not easy. There was strong competition from already established companies such as Cadillac, Oldsmobile, Reo (Olds' company after he left the one bearing his own name) and Maxwell.

Ford used an unusual system for naming his models — only letters of the alphabet. This was typical of his direct and simple approach in an era when other manufacturers were using horse-power or powerfull-sounding names to impress the public.

Ford's cars, however, only vaguely reflected his personality. This is understandable enough as they were built in different factories headed by ex-craftsmen who each tried to impose his habits and point of view. Both the first and second models, the "A" of 1903 and the "B"

of 1904, were of fairly conventional type, though the third in 1905, naturally called the "C", exhibited some originality. For example, two rear seats were provided in a "tonneau" body and could be easily erected or taken down.

The "C" was followed by the flat twin "F" and then in 1906-1907 by the "K", which was an attempt to enter the luxury market. It had a six-cylinder engine (the earlier types had had two or four cylinders) and was put on sale at 2,400 dollars, though the cost of production was considerably more.

Ford at this moment was obviously uncertain which road to follow. The "K" had a six-litre engine and its

OPEL Darracq 1902

Europe continued to progress. Out of experiments and errors came practical vehicles like this 1902 Opel Darracq, the 1909 "Doktorwagen" and the 1902 "Tonneau".

two speeds and reverse foreshadowed the model "T" yet to come. Its appearance was similar to that of the best European luxury cars of the time.

With the model "N", introduced in 1906, Ford set out for the first time to win the mass market. This four-cylinder model was put on sale first at 500 and then at 600 dollars — a competitive price compared with the single-cylinder cars of other manufacturers. Though popular, it did not make much money as Ford had not yet introduced the manufacturing techniques used later for the "T".

OPEL Tonneau 1902

The "N" had certain aspects which were later to gain the "T" its name of "spider" — relatively large wheels of wide track with a small body mounted high above the ground.

In 1907 and the beginning of 1908 two further predecessors of the "T" were introduced. These were the "R" and the "S", de luxe versions of the "N", with which Ford neared his target of a car for the masses. They both followed the general lines of the "N", with the same policy of low price and growing commercial success. Both rear and front suspensions were improved.

Criticism silenced

At last in 1908 came one of the most famous cars in motoring history — the Ford model "T". The "Lizzie"

OPEL Doktorwagen 1909

was to be known to millions of Americans — "Tin Lizzie" at first to its detractors before its fantastic success soon made such jibes ridiculous. It was officially born on 1 October, 1908, with a commercial launch which anticipated the publicity techniques of the future and was master-minded by Flanders, one of Ford's most active colleagues.

Thus before the birth of that first car, which was to be the forerunner of over 15,000,000 others, there had been the tasks of finding and testing new materials, of completely reorganising the machine shops, of setting up assembly lines and of ensuring the full co-operation of sub-contractors.

For this last operation, Ford was not particular about the means he used, preferring to absorb his suppliers to protect himself against commercial antagonism.

A FORGOTTEN BREED FROM SCOTLAND THE ARROL - JONSTON

Nowadays, nobody remembers the Arrol-Johnston. Yet this marque, produced at Paisley until 1913, and thereafter at Dumfries, once enjoyed an impressive following. One of their 18 H.P. models won the first Tourist Trophy of all in 1905, in the recession year of 1907 they turned out 700 vehicles, and as late as 1921 fifty solid tourers

were leaving Heathhall every week. In 1928 the company was — on paper — a Scottish microcosim of B.M.C., offering four different makes and six models, from a modest 12 H.P. to a luxurious and elegant straight-eight. And there lay the rub.
George Johnston was one of Scotland's pioneer motorists, and one realistic enough to design for the immediate home market — he and not his associate Sir William Arrol, of Forth Bridge fame, was responsible for the cars. The dog-carts produced between 1897 and 1905 were primordial Land-Rovers in the best horseless-carriage style, with towering varnished-wood coachwork, a high ground clearance to cope with the abominable Highland roads, and no visible machinery. The big opposed-piston flat-twin engine lived under the floor, as did the horizontal radiator; final drive was by chain. Three rows of bench-type seats were usually provided, the driver being ensconced in the second row of the stalls, as it were. In theory he could start his motor without dismounting. The low-tension ignition was reliable, and Johnston's slogan ("no noise, no dirt, no smell, and no vibration") was true enough at the modest speeds within

the dog-cart's compass. When two of his partners resigned in 1900 to found the still-famous Albion concern, they started with a very similar model.

An odd three-cylinder followed, still on solid tyres, but in 1905 Arrol-Johnston reshaped their entire image with an outwardly conventional type, though this was still a flat-twin, the work of J. S. Napier, who beat one of the earliest Rolls-Royces into first place in the 1905 T.T. Alas, horizontal engines were out of fashion, as Wolseley were discovering to their cost, and the "18" was not a success, any more than were the ordinary "fours" which Napier evolved to replace it. Some of these were enormous — the 1908 38-45 h.p. disposed of ten-odd litres. Nor did their special air-cooled machine built for Shackleton's Antarctic Expedition achieve more than a footnote to history. It was an impressive "first" but it did not sell Arrol-Johnston, any more than did factory support for the French light-car races of 1911 and 1912. The Scottish racers were slow and reliable, whereas the rival Sunbeams were not only reliable, but rapid as well.

None the less, Arroll-Johnston was one of the first firms to offer four-wheel brakes on a standard tourer, these appearing on the Pullinger-designed 2.4-litre "15.9" of 1910 a solid family carriage with Renault-like dashboard radiator, which sold quite well. The uncoupled anchors created more problems than they solved, and were dropped after two seasons, but in 1914 a "15.9" with electric lighting and starting could be bought for only £360. Plans to build the American Detroit Electric under licence misfired: Heathhall had entered this market too late.

Aero-engines were made during the War, but Arrol-Johnston overreached themselves in 1919 with their 2.6-litre "Victory". A 40 b.h.p. overhead-camshaft engine and central gear change sounded promising, but the result was a well-publicised flop, especially after it had broken down with the Prince of Wales on board. In its place came the old "15.9", now with frontal radiator. It was not particularly cheap, and the only thing that distinguished it from its many competitors was a three-piece wrap-round windscreen.

The small, self-contained factory was no longer competitive. They tried a cheap 1½-litre model, the Galloway, and made it in a former aero-engine works at Tongland, staffed entirely by women under the direction of Pullinger's daughter, but this did not prosper, and by 1922 all activities were concentrated once more at Heathhall. For the next few seasons the company made ordinary and ponderous cars, introducing a big 3.3-litre "four" when "sixes" were becoming fashionable. By 1926 overhead valves and front-wheel brakes were standard wear, but sales went on falling.

1927 saw an amalgamation with Aster of Wembley, who built luxury fast tourers — also slow sellers. With Aster came the complex and expensive single-sleeve-valve engine. The Arrol-Aster introduced for the 1928 season was quiet, handsome, reasonably fast, and well-braked. But the valve gear would not sustain anything above 3,400 r.p.m., and this defeated attempts to transform their new straight-eight into a sports car. In 1929 the Arrol-Johnston and Galloway names were dropped; a year later the Aster had gone, but 1928 had been the company's last appearance at a Motor Show, and even a contract to rebuild Sir Malcolm Campbell's "Bluebird" was of no avail. The Arrol-Aster version failed to take the World's Land Speed Record.

Unrealistic policy killed the Arrol-Johnston. Uninspired and barbarous the dog-cart may have been, but it catered for an appreciative market on its front doorstep. Its successors of the 1920s offered nothing that could not be bought elsewhere, either for less money or with a more exciting performance.

An early Arrol-Johnston "dogcart".

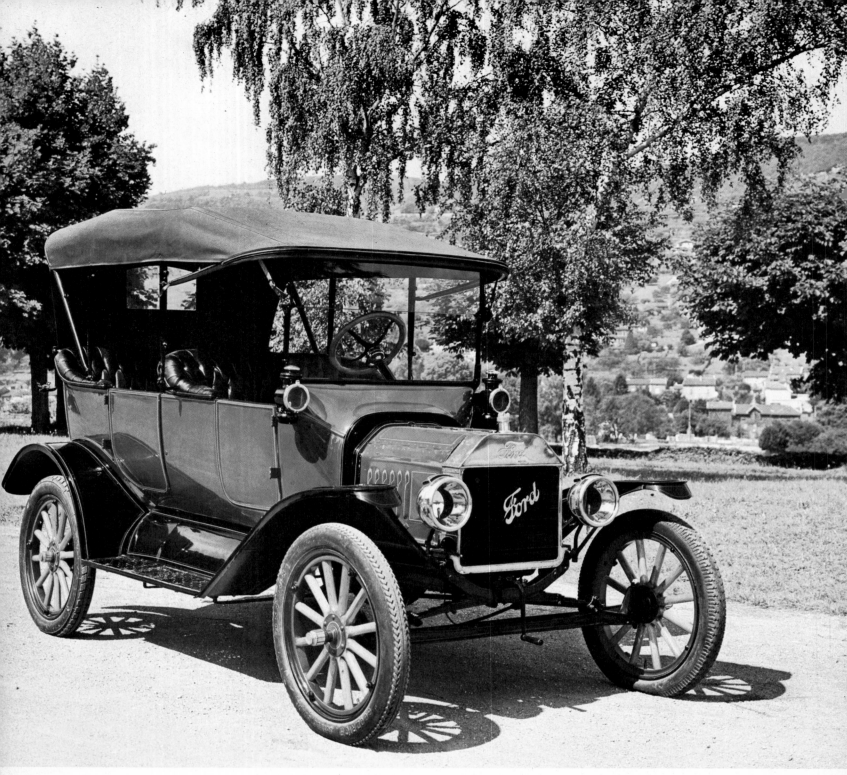

1915 Ford model "T". It cost 440 dollars. The car has non-standard paintwork: by then black was the only colour available.

Road conditions were against this forlorn car; the driver has gone to find a horse for a tow.

This gigantic work of preparation, undoubtedly without precedent, absorbed the last financial resources of Ford and his partners. Couzens, for instance, borrowed his sister Rosetta's last 100 dollars for the launch. Inevitably the crisis raised doubts among some shareholders, especially in the Malcolmson group, and it is easy to imagine the state of nerves in which the "Lizzie" was made ready.

At last the car was launched: from 1913 onwards standardisation was the watchword, and Ford coined his famous dictum — his customers "could have any colour they liked so long as it was black".

The first thing that struck Americans, who had waited with mounting curiosity for the launch, was the apparent fragility of the new car. At first sight the "T"

was disconcerting, giving the impression of little resistance to wear and normal use. It was built largely of vanadium steel, a great technological innovation as it was much stronger than normal steel.

This enabled so much material to be saved that it more than offset its higher cost and gave a bonus in reduced weight. The use of vanadium was one of the most brilliant ideas of C. Harold Wills, a young engineer whom Henry Ford had brought to New York and entrusted with the overall design of the new car. He was responsible for reducing the Model-T's chassis to proportions which could stand up to the buffeting from the American roads of the time. This chassis was supported, front and rear, by transverse leaf springs.

The extreme lightness of the steel, which Wills also used for less essential parts of the car, had a considerable effect on the appearance of other items such as the light mudguards and running boards. But the innovations on the "T" did not stop here.

Above a 1914 Ford "T". Below, veteran cars parked in present-day Virginia City, Nevada.

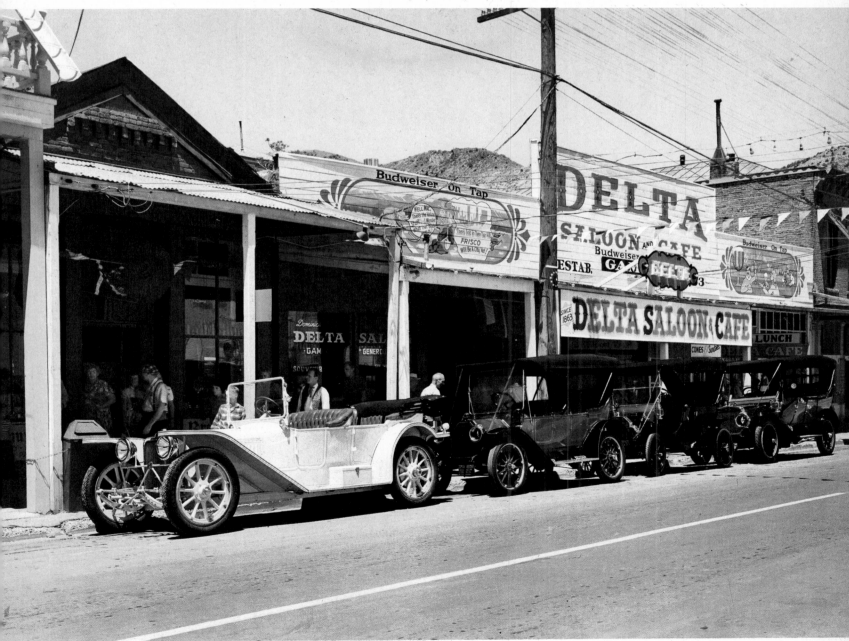

Styling evolution in clothes and cars. A Ford "Thunderbird" and below, a "T". Ford's one-model policy was a great success but it continued too long, and by 1927 it brought the company near to disaster.

The engine, a four-cylinder, 2,898 c.c. (95 × 101 mm. bore and stroke) had its block cast in one piece and the valves were all on one side. The cylinder head was detachable, which allowed much simpler casting and gave easy access to valves and cylinders.

At first it developed 20 H.P.; this was later raised to 22 H.P., which was a reasonable figure for such a light car and which gave it an acceleration that contributed to its commercial success. Its top speed, however, was only 40 m.p.h.; but this, though more than adequate in 1909, was altogether too lethargic by the standards of 1927, when the "T" was withdrawn from production.

Ignition and transmission

The most remarkable features of the "T" were its ignition and transmission systems. Ignition was by fly-wheel magneto running in an oil bath. This system was invented and patented by John Heinze and Ford remained faithful to it for many years, in spite of certain drawbacks.

The transmission was the result of much hard work by Ford technicians, and was revolutionary. It consisted of an epicyclic gearbox with only two speeds, all that was necessary in view of the low top speed of the car and the low revving engine with its maximum of 1,500 r.p.m. (deliberately designed this way by Ford to ensure a long life).

The gear change was by pedal and, to make this possible, the accelerator was a lever placed near the driver's left hand and near the other manual control, the ignition

From left to right — 1910 DFP, 1909 Lion-Peugeot, 1914 Renault, 1914 Benz.

advance/retard lever. The clutch, however, could be operated in two ways, either by the handbrake lever or by the gearchange pedal itself.

To put the "T" in motion a number of unusual procedures had to be followed, the result of Ford's simplification of the various mechanical elements in the case of simplified production. These procedures were to become familiar to millions of Americans — the model "T" owners — while the rest of the world controlled its motor cars in a way very similar to the methods used today.

In order to start the "T", light pressure had to be put on the gear-change pedal, having provided a "neutral". It was then necessary to release the hand-brake lever which worked on the rear wheels. So long as this was

A 1911 Clément Bayard AC2A passing various versions of the Fiat "508 Balilla". Below a 1907 Bianchi Phaeton.

applied it disengaged the clutch, but allowed it to engage as soon as it was released.

With the brake thus released and the clutch disengaged, further pressure on the gear-change pedal engaged both first gear and the clutch. With the car in motion the foot could be gradually raised until top gear was engaged. It was at this point that the inexperienced driver could achieve an astounding series of bounds.

Into swift reverse

To stop the "T" was simple. The brake pedal, which worked on the transmission, was pressed and at the same time the hand-brake was applied to brake the rear wheels and simultaneously disengage the clutch. Two other methods of stopping the "T" were also possible.

The first of these was to stamp on the brake pedal and the gear-change pedal at the same time, thus engaging first gear and so slowing the car down rapidly. The second was used only in the worst emergencies because of the possibility of dire consequences to the machinery. This consisted simply of engaging reverse gear directly by pressing on a third pedal, and at the same time stamping on the brake pedal.

The astonishing fact is that such a manoeuvre, which would result in the immediate disintegration of the gearbox and much else in the modern car, rarely resulted in a breakdown in the "T".

Spanner and hammer

It is difficult to imagine road conditions in America in those days. Whilst it is true that in the period 1908 to 1927, the production years of the "T", there was tremendous expansion of the first-class road and motor-way network, this was anything but true of the second-ary and local road systems.

The U.S. was a relatively young country so that there was nothing like the vast European transport system that served drivers there until roads fit for the motor car were built.

This explains why the Model-T, though uncomfortable and outmoded by later standards, rapidly became a major social phenomenon and stayed so for many years.

Two examples of pre – 1914 styling.

Ford had escaped from the format of the "T" by 1929. A model "A" roadster.

W. R. Morris's garage in Oxford in the early years of the twentieth century, before he launched out into car manufacture.

The motor car has revolutionised land transport but long-range deliveries are now made by rail. From early days road transporters have been used for shorter journeys (below).

The "T" was capable of being driven through mud, over rough ground and through fords and pools. Its legendary robustness and ease of maintenance — for most repairs only a spanner and a hammer were necessary — made it ideal for the conditions in which it operated.

The fact was also important, and unusual at the time, that it came fully equipped not only with body and seats but also with a hood with which to face the weather and a long journey across the prairie. Of course, later the model "T" was also sold as a chassis only, on which a wide variety of bodies were fitted.

Finally, there was its price to convince millions and millions of Americans that at last a car was in the reach of their purses. At the time of its launch the Model-T cost 850 dollars: the price was gradually reduced until a roadster retailed at less than 300 dollars.

These are the reasons why 15 million were sold in 19 years of production and why Ford sales rose from 8,000 in 1908 to 250,000 in 1914.

The commercial success of the "T", and to a lesser extent of the cars which preceded it, would have been impossible in any economy other than that of the U. S. between 1910 and 1929.

In the first year of its production, Ford profits rose from one million to 27 million dollars. In 1914 Ford was able to introduce a 40-hour week in his factories and to pay his manual workers five dollars a day against the 2½ dollars in other factories.

Rosetta's 100 dollars

Alexander Malcomson's 7,000-dollar investment had become 175,000 in three years (the figure is known because Malcolmson was paid after disagreements with Ford); and Rosetta Couzens' 100 dollars, invested just before the birth of the "T", had become 260,000 by 1919.

GAS TO THE RESCUE

The strange variations of cars fuelled by gas is now no more than a memory for most motorists. Such cars, which had their heyday in the wartime 1940s, represented an emergency device which was thankfully given up as soon as circumstances permitted. But when petrol was rationed or non-existent for civilian use in many countries of Europe, the gas-driven cars fulfilled a useful role. The earliest experiments with gas had been conducted in France and Germany by Panhard & Levassor, Renault, D.K.W. and Gepaa. In Italy apparatus was built by Pignone-Hag and Scaglia.

Trials using coal gas as a fuel for motor vehicles were also run between 1920 and 1930. But they were abandoned because of the major drawbacks involved, including the high cost, the inconvenience and the short time that the gas lasted.

Variety of fuels

While these drawbacks were deciding factors in peace-time, they became less important in face of wartime petrol shortages. This was why gas was utilised all over the continent from 1940. The most widespread use was in Italy, which of all the countries at war had the greatest difficulty in obtaining petrol supplies.

In the case of producer gas or water gas, the installation could use a variety of fuels such as peat, anthracite, coal and wood, though the quantity of gas produced obviously varied. Whatever fuel was used, the basic feature was a unit producing gas by distillation.

This was a furnace lined with refractory materials, the bottom consisting of a grill, below which was a cinder tray. A water tank was heated by the fire, and from this tank the water vapour came into contact with the red-hot coals or coke.

Carbon dioxide and hydrogen were formed, and this mixture was conducted to the carburettor and engine via a series of subsidiary devices — the cleaner, cooler, drier and separator.

The use of this gas on a large scale was encouraged by several governments. But it had one defect more important than all the others as far as the motorist was concerned: it was extremely difficult to start a car when it was using gas. It was necessary first to heat the car for a half hour before starting up; it was then difficult to get the mixture to fire the engine until the cylinder block itself was hot.

In theory the engine might have been warmed up on petrol, but this would have led to a serious risk of explosion in the gas system.

Another though less important difficulty — provided the car could operate on gas — was the need to carry around a large quantity of fuel. Towards the end of the war, both wood and coal themselves became scarce in many countries. In many war-ravaged territories heating homes was more essential than moving cars. Nevertheless, the use of gas made possible many thousands of miles of war-time motoring which otherwise would have been impossible.

Some of these journeys were not without incident. It was not unusual to see a bus at rest while its passengers went foraging along the roadside. They were looking for fuel to complete their trip.

Above — a 1968 Chevrolet Corvette. Below — a 1918 Chevrolet saloon, produced a year after the company became part of General Motors.

CHAPTER ELEVEN

THE EMBRYO GIANT

The second big American motor group, General Motors — today one of the most powerful commercial complexes in the world — was officially created in September, 1908. It was the peak of the work of an outstanding individual, William Crapo Durant. The story of his automobile empire goes back to 1904, and parallels that of Ford, but the ambitions and methods of the two men were very different.

Ford was basically an engineer with clear commercial ideas, but all springing from an enthusiasm for the motor car. Durant was, above all, a business organiser and company promoter. He was a man who, like others of

Above — an Oldsmobile of 1908, the year in which Durant formed General Motors and bought Champion and Oldsmobile. Below — a 1916 Oldsmobile. While different from the 1908 model above, car styling has obviously not undergone a revolution.

his time, realised the financial potential of the motor car, and decided to involve himself as deeply as possible in the boom which he so clearly foresaw.

The grandson of a governor of Michigan, in the early 1900s "Billy" Durant was already a millionaire, having founded and successfully developed a carriage factory with his partner and friend, Joshua Dallas Dort, an ex-merchant of fancy goods. Mainly because of Durant's enthusiasm, they decided to turn their plant in Flint — which was a coachbuilding centre — into a car factory. The problem, from a purely commercial point of view, was to find a well-established make of car that was in

financial difficulties and might be revived by the investment of capital. The chance was offered by Buick.

David Dunbar Buick was an ex-plumber, also from Michigan, who had made a small fortune from his patents for vitreous enamelling of cast iron, and then decided to build motor cars as did so many craftsmen of his time. Thanks to his engineering expertise, his first light tourer was quickly accepted. The engine was well balanced, the styling was elegant and the car had some practical ideas such as positively actuated overhead valves.

The financial state of the company, the Buick Manufactur-

ing Company, was not so encouraging. By 1903, only one year after its foundation, it had to reform itself as the Buick Motor Car Company with a large injection of capital from the brothers Vincent and Benjamin Briscoe, who had been among those who had earlier financed Olds.

Buick's association with the Briscoes did not last long, however. Business was bad and the brothers withdrew from the company. Buick, in spite of his ideas and his excellent cars, found himself on the point of bankruptcy. Thus Durant, on November 1, 1904, was able to gain control of his first established motor company. In his capacity of financier, Durant at once increased the capital of 75,000 dollars first to 300,000 then to 500,000. He moved the factory to the wagon works at Flint, with which he had come to an agreement.

Forming a trust

The impetus that Durant gave to this new activity was fantastic. From 28 Buicks built in 1904, production soared to 626 in 1905 and 2,300 in 1906. By 1908 Buick production was so satisfactory that Durant felt strong enough to make another step on the way to the motoring throne which he so clearly coveted.

Instead of looking round for another company in difficulty, Durant's ideas were much more ambitious — no less than a motor trust that would bring together all or nearly all of America's major manufacturers to form a group capable of producing the fantastic figure of 50,000 cars a year.

Without wasting time Durant founded his new company, with the impressive-sounding name of "The International Motor Company", and then sent emissaries to his competitors to propose the union. Ford, clearly the most important objective in this large scale operation, gave a decided no, as did Maxwell-Briscoe and Reo.

Durant, never one to waste his time up blind alleys, at once abandoned the idea and on September 16, 1908, formed another company, the General Motors, with a capital of 12,500,000 dollars. Its job was to shore up any tottering companies — including accessory manu-

A 1903 Cadillac model "A" with 1,609 c.c. engine, two speeds and chain transmission. For many years the name has been associated with luxury cars. In the early days of the company, however, Cadillac was renowned for robustness and low price.

For the first time an English monarch travels in a car. The date is April 12, 1902. Edward VII is at the side of John Scott-Montagu in a new 24 H.P. Daimler. After a ride through the New Forest, the King bought one for his family. Below: a 12 H.P. Sunbeam of 1904.

facturing businesses — in order to form a base for new industrial activity.

The first companies thus absorbed were Dow, a wheel company, Ewing Automobile, the Cartercar Company and Elmore. These were small companies which had previously been grouped in the International Motor Company. Then followed Weston Mott, of Utica (which specialised in axle production) and then the first big purchase, Champion, the sparking plug factory set up by Albert Champion, the French racing driver.

Persisting in his plan to buy up all the accessory manufacturers necessary for his group, Durant absorbed Briscoe, which made mudguards, and then his first big motor car company. This was Oldsmobile, big in reputation though commercially small; like Briscoe, Oldsmobile changed its mind after an earlier refusal.

All these purchases, including also the coachbuilders, W. F. Stewart, took place over four months and Durant distributed 245,000 dollars in dividends — not so much because of trading success as out of necessity to maintain the enthusiasm of his partners. Durant was now in full cry and on July 28, 1909, the famous Cadillac concern was bought at a price of 4,400,000 dollars.

Ill-timed offer

At this point he conceived the most ambitious scheme of his financial career — yet another approach to Ford. "Fabulous Billy", as Durant was already known in Wall Street, offered to buy the Ford Motor Company for the

1901 Columbia, built in the U.S.A. by the Electric Vehicle Company. This car belonged to Queen Alexandra.

astronomical sum of eight million dollars. Naturally, Durant was acting for a group of financiers, and these, as will be seen, were quick to withdraw their support at the first sign of crisis.

The huge offer once again fell on deaf ears, but only for a piece of ill-timing. Ford, in spite of the notable success of the "T", had been having a difficult time, above all because of his dispute over the Selden patent. In fact, Durant's offer arrived just as Ford became certain of winning his legal battle and was free from the nightmare of having to pay huge arrears of royalties to the then holders of the patent.

Ford's refusal was the beginning of Durant's decline. In keeping with what was typical behaviour at the time by American big business, the unlimited faith which it had placed in Durant rapidly turned to uneasiness at the size and ambitious nature of his ideas and then into open alarm. Wall Street turned its back on him and replaced him with Charles W. Nash.

Nash was an old colleague of Durant's, having worked in the cart and carriage factory in Flint, and had set up the first assembly line of the type that was to become typical of every motor manufacturer. Appointed President of Buick after Durant had bought it, he quickly

A 1910 Lion Peugeot on the seafront.

TYRE REVOLUTION GATHERS PACE

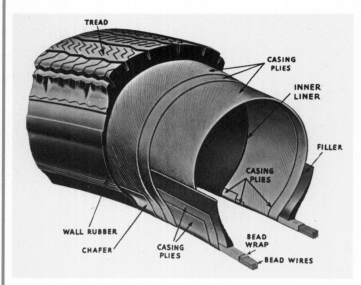

Cross-section cross-ply tyre.

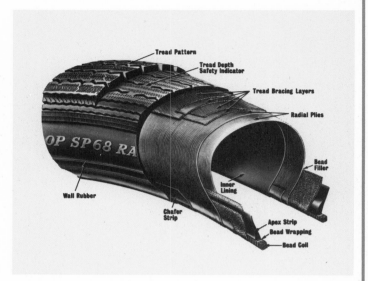

Cross-section radial-ply tyre.

Two dramatic features of tyre design and construction have emerged in recent years, after a long period of steady but slow technological progress in previous decades. Of these, the most remarkable has been the swing to radial-ply casings; the other feature — the trend towards low-profile section — is slower to develop but is now gaining more rapid acceptance.

The radial tyre "revolution" gains impetus every day. In Britain about 20 per cent of the market is now in this type of tyre. The proportion is even higher in Europe, which accounts for about a third of the world sales of 100 million car tyres a year, a figure which will probably double by 1980.

Two factors

The compromise between comfort, Radial deflection, and steerability (sideways stiffness) is not possible with the traditional (cross-ply) tyre structure as with the radial-ply tyre. A radial casing alone offers no improvement, but if it also has a reinforced belt structure, it retains the high comfort factor of its radial-ply nature, with added virtues of steering controlability.

Moreover, it allows the designer to adjust the two factors in relation to each other as required for a particular type of car. In contrast to the radial, the cross-ply is now comparatively limited as far as further development is concerned.

Radials are perhaps 25 per cent more costly than cross-ply tyres, but may give up to 80 per cent more mileage. The cost factor, however, indicates that the two kinds of tyre will sell competitively with one another for some

years to come. Car manufacturers now design certain models for certain types of tyre, but this is a limited tendency and most models can take either type. Mixing of the two types is regarded as risky, especially the use of radials on the front and cross-ply at the back, or different types on each side.

Racing influence

The tendency towards the squat-profile tyre applies to both types. This is accelerated by the adoption of astonishingly wide, flat tyres on the modern racing car, in order to obtain adhesion and endurance with these light, ultra-powerful machines. Such factors are important for road cars, but there is also a strong styling influence.

Designers want wheels of small overall diameter, but they must be big for better braking and suspension; the lowered height-width ratio is the answer. The radial, incidentally, is more easily designed to give enhanced performance at the lower profiles.

Though far from "puncture-proof", the tubeless tyre in cross-ply and radial form continues to gain ground. Steel-reinforced tyres are still popular with many users, though most reinforcement is nylon or rayon. There have also been encouraging results from an all-polyester radial tyre by a British manufacturer.

In North America, there is a current vogue for the bias-belted tyre — a compromise between the cross-ply and radial — though it is likely to be only a matter of time before radials dominate the markets in Europe and the U.S.

1912 La Ponette.

took the old company to a prosperity it had never known before. It is not surprising that General Motors shareholders saw in him a more realistic man with whom to replace the capricious "Billy". (The name "Nash" was to become even more familiar to the mass of American motorists after 1917, when he bought the well known Jeffery factory.)

Not that this was the end of Durant, for five years later he was back at the helm of General Motors as a result of his success with Chevrolet. He left the company finally as the result of a crisis which saw General Motors shares fall from 400 dollars to 12 dollars. He still persisted in the car industry, however, and his name was associated with a number of makes such as Durant, Star and Locomobile, until the world crisis of 1929 sent him finally into obscurity. He died in 1947.

Huge misunderstanding

The "Selden question", mentioned earlier, was a strange affair which had considerable influence on the early American motor industry. The affair has been called a

1909 Humber 8 H.P. It had a 1,525 c.c. twin-cylinder engine with dual ignition and three speeds plus reverse.

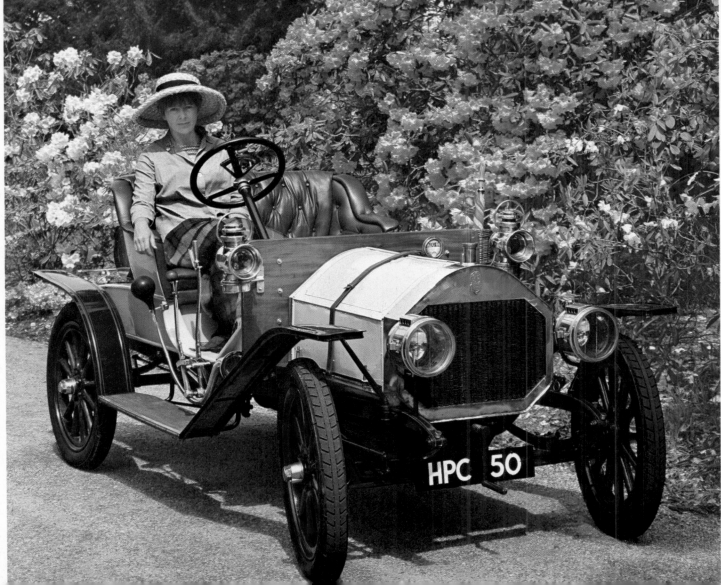

The first Singer, built in 1905.

1913 9 H.P. Hillman coupé.

huge misunderstanding, but others have referred to it as a racket imposed by violence. Its beginnings were at the show held in Philadelphia in 1876 when a young lawyer, George Baldwin Selden, admired George Brayton's i.c.-engine exhibited there; three years later he applied for a patent for a development of that engine, which he had subsequently applied to a vehicle.

As soon as car manufacturing became established on an industrial basis in the last decade of the century, Selden decided to exploit his patent which had finally been granted in November 1895. This patent was possible only because Selden was a competent lawyer and because the patents officials were, at best, incompetent.

1911 Opel "Stadt coupé".

A famous light car: the 1913 "Bebé" Peugeot, which did over 60 miles to the gallon.

Waited for opportunity

The patent covered everything that might be called an automobile. The original text stated "... the combination, in a road locomotive equipped with an appropriate transmission, driving wheels and steering, of a hydrocarbon engine of one or more cylinders, a fuel tank, a transmission shaft designed to run at a speed higher than that of the driving wheels, a clutch and coachwork adapted for the transport of persons or goods..." With considerable foresight Selden was able to have the new patent back-dated to the date of his original application, and he then sat back to wait for an occasion to profit by it.

The opportunity came when Col. Albert A. Pope, of Hartford, in the name of his company, the Electric Vehicle Company, requested a licence to manufacture small cars for use as taxis. The request arose on the advice of Pope's lawyer, who had discovered the existence of Selden's patent.

1903 Panhard-Levassor 7 H.P., a much copied car. The twin-cylinder engine had a capacity of 1,654 c.c. The gear box had three forward speeds, and final drive was by chain. Lord Montagu at the wheel.

Selden, of course, granted the licence and, with the confidence of a first success behind him, did not hesitate to start a legal action to establish his "monopoly rights". The victim selected was the Winton Motor Carriage Company of Cleveland. Winton was a genuine manufacturer, who hardly deserved to be sued in this way, and even less deserved the sentence of the court that he should pay arrears of royalties and damages to Selden. This verdict had the effect of causing 10 manufacturers, including Pope, Winton, Olds and Packard to form ALAM — the Association of Licensed Automobile Manufacturers — to defend themselves against further demands from Selden. Selden agreed, in return for a royalty of 1.25 per cent, to prosecute any competitor who was not a member of ALAM.

This situation, particularly absurd because Selden had no part in the motor industry, was to continue — at least legally — until 12 November, 1912. Cars manufactured by members of ALAM displayed a plaque which said that they were manufactured "under the Selden licence". The final crisis came with Selden's attempts to withhold recognition from manufacturers who were not members of the association.

Soon he found he had to fight on two fronts. On the one hand, there were the European manufacturers who were not worried as long as their products were sold outside America, but who protested strongly at attempts to enforce payment on cars exported to America. On the other, a growing number of American manufacturers were seeking to avoid the threat of legal action.

Ford alliance

These latter, at a critical time, were joined by Henry Ford, against whom proceedings were then taken. Ford's reaction was to form an alliance with some of the major Europeans, including Panhard-Levassor and Jeantaud. They found ample justification for breaking Selden's patent, not the least being the back-dating of the 1895 patent to 1879, and by showing that there were dozens of precedents.

Finally, in 1911, the Federal Appeal Court — reversing a verdict of the District Court — recognized Selden's patent as "valid but not violated". ALAM was at once dissolved and, in spite of the efforts of the owners of the patent, the Supreme Court confirmed the Federal sentence on 12 November, 1912, and finally put an end to a ridiculous legal and technical situation.

The Vanderbilt Cup

The years of expansion of American motoring produced, as might be expected, an important race of international significance in the U.S. This was the Vanderbilt Cup race, which was to have a parallel role to that of the Gordon Bennett Cup in Europe. First held in 1904, the race had many regulations in common with its European counter-part, including one requiring competing cars to be entirely built in their country of origin. The only major difference was in the second clause, which said that the race should always be held on American territory.

The designer and promoter of this race was William K. Vanderbilt, Jr. who was a rich amateur racing driver. The Long Island circuit was chosen for the race and its nearness to New York attracted tens of thousands of spectators right from the start. Though this ensured financial success it also brought organisational problems, most important of which was safety. One incident illustrates the problem. A famous race official, Fred Wagner, once had to use a compressed air pipe on the spectators to force enough room for the cars to pass. Successive Vanderbilt Cup races were to grow in importance. Unfortunately they did not lack tragedy. After being run seven times in the East (first at Long Island and then in Savannah) it was transferred to Milwaukee for 1912. The last two editions, those of 1913 and 1915, were held in California.

'Wrecking race'

The first edition in 1904 was marked by so many breakdowns that it was called the "wrecking race". There were two strong sources of competition from Europe. The French had three Panhards driven by Heath, Teste and Tart, Gabriel in a De Dietrich, and Clément in a Clément-Bayard. The Germans sent five Mercedes, four

A postcard of the 1904 Gordon Bennett Cup.

"60 H.P." and one "90 H.P.", all driven by Americans. There were also two F.I.A.T.s which, however, quickly fell out of the race with clutch failure. America was represented by Royal, Pope-Toledo and Simplex, which were hotted-up tourers, and by the Pope-Toledo Special and "Grey Wolf" racing cars.

Within a few minutes of the start one of the Mercedes overturned, killing the mechanic. Later the other four Mercedes broke down and, with other retirements, the race reduced itself to a duel between Heath and Clément, resolving itself in favour of the former by a small margin. His average was 52 m.p.h. and he won by two minutes. This foreign victory was not isolated and it was not until 1908 that an American car won the Vanderbilt Cup.

Official approval

In 1904 the fifth Gordon Bennett was held in Europe, this time in Germany after the Mercedes victory in Ireland the previous year. The course was near Frankfurt-on-Main in the Taunus mountains where an 87-mile track had to be lapped four times. For the first time the race had official approval marked by the presence of the German Emperor, Wilhelm II. It is said that his interest in motor cars dated from the time when one of his own court, Rausch, overtook the Kaiser's galloping horse in a car.

There was a large number of entries for the race, a possibility due to modifications that had been made to the rigid regulations. Thus there were three French cars, three Belgian, three British, three German, three Austrian, three Italian and one Swiss.

The French entrants were Théry in an 80 H.P. Richard-Brasier, Salleron in a 100 H.P. Mors and Rougier in a 100 H.P. Turcat-Méry. The German drivers Jenatzy, Werner and Warden all had 90 H.P. Mercedes. Among the British were Girling — future brake manufacturer — Edge and Jarrott. Italy had Lancia, Cagno and Storero in 75 H.P. F.I.A.T.s.

This was a breathtaking race. The spectators, were excited by the desperate duel between the French car driven by Théry and the German car driven by the Belgian Jenatzy. At the end of the first lap Théry had only one minute's lead. At the end of the second it was one minute 15 seconds and finally Théry, thanks to the better roadholding of his Richard-Brasier, won by 11 minutes. Wilhelm II himself congratulated the winner and his mechanic, Müller, and sent a telegram of congratulations to the French President, Loubet.

The good performance of the F.I.A.T.s — Lancia and Cagno finished eighth and tenth respectively — was a portent of their excellent showing the following year in the sixth and last Gordon Bennett. In this race Lancia just missed victory due to a radiator fault, while Nazzaro and Cagno were second and third behind the winner, who was again Théry, still driving a Richard-Brasier. It is interesting to explain the death of such an important race as the Gordon Bennett. The rules had been severely

1905 Gordon Bennett. Tracy in the Locomobile 90 H.P.

1905 Gordon Bennett. Jenatzy in the 120 H.P. Mercedes at the Rochefort bend.

1905 Gordon Bennett. The Clifford-Earp team in a Napier 90 H.P.

One of Peugeot's first "Babies", built in 1903. The car was a great success in England as well as in France.

criticised from the start, most of all by the Automobile Club de France which, in particular, wanted a greater number of competitors. This was quite reasonable considering the large number of manufacturers in France,

A 1903 De Dietrich 24 H.P. with a 5,428 c.c. four-cylinder engine. A car such as this took part in the first Vanderbilt Cup race.

and selection there was always a long and bitter process. The British, Germans, Italians, Austrians and Swiss opposed any change, however, and when nominating their team for the 1905 race the French declared that it would be the last they would enter. This automatically decided the fate of the race.

This last race, held in France because of Théry's win the previous year, was on a difficult course chosen by Michelin to the west of Clermont-Ferrand. The circuit had to be completed five times for a total of about 350 miles.

The idolised Théry won after a bitter battle with Lancia. Average speed was 77.7 k.p.h. (about 48 m.p.h.).

The American team had a disastrous race. Of the 90 H.P. Locomobile and two Pope-Toledos entered, only one of the latter finished the race. The driver, Lyttle, was so slow, however, that he finised 2½ hours after Théry, who was just finishing as Lyttle completed his second lap.

MOVING INTO
THE PLASTICS AGE

Ferrous and non-ferrous metals, wood, rubber and leather have been the traditional materials right from the beginning of motor car construction. Metals will always be essential as far ahead as one can see; rubber, though now synthetic, continues to be the best possible material for tyres; leather and wood are still in demand for the more luxurious cars and there is even one highly regarded car — Britain's hand-built Marcos — with a wooden chassis.

Traditional materials are challenged, however, by substitutes or modifications. An important recent example is the development of the substitute body panelling material Prestal, consisting of about threequarters of zinc and the rest mainly aluminium.

At about 260° C this material develops "super-plasticity" and acts like a thermoplastic rather than a metal, so that it can be worked by vacuum-forming and similar processes. It is comparable with steel, but is lighter and has a lower stiffness factor. Experimental body panels and other components have been successfully produced.

Reinforced bodies

Plastic bodies are far from new. Since the early post-war years, smaller manufacturers have been producing glass-reinforced resin bodies, and there have been one or two successful attempts to reinforce plastics with materials such as paper or cloth. Recently Reliant, Bond, Lotus and a few others have produced glass-fibre bodies in considerable numbers, while the Americans have carried out successful semi-automated production in these versatile materials.

New and promising techniques for plastic car body construction have been seen in Germany, where the Bayer Group demonstrated their design exercise for a sports car. The most important feature of the design is the load-bearing base unit, replacing the usual chassis or reinforcing frame. Of sandwich construction, it is made from rigid polyurethane foam, reinforced with epoxy resin-glass facings.

The body shows a variation of the polyurethane system pioneered by Bayer, enabling large and complicated profile sections to be produced by the injection-moulding process. Bayer claim that bonnet and boot lids, roofs and similar items made from polyurethane duromer are commercially possible and are likely to be seen soon on production cars.

Among the advantages of such materials are high strength-to-weight ratios, low tooling and production costs and resistance to corrosion.

The cockpit characteristics of the Marcos 1800, which has a wooden chassis, are highlighted on a runway.

Design and manufacturing concepts for plastic bodies must differ considerably from those of conventional steel bodies. New methods of painting and finishing have to be developed; so do repair methods which are within the capabilities of the ordinary garage.

Conventional sheet steel and in some cases aluminium will continue to be used in great quantities, however, while these new techniques are being developed. The only development likely for such stock materials is that of pre-painting, which is already used in other industries such as building, domestic appliance fabrication and caravans. This is just as likely for some applications on private cars as were the original use of "revolutionary" plastics and anodised aluminium which have been employed in other industries for so long.

It is likely, moreover, that these latter materials would lend themselves well for use in any future utility or town cars which might be developed to meet increasing traffic congestion; such cars might be constructed mainly from flat or single-curvature panels. There is probably a future for coated aluminium as well as steel in the automotive industries, although the non-ferrous metal is always more expensive.

The significant aspect of coated materials is that they reach the manufacturer in the finished state, so that he does not need to have any vast finishing plant. Most pre-coated sheet has been dipped or sprayed with synthetic paint, but some is made by bonding a film of tough plastic to the metal.

Plastics such as polythene, polyether, polytetrafluorethylene, nylon, epoxy resin or p.v.c. are used for coating. The last-mentioned is reasonably abrasion-resistant and has a built-in lubrication quality, in that it has sliding and parting qualities under the shear and compression of bending, pressing and drawing operations. With plastic coatings, the finish can be printed with any kind of pattern and variety of colours. The reverse side of such materials is usually lacquered or galvanised.

Safety incentive

Luxury cars apart, plastics are now almost universally used for car interior furnishings, including door and seat coverings, fascias, headlinings and, in many cases, floor coverings. For safety reasons, manufacturers have developed soft but firm plastics for certain applications including fascia-tops, visors and door handles.

One of the most interesting and most recently developed plastics is polypropylene, which belongs to the same family as polythene but has a higher melting point. It is the lightest of all solid plastics but is almost as rigid as high-density polythene, and can be handled by all the usual methods for thermoplastics.

The life of components made in this material can easily be up to 20 years and perhaps more. For some applications, such as glove-boxes and even accelerator pedals, it can be used to make hinges which can stand up to flexing almost indefinitely. The material lends itself to being moulded with a surface texture, giving an almost perfect facsimile of leather or leathercloth.

Though the craftsmen coachbuilders at the turn of the century might have been unsympathetic to current trends, the synthetic materials of the present age contribute significantly to the appearance and efficiency of the modern car.

Above: the interior of the "DS 21" Citroën and below: the "Blown-open" view of the Bayer all-plastic car.

Above, Fiat Dino Spider. Below, the company's 1952 V8 which reached 129 m.p.h. Over recent years cars' performance has increased only slightly.

CHAPTER TWELVE
EUROPE IN TOP GEAR

Already, towards the end of the first decade of the twentieth century, two quite different but not altogether independent trails were being blazed in the world of motor cars.

There was the normal production industry to supply the needs of the ever-growing numbers of motorists who had no particular leanings towards competitive events. There was the sporting side, which even at that time had started to brand its cars, conceived and built exclusively for racing, with its own unmistakable identities.

So, in the same years that saw the most exciting battles in motor racing fought out in Europe and America — and motor racing will always be romantic and exciting even though the thrills come no longer from catastrophic breakdowns but more from fantastic speeds and brilliant driving — equally important events and developments were taking place in the motor factories, out of sight of the public.

It was here that technical progress took its greatest strides, here that cars even nearer to perfection were born and continually brought up to date in the light of research directed towards the future. Evolution was even more rapid then than now. The cars of today are, perhaps, too near mechanical perfection to admit of rapid change, other than in detail and styling modification. This early progress cannot be traced in all of its detail, since this would involve extensive technical descriptions. The interest and, it might be said, the charm of those

Wolseley 6 H.P. 1,302 c.c. single-cylinder engine with three speeds and chain drive, built from 1904 to 1906.

A 1911 Austin in front of the Grand Palais, Paris.

cars of long ago are best experienced by standing in the presence of a "veteran", and for preference one which is in working order. The now numerous veteran car enthusiasts have for many years understood this.

In the first decade were born models and marques which stand as pointers in technical evolution, and many famous factories came into being.

Two makes dominate

Because of the legislation of the Locomotives Act of 1865, Britain was deprived of the honour of inventing the first effective petrol-engined car, although she had pioneered steam cars.

It can, however, be said that the first British petrol-driven four-wheeled car — the 1895 Lanchester — was advanced and individual in design with its worm drive, epicyclic gearing, pneumatic tyres and racy appearance.

186

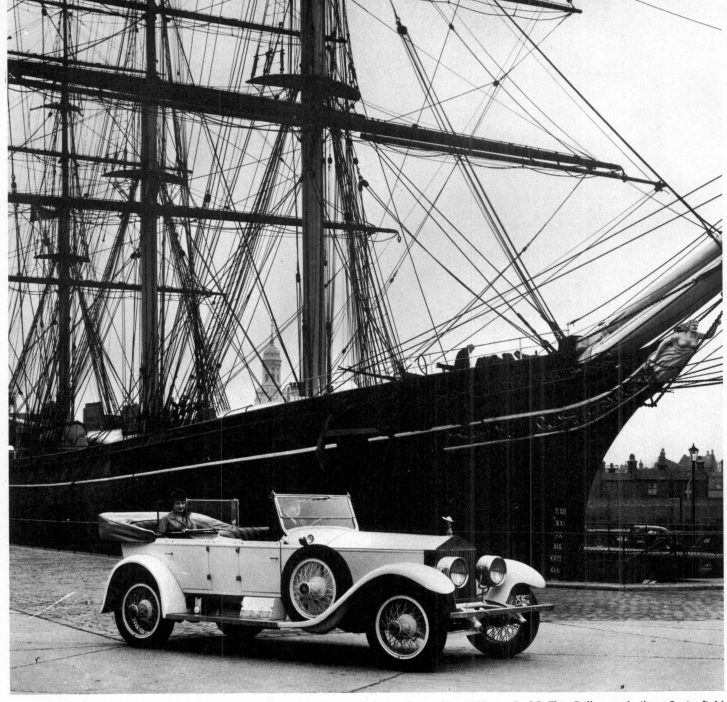

Two splendid survivals — a 1925 "40/50 Silver Ghost" Rolls-Royce in front of the clipper "Cutty Sark". This Rolls was built at Springfield. Massachusetts, where the company had set up a factory.

Meanwhile the British Motor Syndicate started to make Daimlers, and the two names Lanchester and Daimler dominated the early history of automobilism in Britain. Today they both belong to another "syndicate" — British Motor Holdings. Among the names of individual men who really founded the industry were those of the Lanchester brothers, F. R. Simms, Henry Hewetson, J. H. Knight, Sir D. Salomons and H. J. Lawson, while the editors of the motor Press and executives of motoring associations had no small influence.

By the end of the century it was clear that the petrol motor was to reign supreme, although steam and electric vehicles still had a stake in the business for many years. Moreover, the general specification of the car seemed fairly well established, at any rate in respect of the broad principles of having an internal-combustion engine, electric ignition, wheel steering, pneumatic tyres, chain or shaft drive and sliding-pinion gearbox.

The British motor industry was becoming more influen-

tial because of the formation of administrative and representative bodies. In 1897 Simms founded the Automobile Club of Great Britain and Ireland, which was, in 1907, to become the R.A.C., and in 1902 he established the Society of Motor Manufacturers and Traders, as watchdog of the expanding industry.

With the start of the 20th century, motors and affairs began to move forward more rapidly, and competition became more vigorous. Since no history of automobilism can be complete without reference to Rolls-Royce, let us refer to the immortal designer Henry Royce immediately. The brilliant, painstaking Northamptonshire miller's son put the firm on the map with the 40/50 Silver Ghost, and over 6,000 of these hand-built quality cars were made between 1906 and 1925, when the Phantoms and smaller cars were introduced.

Large quality cars such as the Rolls-Royce are still in considerable demand, but today mini-cars are more acceptable to most people than large limousines.

B.M.C.'s Mini is descended from the Austin Seven of 1922, a product of Herbert Austin's genius that made as much impression in its day as did Alec Issigonis's 1959 creation.

Herbert Austin, who later became Lord Austin, was born in 1866 at Little Missenden, Buckinghamshire, but at the age of 18 emigrated to Australia to work as a foundryman. After richly varied technical experiences, during which he pursued his studies in engineering, Austin returned to England and built a number of experimental prototype cars almost single handed. He started with a lightweight three-wheeler in 1895, following it with a further car, this being exhibited at the Crystal Palace.

Royal patronage

In the meantime he had been made general manager of the Wolseley Sheep-Shearing Machine Co. In 1899 he brought out the first four-wheeled Wolseley car and this single-cylinder machine was a prizewinner in the Thousand Miles Trial of the Automobile Club — an event which went far towards establishing motoring in Britain — especially as King Edward VII (then Prince of Wales) followed it enthusiastically and soon took to motoring himself.

Austin produced the first car to bear his name in 1906 and built the nucleus of the Longbridge factory that is still there today and which is indeed the nerve centre of the Austin-Morris Group. In the same year the first Austin — a four-cylinder 25-30 H.P. — was put into production. This first Austin was followed by other models, a wide range being offered in 1908 — the largest was a 60 H.P. six-cylinder.

A 1914 Standard. Below a 1907 Daimler "Open Tourer" with a 10,604 c.c. 45 H.P. side valve engine, four speeds and chain drive.

There was even an "Austin Seven" in 1909 but this single-cylinder utility car only theoretically anticipated the historic best-seller of 1922 — the famous Chummy, a four-cylinder 10 B.H.P. car which stayed in production until 1938-9, with progressive development.

Daimler is another marque that now serves under the B.M.H. banner. Originally the Daimler car was German, but H. J. Lawson founded the British company in 1896 and bought a factory site in Coventry. Jaguar-Daimler themselves have said; "This represented the laying of the British motor industry's largest foundation stone". From 1897 onwards, new Daimler models — Coventry-built — appeared in rapid succession, and between that year and 1903 twelve different power units were used, varying in size from one to 4½ litres, and of two or four cylinders. It has been noted that the Prince of Wales interested himself in the Thousand Miles Trial and it was the award-winning Daimler cars that interested him most — so much so that he bought a British Daimler with Hooper body, a four-seater mail phaeton. This was the beginning of a long association between Daimler and the British Crown.

Daimlers took 11 awards in the Thousand Miles Trial; their 13 cars all finished the course. This success in competitions became a habit and continued until the adoption of the Knight engine in 1909.

A particularly interesting Daimler model — again bought by Edward, now on the Throne — was the 1904 28/36 which was offered with the option of coil ignition or the Eisemann magneto, which was then very modernistic,

In 1902 the magazine "Nature and Art" showed an illustration of a "dog and cat ambulance" for English animal lovers.

Designer, Louis Coatalen, at the wheel of the 1907 Hillman.

but the engine still had an exposed camshaft! The King's particular car had revolving chairs in the back.

An interesting sidelight on Daimler history is that even the very early cars wore the fluted radiator which is now still simulated on "Jaguar-Daimlers".

Daimler adopted the sleeve-valve engine in 1909, with great success, and retained it until the middle 1930s. The 50 H.P. Double Six of 1926 was probably the most impressive Daimler ever made.

Some of the earliest automobile manufacturers bear the great names of companies now in the Chrysler-controlled Rootes Group. The famous Humber Company made superb bicycles for some years, then started on the production of equally excellent light cars, with the lovely little 5 H.P. Humberette in 1903. Dozens of these early "minis" still take part in veteran car events, and are among the most reliable and economical of the real veterans. The company soon started making bigger cars, such as the 1909 20 H.P. model, but they brought back the name Humberette for their small-wheeled cycle car in 1912.

Rootes's "Imp family" now embraces Sunbeam, Singer and Hillman models, and as rival companies these were all going strongly in the early 1900s. Typical of early Sunbeams was a 12 H.P. four-cylinder tourer of smart appearance and "upright carriage". This was a conventional car; hardly the same can be said of the 1901 Sunbeam-Mabley light car, the machine with one wheel at front, one at the back, and two wheels abreast in the middle! The famous designer, Louis Coatalen, worked for both Sunbeam and Hillman. Singers made their first car in 1905 and it had a White and Poppe engine; their most successful early car, however, was the 10 H.P. of 1912, and this was where Rootes came into the picture for the first time, the Maidstone agent William Rootes taking the entire first year's production.

The motoring fraternity nowadays tends to lose sight

Henry de Rothschild's 21 H.P. Daimler at the start of the Chantaloup hill climb in 1900.

1912 25 H.P. Lanchester. It was the first British car to have electric lighting as standard. The foot brake actuated a disc on the transmission. The handbrake worked on the rear wheels. 4-cylinder 3,299 c.c. engine with preselector epicyclic box.

of the importance of the earliest Vauxhall cars, although vintage enthusiasts venerate the big 30/98 cars of later years. The Vauxhall Iron Works of London made engines and pumps only, at first, and they were very successful. Then Vauxhall came out with a remarkably advanced small car in 1903, followed by a three-cylinder version a year or two later. The little 6 H.P. had an automatic inlet valve and even had a hot-spot system for the carburettor. Speed control was by varying the tension of the inlet valve spring. Coil ignition was employed and pump cooling was a feature.

Ahead of its time

The car had a two-speed and reverse transmission and — wonder of wonders! — a steering-column gear-shift. Admittedly it had a tiller instead of a steering wheel, but the column-change represented a fashion of the period that was not to be revived generally until the 1940s. Another interesting fact was the use of hub-type free-wheel mechanism instead of a differential.

In 1905, moreover, the company moved to Luton, where it nowadays has a whole town of its own; there one of the first-ever thoroughbred sports cars worthy of the name was surely the Prince Henry 3-litre car, from which was derived the 30/98 — that beloved, imposing piece of historic machinery so well represented in vintage events.

Already, in 1905, one saw the beginnings of those well-known flutes on the bonnet of the Vauxhall, which were retained in some form or another until a few years ago. The Napier story is an important one, although the name passed out of the automotive field many years ago. The Napier concern made a highly successful car in 1900. In fact, an example was entered in the Thousand Miles Trial and did well. This event itself was an extremely important one; in fact, it really put the whole industry on a firm footing at a time when it was very shaky, due to prejudice and hidebound tradition, associated with an undue reverence for the horse.

The Thousand Mile Trial was organised by the Royal Automobile Club — a body which also was responsible for getting the new craze for motoring accepted in circles that mattered — with the twin objects of letting people up and down the country see the incredible monsters, and proving that these devices could travel great distances without breaking down too often. The route was from London to Edinburgh via Bristol, Birmingham, Manchester, and Carlisle on the outward leg and Newcastle, Leeds, Sheffield and Nottingham on the way back.

One of the most enthusiastic supporters of the great trial was the Prince of Wales, later King Edward VII. Indeed, this member of the Royal Family was keen on every aspect of motors, and without his patronage the industry might have been much slower to develop.

It was the Australian pioneer motorist S. F. Edge who got Napiers into the "big time" and out of their little works in Lambeth Walk. Persuaded by this far-sighted extrovert, the company went racing in Europe with great success, their crowning achievement being to win the Gordon Bennett Cup Race in 1902. Then in 1907 S. F. Edge took a Napier to the already famous Brooklands track — now "underneath" an aircraft factory — and established a 24-hour record of 1,581 miles at an average of 65 m.p.h., which no one managed to crack for nearly 20 years.

Type of caravan

From 1904, when the company introduced their 18 H.P. model, the name Napier became associated with precision-built luxurious six-cylinder cars, right up to the years just after the First World War, when they went over to aero-engine production. But even just before the Second World War, lordly Napiers were to be seen in use as hire cars, hearses, etc. The company, incidentally, made an export model — a kind of motor caravan.

fitted with a hood that could be converted into a tent, and seats that could be made into bunks.

Among the names of all the historic marques that now come under the banner of Leylands is that of Morris, and many people think that it is the oldest. This is not so — not by a long way, for William Morris was selling and making cycles when the earliest cars began to take to the roads, and he did not start manufacturing until much later. The famous Bullnose Morris, in fact, did not delight the motoring world until 1913, but Morris had a profound influence on the motoring scene thereafter. Morris, later to become Lord Nuffield, still attended new model presentations until the middle 1950s.

Leylands were pioneers in the steam wagon business rather than in cars, but it should not be forgotten that one of the directors of the firm that became Leylands actually built a steam tricar in 1895. And, of course, there were Leyland and Trojan cars later on, in the early 1920s.

Rover and Riley (also now Leyland names) were pioneer cars. There were Rover tricars and a single-cylinder four-wheeler in 1904. The latter boasted a tubular backbone type chassis, rack-and-pinion steering and three-speed gearbox. In 1907 a Rover car won the classic Tourist Trophy race, and the marque has always had a reputation for quality and performance. One of the nicest cars of the early 1920s was the Rover 8 air-cooled twin — a real sporty little disc-wheeled roadster that caught the eyes of the motoring enthusiasts.

There was a Riley car as early as 1898, and although

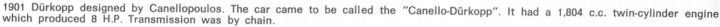

1901 Dürkopp designed by Canellopoulos. The car came to be called the "Canello-Dürkopp". It had a 1,804 c.c. twin-cylinder engine which produced 8 H.P. Transmission was by chain.

1905 Prosper-Lambert, the firm disappeared in the 1907-08 crisis. This car had a 2,545 c.c. engine, 3 speeds and shaft transmission.

it was a prototype, the Riley company had fair justification, later, for coining the catchphrase "As old as the industry, as modern as the hour". Various three- and four-wheeled models followed, and led to the exciting Redwing and the illustrious Nines of later years.

It is not always appreciated that Standards bear one of the oldest names, or that they had a vital influence on the progress of the industry. They introduced a 6 H.P. single-cylinder model as early as 1903, and it had a three-speed gearbox, sloping steering column, flexible couplings for the shafting, drum-type rear brakes and leaf-type suspension, front and rear. "Quantity" production began in 1905 with the 16-20 H.P. tourer, subsequent developments included some of Britain's first inexpensive six-cylinder cars, and the very successful 9.5 H.P. two-seater of 1913. Today's Standard-Triumph concern is part of the Leyland Group.

The Lagonda car — or tricar, as it was then — first saw the light of day at Staines in 1904, where an American opera singer took the mellifluous name of the marque from the Indian-sounding Lagonda Creek, Ohio. One could still obtain Lagonda spares at Staines in 1950, and the cars were being made at the old Hanworth aerodrome when Prince Philip bought one in 1954. They were to be seen there with their sister Aston Martins until only a few years ago, when Aston Martin Lagonda took over the historic Tickford coachbuilding works at Newport Pagnell.

The first taxis

The contribution of France to motoring started with the remarkable steam carriage made by Cugnot and often claimed as the first "car" but one of the most important events of the pioneer motoring years was De Dion-Bouton's launching of the "Populaire" in 1903. It had a rear axle and transmission arrangement which has become a classic and is still in use on some of the finest cars today.

The Renault history is an important one, of course, and Louis Renault's car designed in 1898 bristled with advanced characteristics, including shaft drive, direct-drive top gear and a tubular chassis. Louis and Marcel,

193

DYNAMO AND ALTERNATOR

A small technical revolution — the advent of the alternator — has been taking place in the contemporary car. The majority of motorists are beginning to realise that the dynamo, that good old faithful servant whose duty for many years has been to supply electricity to the battery, it being ousted by the alternator.

It is generally agreed that this development carries with it certain technical advantages, but it is not always obvious what they are.

Perhaps the first questions are why this replacement of the dynamo by the alternator should be proceeding so slowly and why, considering the advantages claimed for the alternator, not all motor car manufacturers have yet been persuaded to fit it. The alternator and control gear assembly at present costs more, but it is likely this will cause little difficulty, as the difference in cost is fairly small.

Paradox

Before illustrating the technical advantages, it would be useful to run over the operating principles of the dynamo and compare them with those of the alternator.

The role of both is that of battery-charger. The battery is a large reservoir of electrical energy. Both dynamo and alternator replace in it the "deficit" of electricity used in supplying the car's various electrical apparatus. The battery accepts and delivers only direct current. Here we strike an apparent paradox, since it would be thought that the most suitable device would be the dynamo, by its very nature generating direct current, rather than the alternator, which, as its name implies, produces alternating current that must be rectified before being put into the battery.

In fact, this complication does not exist. Indeed, there is a considerable simplification in using the alternator, because of the type of input system which it requires and because of the transistors, which perform two essential tasks in the control gear.

The dynamo works on Faraday's and Pacinotti's principles. Electro-magnetic induction generates a direct current in the copper wire coil wound on a soft-iron armature, which rotates in the electro-magnetic field provided by an electro-magnet (the inductor). Since the coil is continually in rotation, the electric current generated in it is collected by brushes in contact with the commutator, which is integral with the armature.

The voltage of the current supplied by the dynamo is, roughly speaking, directly proportional to its speed which, in turn, is strictly related to the engine speed. Hence, at low speeds, the induced voltage is very low. To prevent a current reversal, in which the higher voltage of the battery would drive current through the dynamo — which would then act as an electric motor — it is necessary to insert an automatic cut-out in the circuit. At high speeds, however, the voltage of the current supplied by the dynamo is excessively high, so it is also necessary to insert a voltage regulator in the circuit to avoid burning out the battery.

These complications do not arise with the alternator. Theoretically speaking, the mode of operation of the alternator is different from that of the dynamo. The induced current is not generated in a rotating coil but in the winding of a stationary element (the stator), inside which a concentric inductor rotates, so that the commutator and brushes are no longer necessary.

Apart from the fact that in dynamos these are the parts which are most subject to wear and which therefore demand the most frequent maintenance operations, the substantially greater robustness of the alternator also assists the saving in maintenance.

There is, of course, the question of rectifying the alternating current. This is done by using silicon diodes (transistors), which have the property of allowing current to pass in one direction only and so act as current rectifier valves. But the transistors in the alternator also perform the function of the automatic cut-out.

Because of their semi-conductor properties they effectively prevent any counter-current flowing from battery to dynamo.

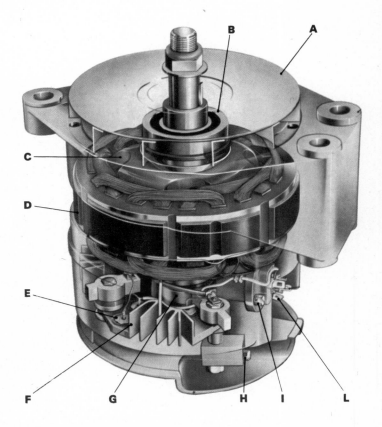

Section of C.A.V. Alternator
A - fan B - bearing C - rotor D - stator E - silicon diode F - wing G - contact ring H - positive terminal I - brush mounting L - negative terminal.

A - belt.
B - retaining bolt.
C - hinge.

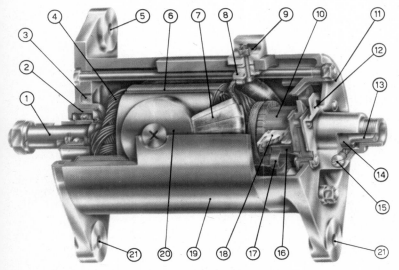

Section of Magneti Marelli Dynamo
1 - pulley shaft 2 - ball bearing 3 - end plate 4 - induction windings
5 - mounting holes 6 - field stack 7 - field windings 8 - earth terminal
9 - terminal 10 - commutator 11 - end plate 12 - positive terminal
13 - tachometer drive 14 - bush 15 - oil nipple 16 - brush 17 - brush
spring 18 - brush holder 19 - body 20 - earth 21 - mounting hole.

The voltage regulator is also simplified because the alternator and dynamo have different input curves; changes in voltage between low and high speeds are smaller in the alternator. Furthermore, the voltage is already satisfactorily high when the engine, and therefore the alternator, is running slowly.

Increased demand

This is one of the useful advantages of the alternator, since it means that the battery does not discharge so quickly under particularly heavy conditions of working. These include urban use in winter when, apart from the inadequate charging, there is increased demand by the electrical installations of the car (the lighting system, windscreen wipers, fog lamps, radio, heater, etc.). There is no doubt that the use of alternators is becoming more widespread, not only because of the progressive reduction in manufacturing costs, but also because of the electrical "extras" now available in many cars.

his brother, slaved away in a tiny shed in their father's garden. It is still there — in the forecourt of the great Renault factory in Paris — with the bench, lathe, drilling machine etc. In March 1899 Renault Frères was founded.

A highlight in the fortunes of the company was the production of the first taxis in 1905, and some of the popular Renault cabs were used in London, too. The Paris cabs were "enlisted" in the First World War and did great work at the front.

French and Italian Pioneers

In those early years Renault also produced a two-cylinder 10 H.P. car and a four-cylinder 14 H.P. model developed from the prototype that won the Paris-Vienna event. Luxurious coachwork was mounted on this chassis and it came to be adopted for many official functions. Other firms that came into the picture early, were Sizaire-Naudin, and Delage. The former specialised from the start in making sports cars; one of the first — the 8 H.P. — had independent front suspension. Louis Delage's firm produced both tourers and racers. Both these firms did quite well in competitive events. Panhard-Levassor were among the pioneer concerns, of course, and made cars as early as 1891. Levassor was

Pages from the Lancia catalogue.

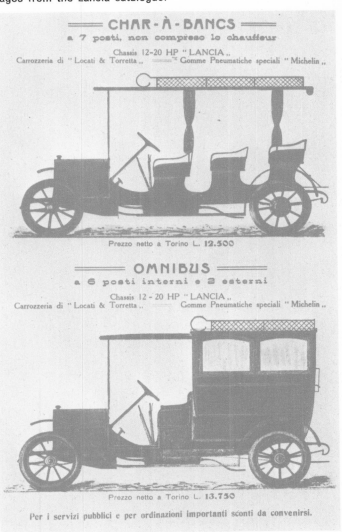

responsible for the first sliding-pinion type of gearbox. The marque was noteworthy for its racing record, right up to the early 1900s.

Other important French pioneer marques were Peugeot, Decauville, Gobron-Brillié, Gladiator, Delahaye, De Dietrich, Bugatti, and Panhard.

Among the earliest Italian cars was the Giusti & Miari which was designed by Bernardi and built in 1896, whilst in the same year, the first cars were constructed by Michele Lanza. In 1898 Ceirano (later associated with the Itala) manufactured the Welleyes.

Died in poverty

A year later, the Fiat concern — now the largest European motor manufacturer of all — was founded, on the first day of July.

In November of 1899, ten 3 H.P. cars were completed

A superb racing car — the 1911 Fiat S74, which weighed 3,300 lbs. and had a four-cylinder 190 H.P. engine of over 14 litres.

The famous 1909 Itala "Palombella" complete with steps.

Nazzaro in the Fiat F2 on the Landinier straight, in the 1907 French Grand Prix.

and work was about to start on 6 H.P. models. This was the beginning of a great endeavour, and it was unfortunate that the designer of the Welleyes car — the earliest Fiat — died in poverty after giving up his profession.

Giovanni Agnelli was the industrial genius behind Fiat and its employees included Lancia and Nazzaro, themselves soon to become famous.

From that early start in Corso Dante, the Fabbrica Italiana Automobili Torino grew steadily during the first decade of the century, and a good deal more quickly after the First World War. Much of its early success was due to racing, even as early as 1902, and a Fiat racing car did 128 m.p.h. in 1906. The firm went on racing for another 20 years, then withdrew, like most mass producers, but continued to build sports cars.

The company also expanded into other spheres, among them aviation, railway rolling stock, marine engines.

In the three major motor races of 1907, Agnelli entered three different models with quite different features. The car for the Targa Florio was the 28-40 H.P. model, of 7,358 c.c. with a maximum speed of 60 m.p.h. The Taunus model, with which Nazzaro won the Kaiserpreis was an eight-litre machine with a maximum of 80 m.p.h. For the Grand Prix of the French Automobile Club the

A 1909 Alfa in a racing guise. Below Merosi, the designer, at the wheel of the 1914 Alfa "Grand Prix".

entry was a spectacular vehicle of 16-litre capacity and a 110 m.p.h. maximum.

The illustrious Lancia concern was founded in November 1906 by Vincenzo Lancia and Claudio Fogolin. There was a disastrous fire almost immediately, but this did not deter the pioneers, who soon launched a series of cars designated by the letters of the Greek alphabet, starting with the 24 H.P. "Alfa". This was followed by the six-cylinder "Dialfa" and thereafter by the "Beta" and Gamma.

The firm then moved to a larger factory and from the new premises emerged the first Lancia to achieve real commercial success. This was the Theta, which had a capacity of almost five litres and developed 70 B.H.P. at 2,200 r.p.m. Lancia was always on good terms with

Fiat's Agnelli and in the early years of his own industrial efforts, still raced for Fiat.

Darracq Italiana was founded in Naples in 1906, for the purpose of building the same models as the parent company in Paris. In fact it was really an assembly plant. The company ran into difficulties and was rescued by a Milan bank which insisted that a new car be designed, suitable for touring and racing. The new company was called Anonima Lombarda Fabbrica Automobili, hence Alfa, and the designation Alfa Romeo came in 1920.

The fame of Itala — another notable name in Italian early history — was consolidated after the epic Pekin-Paris race, which was won by one of the marque, driven by Prince Scipione Borghese. The firm had been set up in 1904 by Matteo Ceirano. A very special Itala was

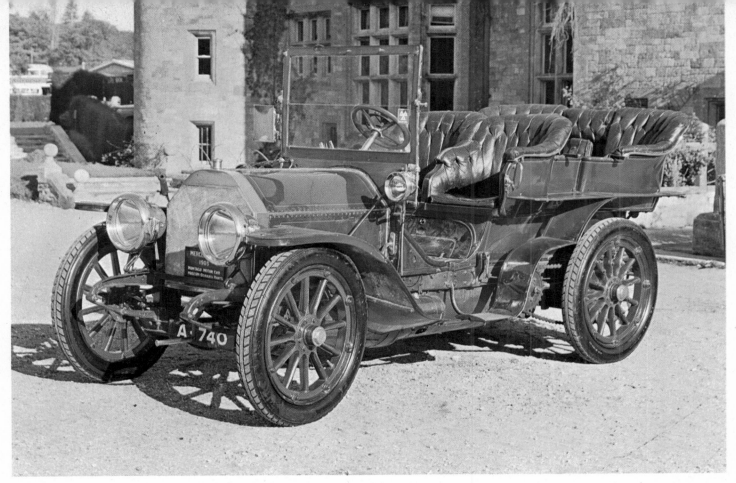

A much admired G.T. car—a 1903 Mercedes 60 H.P. with a 9,230 c.c. four-cylinder engine. The electric lights on this car were fitted in 1910.

that owned by the Queen of Italy and nicknamed by her Palombella. It can be seen in Turin's motor museum. Apropos of Italian Royalty and the motorcar, King Victor Emanuel III rivalled the Kaiser and King Edward VII as a motoring enthusiast. Emanuel and his Queen Elena were involved in a somewhat sobering incident when they tried out an electric car and it got out of control and went backwards, hitting a tree and flinging them out. The Queen sprained her ankle but they both remained enthusiasts.

In 1906 the firms of Brixia-Zust, Aquila Italiana and Legnano came into existence. The first of these distinguished itself mainly by reason of its vertical three-cylinder engines, built in various sizes. The 1500 c.c. example powered a fine touring car and gave it a maximum speed of 40 m.p.h. In 1918 Brixia-Zust and Officine Meccaniche of Milan merged and this resulted in a new company later called O.M. - Fabbrica Bresciana di Automobili. This, still later, became a part of the Fiat group Aquila Italiana of Turin made sports cars under Ing. Cappa. Some of the cars boasted such advanced features as monobloc engines, aluminium pistons, ballbearing crankshafts and engine sub-frames.

The Legnano company had a somewhat short life but produced some excellent cars, including the 6-8 H.P. twin, with a circular radiator well-known to veteran enthusiasts.

The most interesting German machine of the first decade of the century was the 60 H.P. Mercedes, the excellent qualities of which were demonstrated in the fourth Gordon Bennett Cup Race. At this time, the firm had lost their new 90 H.P. models prepared specially for the competition to be held that year in Ireland, because fire

had swept through the factory. But they wanted to see a team at the starting line so they hurriedly converted three of the 60 H.P. tourers and these did well in the event. The model had a four-cylinder 9200 c.c. engine.

Elegance in the Valentino Park at Turin.

Smoother lines all round. A Hillman "Californian" with feminine appeal. A similar setting below for a Citroen and lady driver of the 1920s.

CHAPTER THIRTEEN
BY CAR ROUND THE WORLD

The long-distance motor races and trials are already legends, heroic achievements of a time never to return, though hardly fifty years have passed since they were run. Already it is almost impossible to imagine the enthusiasm, admiration and worship for the drivers who took part in those long, long drives over impossible roads in far-away and exotic places.

These exploits not only tested cars to their destruction, but also demonstated their ability to serve as reliable transportation anywhere in the world. They attracted the interest of many people who were by no means potential customers, while women tended to regard motorists as the knights of a new mechanised civilisation.

Brief mentions have been made of some of the early exploits of this type — Winton's adventurous journeys from Cleveland to New York in 1897 and 1899; Chapin's eventful drive between Detroit and New York in 1902; the first coast-to-coast drives by various Americans in 1903; the "Passe Partout" trip of Lehwess and Cudell; and the fantastic journeys made by Charles Glidden of 50,000 miles round the world in his indefatigable series of Napiers.

Glidden's travels between 1902 and 1907 touched continental Europe, Scandinavia to the Arctic Circle, North America, Australia, Malaya, New Zealand, China and Japan.

One may well wonder if the roads of many of these places were in a sufficiently good state to allow a car of those times to survive such a severe mechanical test for five years. The answer is obviously that they were not; the prudent Glidden had the foresight to equip

his Napier with a set of interchangeable wheels by means of which it was possible, when the roads were too bad or when they did not exist at all, to continue by another means — on the railway track. He fitted his car on the rails and boldly forged ahead like a small locomotive. In Glidden's honour (he was a native of Lowell, Massachusetts) a number of transcontinental trials were held in America which provided a splendid opportunity for the leading transatlantic motoring figures to meet periodically. The name "Glidden Tour" has been revived of recent years by the Antique Automobile Club of America for their biggest annual road rally.

R. L. Jefferson was another who figured in an exploit similar to Glidden's, also impressive and exciting even though it was shorter in time and distance. Like many other motorists he was attracted by the prospect of adventure which the Balkans and above all the Ottoman Empire still held at the beginning of the century for European eyes. In 1905 there were only two cars in Serbia and none in Bulgaria, while in Turkey they were

For years roads in America were terrible. It was not until 1912 that the first bitumen road was built. In the picture — the official parade at the opening of the road to the New York State Fair.

The development of motor roads has changed the aspect and sometimes the geography of the countryside. This photograph and the photograph on the preceding page are of the same place.

completely prohibited for reasons which were partly religious and partly political. Not only mechanical and logistic difficulties but also major diplomatic problems had so far prevented any Balkan trial, but the tenacious Jefferson set out to overcome them.

Pleasant surprises

Firstly, he got Rover to build him a strengthened version of their 8 H.P., a car whose mechanical elements had a suitable strength and simplicity, including a single-cylinder engine. He then got into contact with the countries through which he was to pass and soon obtained permission to drive across Serbia and Bulgaria — though in neither country was it possible to find petrol. The Turks were much more obstinate, however, and to get anywhere Jefferson had to ask the British Ambassador to intervene.

The Rover set off from Coventry and after crossing that part of Western Europe which had decent roads quickly reached the Hungarian frontier. Here Jefferson encountered the first of two pleasant surprises — the plain which had no roads whatsoever, where he had envisaged tremendous difficulties, proved to have a firm, hard surface over which he could boldly make his way. His troubles began when he had to cross rivers or swamps and more than once the courageous driver was put to a severe test of his ingenuity.

He continued his way across the frontier, which he passed at full speed, giving a military salute to the startled guards (this inevitably ended up as a diplomatic

Rover has maintained its traditions for solidly built cars since the days of Jefferson's journey. A Land Rover is particularly suitable for difficult terrain.

1904 Renault. Note the functional but elegant clothing. Below the 1906 Renault "Grand Prix".

From top to bottom — 1904 Humberette. 1904 Vauxhall and a 1903 Panhard-Levassor. The three cars were photographed at the 1964 Prescott hill climb.

incident). When he reached the Turkish frontier, however, things took a turn for the worse as the frontier guards had not been informed of his special permission to enter Turkey. In the end this matter, too, was resolved and then Jefferson had his second pleasant surprise — the Turkish roads were unexpectedly smooth and well-maintained, though this turned out to be true only of the frontier zone.

The journey towards Constantinople quickly took on the more normal character of cross-country "navigation" but it aroused delirious enthusiasm among the local population, who were able to see the first car ever to enter the Ottoman Empire. It was only when in sight of the Turkish capital that the Rover had its first serious breakdown — a broken valve — but the conquest of the Balkans was already achieved.

The fantastic Pekin-Paris

The greatest and most exciting of all the long-distance trials was immortalised in the reports of Luigi Barzini, who took part as special correspondent of the "Daily Telegraph" and the Italian "Corriere della Sera", and in reports by Edgardo Longoni of "Secolo", Jean Taillis of "Le Matin" and of one of the competitors, Georges Cormier. To try to drive from the Chinese capital to Paris in 1907 was considered sheer madness, considering that to the lack of roads and bridges were added other obstacles unknown in early trials — swamps, mountains, narrow gullies and unknown territories where the only means of passage were doubtful tracks. Nevertheless, there was an immediate and enthusiastic response from several keen motorists when "Le Matin" proposed the idea to all the countries of the world. Soon after the announcement the editor received entries from 25 volunteers, but later when the entries had to be confirmed in a more tangible way — by the payment of 2,000 francs — they dropped to five.

A lone italian

There were four Frenchmen — Cormier and Collignon, both with two-cylinder 8-10 H.P. De Dion - Boutons, Godard with a four-cylinder 15 H.P. Dutch Spyker and Pons with a Contal tricycle — and one Italian, Prince Scipione Borghese with a 35-45 H.P. Itala. The drivers quickly paired with journalists, for the big newspapers were aware of the interest such a race would arouse in the public. Barzini travelled with Borghese, Longoni with Cormier and Jean Taillis with Godard.

At once their respective newspapers began the pre-race publicity and diplomatic channels hummed with activity as the French, Dutch and Italian authorities made contact with those of Pekin. The latter exhibited great diffidence towards the undertaking which to them was quite inexplicable. As Luigi Barzini was to be told later when in China "The reactionary Mandarins, who hold the power at Court, are afraid that the race is really an

effort to see how long it would take to invade China by car".

Nor was this the only suspicious interpretation of the race. Some Chinese officials saw the competitors as saboteurs who were to discredit the Kalgan railway, and still others saw them as military spies under the command of Prince Borghese.

Getting permits to cross the various frontiers proved a difficult task and was a test for the nerves of the organizers. One minor incident occurred when the request for the translation of a permit into Mongol was turned down by the Chinese for fear of the effect on their uneducated soldiery of the word "fire-cart" — the only way of translating the words "motor car". In the meantime logistic problems seemed almost insurmountable. All the competitors had renounced any sort of comfort during the race, but petrol had to be made available en route. Finally, dumps were formed by mule and camel transport. Meanwhile the vehicles were shipped from Marseilles and Naples for the long sea voyage to Shanghai and then by Trans-Siberian railway to Pekin. The race started on 10 June, 1907, at 7 a.m., saluted by the band of the French garrison at Pekin. Paris was

1899 De Dion-Bouton and a 1902 experimental Royal Enfield quadricycle, fitted with a single-cylinder 244 c.c. De Dion-Bouton engine.

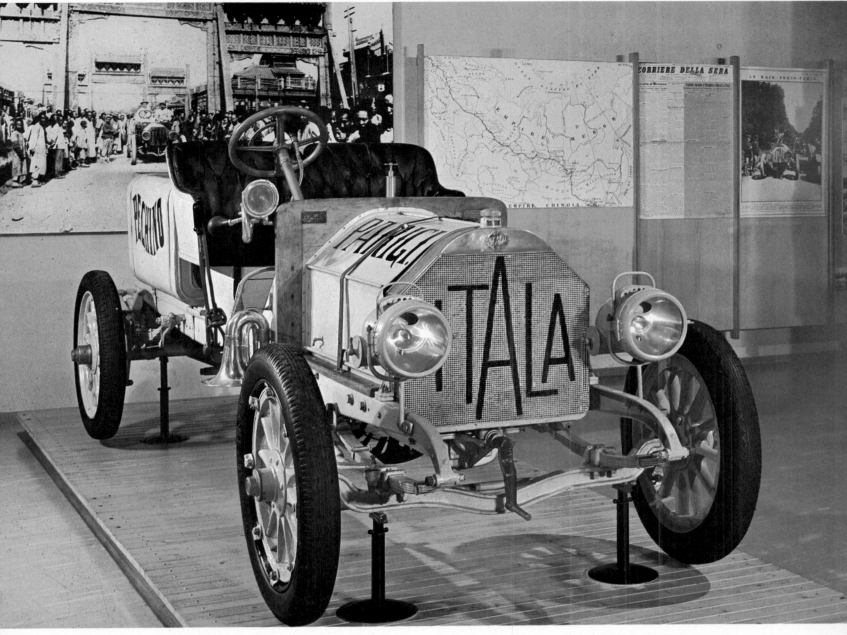

The famous Itala of the Pekin-Paris race. It had a 7,433 c.c. four-cylinder engine which produced 45 H.P. at 1,250 r.p.m.

10,000 miles away. Right from the start Prince Borghese took the lead which he was never to lose. Thus began the impressive performance of his Itala, and its enthusiastic driver who was incapable of driving a cautious race such as the innumerable and unknown difficulties ahead might have suggested.

The first region to cross was the terrible, mountainous area of Kalgan, 800 miles of impossible "road". When mountains were met, it was necessary, wrote Barzini, "to haul the cars up — the way a cannon is manhandled into place". Boulders had to be moved; undergrowth and roots blocked the way and had to be wearily cut through with axes. The steep slopes were too much for the brakes and it was necessary to call on local peasants to fasten ropes to the rear of the cars and slow their downhill progress.

If one of the objects of this race was to spread knowledge of the motor car in those out-of-the-way places, it was not achieved. There were plenty of acts of generous

The Itala driving on the track of the Trans-Siberian railway.

VLADIMIR
MOSCOW
COMPIEGNE
SNOSSIOS
CHARLEVILLE
PARIS
HANNOVER
AIX-LA-CHAPELLE
BERLIN
POZNAN
WARSAW BREST

hospitality and spontaneous help from the local population, but the Chinese peasants were entirely incurious.

Across the Steppes

Finally they were through the mountains, with the immense Mongol plain to cross. Pons' tricycle dropped out of the race and one of the five competitors was gone. Behind the Itala, which continued to forge ahead, the two De Dions ran in convoy, experiencing no serious mechanical troubles (nor were they to do so, finishing the race in fine style) while the Spyker was already in trouble.

On June 25, two weeks after the start, the long awaited frontier between Russia and China was reached at Kyakhta — and three days later Cormier and Collignon saw their first "civilized" bed since they had set off. In the meantime Borghese was galloping over the horizon. Now the cars began to use the only road available to them the Trans-Siberian Railway, alternating with short stretches of Siberian road where the simple sign-posting prevented the drivers from losing their way in the Steppes. It was, in fact, in the Steppes that an accident that was to become famous in the annals of motoring befell the Itala.

A wheel collapsed, the ends of the spokes coming out of their seats in the rim. It seemed impossible to go on, but Borghese had a bright idea. Remembering the famous cry "Water on the ropes!" he thought he could effect a repair by swelling the wood in water.

The only suitable place for this operation was in the public baths of the small town where they happened to be. That night he booked a cabin and the Italian wheel went into the Russian bath. The repair did not last and the wheel finally gave up after a few miles. Only the work of a Siberian blacksmith enabled the Itala to carry on to victory.

As they reached Kazan the drivers began to find roads

The Itala in difficulty.

One of the early stages.

KAZAN

ELABUGA

BIISK

ZLATOUS

KURGAN

VOLGA

URAL Mts.

SIBERIA

SIBERIA

TOMSK

KRASNOYARSK

KANSK

IRKUTSK

Lake BAIKAL

KYAKHTA

GOBI

PEKIN

that gradually became more and more "civilized". Cormier told how he nearly fainted when he found a road-roller at the entrance to one city!

Nijni-Novgorod, Moscow, Warsaw... Borghese dashed towards the finish while the others were still on the Russian plain, and on the 10th August the Itala was in Paris — to be received with delirious enthusiasm. Borghese had covered 10,000 miles in 60 days exactly and the other three competitors arrived together 21 days later!

Found in warehouse

Let us see how this wonderful Itala was built. It had a front-mounted, vertical four-cylinder engine which developed 45 H.P. at 1,250 r.p.m. from its 7,433 c.c. It had a four-speed gearbox, and the whole car weighed about 27 cwts. The car did just over 8 m.p.g. a single rear seat was squeezed between the two supplementary petrol tanks which contained a total of 70 gallons.

Behind the tanks was a large box full of tools and spare parts, but most of these were thrown overboard during the race to lighten the car. Hidden away were two other tanks of 12 gallons each, one for oil and one for water. Pirelli had manufactured special tyres for the Itala, capable of lasting "as much as 2,500 miles".

Today the 35-45 H.P. Itala of Prince Borghese is preserved in the Turin Motor Museum. Even after the great race it had a romantic history. Abandoned in a disused warehouse by Itala, it was found almost by accident in 1923. Carlo Biscaretti, later to found the museum that bears his name, was then Itala's director of publi-

BLENDING IN THE QUALITY

Petrol is a cocktail of many hydrocarbons and additives tailor-made to the needs of the motor engine as a good whisky is blended to suit the individual palate. Petrol is probably the most complex and sophisticated product in normal daily use by the public, and a vast amount of know-how and skill enters into its formulation.

A satisfactory petrol must meet the needs of a large variety of cars, each with its own particular performance chacteristics, driven by a wide variety of drivers in towns, on motorways, in hilly country, in all types of climate. Wherever and whatever he is driving, the motorist expects to have instant starting, rapid warm-up and quick acceleration from cold, freedom from knock, good fuel consumption, smooth engine running, little power loss as the car grows older, and good performance in all weathers. It is no easy matter to build all this into a petrol, at a reasonable price, but this is precisely what is done in top-quality petrols.

Birthplace of high-grade motor spirit — catalytic cracker at Shell's Stanlow Refinery in Cheshire.

A 24-hour job — pumping units in typical Dutch countryside.

Petrol is essentially a mixture of hydrocarbons, but the mixture can vary widely both in the types of hydrocarbons and in their relative proportions, depending upon the crude oil from which it is derived, and the process used to manufacture it. There are at least ten different processes, ranging from simple refinery distillation to complex cracking and reforming, and there are more kinds of crude oil than there are of the famous brand of soup.

By judicious selection and blending of petrol components produced by these various processes the characteristics of a petrol can be determined. But the product will still be lacking in certain essential requirements that can be achieved only by the addition of various non-petroleum products. It is this inherent variability of the basic petrol fractions and their sensitivity to additives that makes the formulation of a top-quality petrol so complex.

The refining process

Petrol, as it flows from the crude oil distillation columns in an oil refinery, is a mixture of hydrocarbons with a boiling temperature range between about 30° and 200°C. The vapour of this mixture burns in the presence of air to form carbon dioxide and water, a reaction which releases energy to power the engine.

In the early days of the motor car at the turn of the century, it was this petrol fraction straight from the distillation columns that was sold to the motorist. As the population grew, straight distillation did not produce enough petrol to meet demand without creating a large and wasteful surplus of other oil fractions such as paraffin and fuel oil.

Refiners had to find a way to convert surplus oil fractions into petrol, and so balance supply and demand for all their products. Cracking techniques, first thermal and then catalytic, proved to be the solution. Single hydrocarbon molecules of heavy fractions such as gas oil are broken down — or "cracked" — to form two molecules of lighter fractions such as petrol. Cracking not only produced more petrol, but also of the superior quality (higher anti-knock rating or octane number) needed to fuel the newer engines with higher compression ratios. The engine designer and the fuel designer have worked together to raise performance over the years.

Petrol tailor-made

Most modern refineries are also equipped with reforming plant which improves petrol quality without increasing the volume yield. In such plant individual molecules of the feedstock (petrol from the distillation column) are re-arranged to give a product with a much wider boiling range and a higher anti-knock value.

Petrol from the pump is a blend of components to which are added various chemicals to improve specific aspects of car performance. It is at this stage — in the blending and use of chemical additives — that the petrol is tailor-made to meet the diverse needs of modern cars.

The proportions in which the components are blended to make a petrol are determined by a number of performance criteria. For a car to start from cold, a combustible petrol/air mixture must be present in the cylinder. Thus a very volatile fraction such as butane must be incorporated in the petrol, but not too much or it will create problems of vapour locking and hot re-starting.

Freedom from knock

For quick warm-up and acceleration, the fuel must contain petrol fractions in the lower and middle boiling range; and, for good fuel consumption over a long period, fractions with higher boiling points and greater energy release are needed. Petrol has therefore to be a correctly-proportioned blend of fractions covering a wide range of boiling temperatures.

Another important aspect of performance is freedom from knock. This phenomenon stems from irregular combustion of the petrol/air mixture in the cylinder; it causes loss of power and can damage the engine. Although the steady increase in compression ratios of engines develops more power for less fuel, it also leads to a greater tendency to knock; therefore modern cars require fuels with a very high anti-knock rating. Refinery processes such as cracking and reforming improve anti-knock properties of fuels. Addition of such compounds as tetraethyl lead also produces marked improvement.

Fractionating tower at BP's Gothenburg Refinery, Sweden.

Forerunner of today... this Paris taxi-driver serves himself with petrol during the first World war. Each driver had his own hose and key to the pump; by putting in a disc he released a set quantity of petrol. The pump was invented by a French taximan.

But the anti-knock properties of the finished petrol depend upon careful blending.

Originally the knock rating of a fuel was assessed in terms of a single rating number — in a laboratory test engine, with full throttle knock at low speed. A much higher degree of control has been achieved by the introduction of two more ratings that give a better guide to anti-knock performance at high speed and where segregation of the fuel/air mixture occurs in the inlet manifold. Fuels are also tested for knock in all standard makes of car engine.

By blending components in the correct proportions, it is possible to produce petrols which have high anti-knock ratings in all motoring conditions and which, at the same time, have the desired volatility range. Petrol performance will, of course, be influenced by climate, and therefore the proportions are amended from summer to winter. So many variables are involved that nowadays it is normal practice to work out the proportions on a computer.

Quality control

To the fuel blend, chemicals are added to control various aspects of long-term engine performance. These additives vary with the brand of petrol, but fairly typical are organo-phosphorus compounds which modify deposits on sparking plugs. Deposits of this kind, which are more likely to form on engines with high compression ratios and in congested driving conditions, lead to spark plug misfire and random ignition.

Elaborate quality control tests are carried out during manufacture, storage and distribution to ensure that the petrol conforms to the prescribed specifications. Ultimately, the reputation of the petrol depends upon specifications being kept up to date with, or ahead of, current motoring requirements.

A customer serves himself at the pump island and another pays at the kiosk in a modern self-service station.

A 1903 De Dion-Bouton and a 1909 Humber.

city, and he arranged for its restoration. Unfortunately today it lacks the four famous mudguards which played an important part in the Pekin - Paris race. Made out of strong steel, they could be detached and placed under the wheels to cross streams and marshes.

Somewhat unjustly history has neglected the third member of the team, Ettore Guizzardi, the mechanic. "When he had nothing else to do he would stretch out under the car and examine it all, nut by nut, bolt by bolt, piece by piece", wrote Barzini, "and he would spend a long time in this strange communion with his machine".

As was inevitable, the Pekin - Paris generated a spirit of emulation. Thus the "New York Times", planned an even more ambitious race all round the world. The idea was for the competitors to leave from New York and, after having gone north-west across the American continent, to cross the Bering Straits from Alaska to Asia. From there, covering much of the route of the Pekin - Paris, they would arrive in the French capital. The distance to be covered was 18,341 miles and there was a terrible enemy to conquer — the North American winter.

The start was fixed for February 12, 1908 at 10 a.m. and there were present — after the inevitable withdrawals — six cars. There were three French (Bourcier, Hansen and Autran's De Dion, Godard, Hue and Livier's Motobloc, and Pons, Deschamps and Berthe's Sizaire-

The start of the New York-Paris race on the morning of February 12, 1908. Below a 1907 20-30 H.P. Spyker.

Naudin), one Italian (Scarfoglio, Sartori and Haaga's Züst), one German (Koeppen, Knappe and Maag's Protos), and one American (Schuster, Roberts and Williams' Thomas "Flyer").

Once again quite a few of the competitors were journalists for whom these great adventures were beginning to offer opportunities for a type of story sure to attract the public as proved by Barzini.

At least 50,000 people were present at the start from Times Square and another 150,000 lined the streets of Broadway between 42nd and 20th Streets. Similar enthusiasm had been shown for European competitors when leaving their respective capitals and the Kaiser himself had sent his best wishes to the German team. Most of the press, both American and European, criticized the choice of the time of year for the race. Everyone forecast its premature end on the outskirts of New York or at least in Illinois. They underestimated, however, the spirit of the competitors who, amidst every kind of difficulty (snow chains were used for the first time in this race) advanced slowly across the continent, over vast expanses of snow where tracks were barely visible, and on the railway track when necessary, as they

were authorized to do. Competitors even helped one another out of difficulty in a spirit of understanding though occasionally less orthodox methods were used, Koeppen being literally forced to help Schuster on one occasion.

Guidance in the snow

The inhabitants of the areas which were crossed, watched the progress of the competitors with ever-increasing amazement as the race went on relentlessly. They also gave tremendous help of all kinds. In Schenectady they showed the way after a particularly heavy snowfall by laying coloured streamers across the snow.

In spite of all this only four machines reached the Pacific coast at San Francisco. The Sizaire-Naudin had never even left New York State and the Motobloc fell out finally at Cedar Rapids, Iowa. The first to enter San Francisco was the Thomas, 42 days after the start, six days ahead of the Züst and 14 days ahead of the De Dion. The Protos was out of the race for the time being, stuck in the mud in Wyoming.

Schuster's team at once set sail for Valdez in Alaska,

from where they were to drive to Nome. The team had been changed to: Schuster, driver; Miller, mechanic; Hansen, navigator; and Macadam, a journalist from the "New York Times". While the team was on its way, however, the organisers changed their minds, afraid of the terrible state of the roads between Valdez and Nome.

Ship recalled

Thus the ship was recalled to Seattle, where the American team was joined by the other three to sail for Japan. The Germans had been hauled out of the "quicksand" and had been sent on by train to San Francisco. While the teams were sailing to Japan there was tremendous supply activity in Siberia as sledge teams hauled drums of petrol to supply points. The experience of the Pekin - Paris race proved very useful, indicating what to do and what not to do and when the race began again after another sea crossing between Japan and the Asian continent, it turned into a speed competition between the Thomas and the Protos. First prizes of 1,000 dollars each gave an excellent incentive on the successive stages into which the race was divided. Almost at once the American car was delayed by a series of misfortunes. First the transmission broke, causing the loss of precious lubricant which they tried to replace with tallow. Then the gearbox broke down. Schuster had to leave his car and go on horseback to the nearest town to try to get an emergency gear made. Almost at the same time the Protos became stuck in a sea of mud; the same thing happened to the Züst and the De Dion, both of which had to give up the race.

Getting free once again, the Germans set off before Schuster was able to get his machine going and, arriving in China first, won the 1,000 dollars affered by the Trans-Siberian Railway. Then, alternately passing and re-passing, the Americans and the Germans reached the area of Lake Baikal, where the Germans arrived first and the Americans had the misfortune of seeing their adversaries disappear into a ferry while they had to wait another 24 hours. Although he recovered the time lost in a dash to the Russian frontier, Schuster had once more to give way to the Germans, who thus won the 1,000 dollars offered by the Russian Automobile Club.

The Protos was already on good European roads and the Thomas had no more chance to catch up. Thus the Germans arrived in Paris on July 26 at 6.15 p.m., just at the time when the Americans were leaving Berlin. All the same, the victory was quite correctly given to the Thomas, which arrived four days later. The Protos received a thirty day penalty for having crossed part of America by train and for having refused to go to Alaska — it was because of the German refusal that the organisers had changed the route.

Amid delirious scenes of welcome the four Americans, bedecked with a huge "Stars and Stripes", arrived at the finish to be proclaimed the winners of the toughest of races.

Back to the factory

The winning machine, which had been in the race for 170 days — 88 of which it had been on the road — and had averaged over 150 miles per day (with a maximum of 400 in 24 hours), stayed only five days in France before being shipped back to the factory in Buffalo. There the bonnet was sealed and it did a 600-mile test run, after which the bonnet was opened. In the presence of witnesses, it was shown that the valves, spark plugs and bearings were those fitted before the race.

This remarkable technical achievement did not give the hoped for prosperity to the small American company. It was a victim of large-scale competition and four years later it was closed down.

The triumphal arrival of the Protos team on the 26th July, 1908.

The car has become an instrument of daily living, but as a social symbol it accurately represents the public taste of its time. Above, the 1967 Oldsmobile convertible complete with model passenger and umbrella. Below, a 1930 Bentley 4 ½-litre with Gurney Nutting body.

CHAPTER FOURTEEN

THE GRAND PRIX MONSTERS

In 1905 the last race for the Gordon Bennett Cup was run on the Auvergne circuit; in 1906 was born the Grand Prix of the Automobile Club de France. The succession was a natural one.

There was much opposition to the Gordon Bennett Cup rule that required that every part of a competing vehicle be made in the country it represented; many manufacturers who were excluded from taking part suffered material damage by not being able to share in the publicity created by the races — publicity which was an important commercial factor. These considerations had led the Automobile Club de France to announce that, after 1905, it would take no further part in the Cup races. This withdrawal, which deprived the race of its most important entries, brought about its demise, and it was natural and logical for France to create another major competition to replace it, the Grand Prix. It is said that this competition signalled the birth of "formula" racing

Two racing Wolseleys. The one above was photographed in 1905; the one below, in less formal pose, was photographed the year before.

in the modern sense of the word. For the first time in a major international race, technical limits were laid down for participating cars in a very similar way to the method used today.

As previously the most important requirement was that weight should not exceed 1,000 kgs. (about 2,200 lbs.) though an extra 7 kgs. were allowed for cars with electric ignitions. The driver and mechanic had to weigh at least 60 kgs, (132 lbs.) each and, as in the Gordon Bennett races, no manufacturer could enter more than three machines.

There were also more severe regulations, such as the rule that breakdowns could be repaired only by the driver and his mechanic. The race was to be over a distance of 1,248 kilometres (almost 780 miles) run in two days, with the machines in a *parc fermé* under the control of three inspectors during the intervening night.

The course was unusual — a large circuit near Le Mans, created by building new wood-paved roads through Vibraye forest and near Saint-Calais. All the rest of the 65-mile circuit was thickly paved with asphalt to avoid the terrible dust which was characteristic of other race tracks.

The asphalting was one of the earliest of its kind and derived from the attempts of the Swiss doctor, Gugliel-minetti and an engineer, Legavlian, to contain the dust under a covering of tar. The first roads so treated showed encouraging results, leading to the use of the method for the first time on a large scale at Le Mans. In practice, the remedy for dust proved to be worse than the complaint as high road temperatures played havoc with tyres on a hot June day.

The new race created a new craze among the public. For the first time tens of thousands of enthusiasts came

A 1904 Turcat-Méry racer. Note the finned tube radiator.

to Le Mans, then almost unknown, though later to play an important part in the story of European motoring. There it was possible, from dawn on 26 June until dusk the following day, to admire the most beautiful cars of the time. Hotels and inns were invaded for miles around and special trains poured visitors into the local stations.

At the start there were 32 cars (23 French, six Italian and three German). It was a surprising array, with nearly all the most important French and Italian makes represented, but not one from England, where it seemed the new race had aroused little interest. Among the makes taking part were Panhard-Levassor, Hotchkiss, Lorraine-Dietrich, Darracq, Renault, Clément-Bayard, Brasier, Itala, Fiat and Mercedes.

Because the regulations put no limitation on engine capacity or power, many manufacturers had built monster prototypes with very light chassis and huge engines with capacities ranging from 12 to 18 litres and outputs ranging from 90 to 130 B.H.P. These unusual vehicles were typical of racing cars for some years, until they were defeated by much lighter vehicles of a new technical age. An example was the 90 H.P. Renault with its 13-litre four-cylinder engine which had magneto ignition, side valves and a three-speed gearbox. There were brakes on the rear wheels only.

The race was won by a Renault and one of the reasons was that the machine, like the Fiats and Italas in the race, had detachable rims which could be removed by unscrewing eight nuts. This was a Michelin invention

Collapse of a car. What happened to one of the 1903 Gordon Bennett Napiers at a hill climb in 1933. The car still exists in America.

A 1908 G. P. Austin. It had a 9,677 c.c. six-cylinder, 100 H.P. engine with h.t. magneto and 4 speeds.

which in those days was revolutionary. In fact, a number of people had no faith in removable wheels and considered them very dangerous.

Changing a tyre

The most frequent repair, which regulations stipulated should be done only by the driver and mechanic, was changing the tyres. This was always a battle against time. First the remnants of the old tyre had to be removed from the rim — often a knife was necessary — and the new tyre had to be fitted with safety bolts. This often caused difficulties. Then followed the inflation of the tyres; and finally an 18-litre engine had to be started by hand! When it is remembered that this process might be necessary ten or twelve times (in that first Grand Prix Rougier took the record with fourteen changes) some idea can be gained of the strain imposed on crews of these early racing cars.

At the start, at 6 a.m., the race was led by Gabriel in a Lorraine-Dietrich followed by Lancia and Nazzaro in Fiats, Szisz in a Renault and Héméry in a Darracq. The first part of the race was marked by the high speeds of the three Brasiers driven by Barillier, Baras and Pierry (Baras did the first lap at 75 m.p.h.) but they

Make a rule and someone will find a way round it! When the regulations limited the bore to 80 mm, manufacturers increased the stroke to exaggerated lengths. One result was this 1910 racing Peugeot.

began to have mechanical troubles at the beginning of the second lap and quickly disappeared from the scene.

Nazzaro in the Fiat did the second lap at 80 m.p.h. but then he had to stop and Szisz in a Renault went into first place, which he held for the rest of the day, covering the course in 5 hours, 45 minutes and 30 seconds at an average of just over 65 m.p.h. He was followed by a Clément-Bayard, Nazzaro in a Fiat and Shepard in a Hotchkiss.

On the second day the duel between Szisz and Nazzaro began at once, and the whole of that day's race consisted of a vain attempt by the Italian driver to overtake the leader. At the finish less than a minute separated the two machines and the Renault was given a winning total time of 12 hours, fourteen minutes and 7 seconds at an average of just over 63 m.p.h.

The blinding tar

Photographs of the race show another torture undergone by the drivers, blinding by hot liquid tar thrown up by the wheels on those two extremely hot days. Szisz had actually to be led by the hand at the finish to the prize-giving with his eyes covered.

It is a curious fact that the second French Grand Prix

The helmeted driver of a 1910 Wolseley rounds a bend in a veteran car trial.

In 1912 Leslie Hounsfield built two prototype "people's cars" named Trojan. One of these still exists. Shown here, it had a four-cylinder 1,523 c.c., 10 H.P. engine, with two epicyclic gears and h.t. magneto.

Foreign influence. This 1904 Brush, made in England, was built to American ideas with an under-floor-mounted single-cylinder horizontal engine and central chain drive.

had the positions of the leader and runner-up reversed, Nazzaro winning in a 16-litre Fiat with Szisz, still faithful to Renault, coming in second. Fiat attached a growing importance to racing in those years, having prepared three prototypes for the major races of 1907. The lawyer Carlo Cavalli, who despite his profession was the designer of all racing cars for Fiat at that time, had designed for this Grand Prix the 130 H.P.

monster which could reach 100 m.p.h. at 1,600 r.p.m. The choice of this car was due to the new regulations for the 1907 race. In addition to the weight limit, fuel consumption was not allowed to exceed 30 litres every 100 kilometres (about 9 m.p.g.) and the drivers had to do 10 laps of a 47-mile circuit without an interruption, the two-day formula having been abandoned. Cars were to start at one-minute intervals.

A Fiat 130 H.P. prepared for the 1907 French Grand Prix.

High bonnets

The first to start was Vincenzo Lancia, who at once went into the lead and stayed there for most of the race. On the last lap clutch trouble caused him to lose some minutes and cost him the race. The race was won by Nazzaro who, following his usual practice, had started cautiously, partly to save petrol in view of the regulations, then becoming faster and faster to a final lap at almost 75 m.p.h. After Nazzaro had won, at an average of about 71 m.p.h., his petrol consumption was found to be 3 gallons less than the limit required, which is another indication of the driver's prudence. The Grand Prix was the third of Fiat's great victories in 1907, having been preceded by wins in the Targa Florio and the Emperor's Cup.

Henri Cissac's Panhard-Levassor before the start of the race in which he was killed. Below the French Grand Prix driver Szisz is escorted from his car with his face burned by the hot tar on the course.

Renault's gas turbine car, the "Etoile filante".

TURBINES FOR THE FUTURE

Over the past 20 years, several important automotive concerns have built and tested gas-turbine cars or commercial vehicles, whilst in long-distance racing, as well as the land speed record, the turbine is already established as an effective prime mover.

The Rover Company made world news with JET 1, the first practicable turbo-car, in 1950. There was a notable Fiat turbine sports car in 1954 and Renault set new standards of performance with their Étoile Filante race car a few years later. Rover produced later versions of their car, which were driven by Prince Philip and Princess Margaret.

Test driving

Other manufacturers, including Leyland in the commercial field and Austin with both cars and lorries, have developed the gas turbine. The result is that it is now a production possibility, if not today at least in the reasonably near future.

Wide research has been carried out by Ford and Chrysler, as well as General Motors. Ford and GM have concerned themselves mainly with the turbine's application to heavy vehicles but Chrysler have produced saloon cars with this type of engine. By 1964, in fact, Chrysler had made a preproduction run of 200 such cars, derived from an unusually handsome Ghia-styled prototype which has been demonstrated all over the world.

These cars were lent to 200 ordinary motorists who undertook to use them in certain conditions and to keep records on their working, defects, breakdowns, etc.

More than 1000 drivers were in fact involved, because after 12,000 miles each car was passed to a new user. The basic principles of the gas turbine are very simple, though there are a number of possible ways of building such units in practice. The principal element is a kind of fly-wheel on the circumference of which is fixed a large number of vanes. A mixture of hot air and burning gas is directed on to this, causing the wheel to turn. In practice, the gas turbine is a much less simple affair and there are various types, provided with one or more compression stages or turbine wheels or combinations of these multiple units. In the most commonly adopted layout of such an engine for use on land the air is first compressed and then mixed with vaporised liquid fuel, which is ignited in a burner.

As the mixture issues at high velocity from the burner it strikes the blades of the twin turbines, of which the first stage serves to drive the auxiliaries and the second initiates movement of the transmission. There are also devices to make use of the high temperature of the exhaust gases, whereby a heat exchanger passes heat to the air as it is taken into the compressor. The exhaust gases themselves pass out through the exhaust cones.

Easier construction

The principal problems of a motor car or lorry turbine lie in the method of controlling the power developed, to produce acceleration or deceleration. In the Chrysler car a double system is used. The angle of incidence of the turbine blades to the income gases is variable, while

The experimental Rover "Jet 1" of 1950, the first gas turbine car.

Interior of the Chrysler gas turbine car.

it is also possible to vary the direction of entry of the gases. This system even enables the direction of rotation of the turbine wheel to be reversed, producing a deceleration or braking effect.

The advantages of the gas turbine for land use compared to a reciprocating i.c. engine lie in its lower weight and smaller engine, in the "cleanness" of its exhaust gases, its silence, and its greater simplicity for production as there are no valves or clutch and the electrical circuit is much simpler.

There are fewer moving parts (about one fifth of those of a i.c. engine) and there is no vibration, making the design inherently more durable. Moreover, the gas turbine has greater torque and crude fuels can be used. The principal obstacles concern the major technical problems involved. Temperatures of 2,200°C are reached in the burner and the turbine wheels revolve at around 50,000 r.p.m. Production costs are high, and other disadvantages include a flat power curve and lag in response in application of power.

The Fiat gas turbine car of 1954.

The winner of the second Targa Florio on the Madonie circuit on 21 April was the "20-B", the 28-40 H.P. which had a top speed of 60 m.p.h. This car was designed particularly for the "Targa" in view of the limits placed on cylinder bore by the race regulations. This led to long-stroke engines and very high bonnets to contain them, thus giving this type of car its distinctive appearance.

Vincenzo Florio had received forty entries for the race and among machines represented were Fiat, De Dietrich, Isotta-Fraschini, Clément-Bayard, Itala, Darracq, Gobron-Brillié, Benz and Berliet. The list of drivers included Wagner, Héméry, Duray, Gabriel, Hanriot, Opel, Sorel and Rigal — all famous at the time. Some of the cars had the new shaft drive, but it was generally considered less reliable than chains.

The race, which also adopted interval starts, was exciting from beginning to end. At the finish Duray led, followed by Lancia and Nazzaro, and the public acclaimed Duray as winner. Then it was announced that Felice Nazzaro had registered the shortest time to cover the 280-mile circuit, followed by Lancia 15 minutes behind, Fabry 10 minutes later and Duray at 26 minutes. Nazzaro's average was just over 35 m.p.h. and Lancia did the fastest lap.

This second Targa Florio was notable for the consistent timing of some of the drivers. For example, Nazzaro showed 23 seconds difference in lap times and Lancia even fewer, 20 seconds. This may serve to correct the

A 1907 Hispano-Suiza, one of the first cars built by the company.

1907 La Buire, particularly interesting for its six-cylinder engine with twin carburettors. The model shown is a "double phaeton".

The winning Mercedes in the third French G. P. in 1908. Lautenschlager is changing a wheel.

A laden Daimler seen in the 1907 Herkomer Trophy.

1905. Siddeley 100 H.P.

impression of the latter as having been too impulsive and undisciplined as a driver.

Fiat's and Nazzaro's third success in 1907 was in the "Kaiserpreis", the Emperor's Cup. The "Taunus", a 72 B.H.P. 8 litre (the maximum capacity allowed by the regulations) was used, which also conformed to the weight limit of 1,175 kgs. (about 2,585 lbs.).

The race was run less than two months after the Targa Florio on a circuit in the Taunus mountains in Germany, on roads very similar to those which had seen Théry's victory in the fourth Gordon Bennett Cup in his Brasier. The organization of the race was carried out with a precision that was unusual for the time. For example, for 200 yards before every curve the tree trunks were painted white to a height of six feet and a series of white discs on the side of the road indicated dangerous inclines. The Emperor's Cup was held on 14 June in the presence of Kaiser Wilhelm II. There were 33 German, 20 French, 19 Italian, 10 Belgian, four English, three Swiss and two Austrian cars, representing practically every make of the times.

The large number of entrants at once gave rise to safety problems. It seemed unwise to allow so many competitors to race on such a twisting circuit, made even more dangerous by two narrow sections. So it was decided to run two heats, the first 20 in each of which were to enter the final, consisting of four laps of the 75-mile circuit. The heats consisted of two laps only.

Nazzaro won heat and final — and the useful sum of £ 2,000 in special prizes.

Racetrack in the pines

The circuit of Le Mans, one of the first in Europe specially designed for car racing, was built in 1906. In 1907, on our own side of the Channel, another track was inaugurated, at Brooklands in Surrey. This had very different characteristics from Le Mans because it was intended for record attempts and out-and-out speed racing. It was to be one of the most important tracks in Europe up to the outbreak of the Second World War. The track was built in a forest of pine trees through which ran the small river Wey: it was first used by S. F. Edge's Napier for the double-twelve-hour record, and Edge also used it for challenge matches. One of the most famous of the challenges was that given by S. F. Edge, Napier's official driver, to Fiat.

A line-up of Austins — from left to right 1911 7 H.P., 1908 100 H.P. "Grand Prix", 1936 "Twin Cam" 750 c.c., 1926 "Gordon England" and a 1931 "Swallow" 7.

Before the start of the 1960 Prescott Hill Climb — a 4½-litre Vinot-Deguingand and the 12,076 c.c. Itala G.P., both built in 1908.

Felice Nazzaro was chosen to defend the honour of Fiat in the race, which took place on June 8th 1908.

He won in his "SB-4" (Mephistopheles) after a broken crankshaft had put the Napier out of the race. The "SB-4" had a four-cylinder oversquare 18,146 c.c. engine with bore and stroke of 190 mm. and 160 mm. — a rare formula for an engine of this size. It developed 175 H.P. at 1,200 r.p.m. and the car weighed 23½ cwts.

At Brooklands in June the previous year had already been sensational when Edge, in a six-cylinder Napier, set up a record by running for 24 hours at an average speed of 65 m.p.h. — over 1,500 miles covered in spite of 1 hour and 40 minutes spent in the pits changing tyres. The Press of the time showed imaginative illustrations of the great car hurtling through the night in its race against time, with the edge of the track picked out by torches.

After this successful attempt, Brooklands was host to many outstanding motoring events for more than thirty years. Here may be mentioned the flying kilometre of the Frenchman Goux in a Peugeot at a speed of 170.868 k.p.h. (nearly 106 m.p.h.) and the "one-hour" record set by Percy Lambert in a Talbot 4½-litre at almost 105 m.p.h. During the Second World War, Brooklands was taken over for military use and was considerably damaged. Afterwards, for a number of reasons, it was unfortunately lost to motor racing, and today is the site of an aircraft factory although parts of the circuit can still be seen.

The "Blitzen Benz".

W. O. BENTLEY

To the modern layman, the term "Vintage car" symbolises a green open four-seater with outside gear and brake levers, bearing a winged "B" on its radiator, and emitting the purposeful burble of four big cylinders.

The man who created this legend, Walter Owen Bentley, was born in 1888, and trained as a railway engineer in the C.N.R. shops at Doncaster before managing a fleet of taxis in London, and taking on the agency for the French D.F.P. car, which he transformed into an effective sports machine, as his sixth place in the 1914 T.T. testifies. By the time the first 3-litre Bentley appeared in 1919 he was famous, too, in another field — as the creator of the B.R.2 rotary aero-engine, the "Merlin" of the First World War, and the power behind Sopwith's "Camel".

The next decade saw five wins at Le Mans, including tthe legendary 1927 race in which Davis and Benjafield nursed a crippled 3-litre to victory. Though there was never enough money, the three-thousand-odd "old-school" Bentleys that left Cricklewood put a new name on the map. If the luxury sixes were never a commercial success, they culminated in the magnificent 100 m.p.h. 8-litre of 1930, a car good enough to induce Rolls-Royce Ltd. to purchase Bentley after the finances finally ran out. Bentley did not stay long with his company's new owners, but he was back in 1935 with a more refined version of Lagonda's 4½-litre. This was followed by a modern and rapid V-12: the Second World War put a stop to development, but not before its first competition outing (appositely at Le Mans) resulted in third and fourth places for the marque. After the war Bentley designed a smaller all-independently-sprung six for Lagonda, but though this one never matched the succes of its forebears, it provided the engine for the brilliant Aston Martin DB2 series.

Bentley now lives in retirement in Surrey, but the cars survive as a monument to a great Englishman and a great designer.

Six-cylinder engines began to be built in 1908. The fact that the four cylinder is more common in Europe is due to present and past fiscal measures. Above — the V6-cylinder Lancia "Flaminia". Below — the eight-cylinder Lancia "Dilambda Speciale".

CHAPTER FIFTEEN
COMFORT AND CONVENIENCE

The year 1907 was important for major sporting events. In another sphere of motoring, however, it was important as it marked the perfection of the "valveless" engine by the Wisconsin agriculturist Charles Knight. Its primary object was the elimination of valve gear, which was then very noisy partly owing to the considerable "play" between cams, tappets and valves, which the techniques of the times demanded to cope with expansion caused by heating.

After early studies that began in 1901, he built his first experimental engine with a friend, L. B. Kilbourne. It had a somewhat rudimentary system of letting in the mixture and letting out the exhaust gases by alternately raising and lowering the cylinder itself, and in so doing uncovering inlet and outlet ports. The device was over-complicated and Knight devised an improved system. His first production engine saw the light of day in 1907.

In this engine a sleeve was introduced between piston and cylinder. The sleeve was windowed and it reciprocated in such a way as to cover and uncover inlet and outlet ports. The first of these sleeve-valve engines was fitted in a Panhard imported into the United States,

and performed well both from the points of view of silence and of general performance.

In 1908 Knight and the English Daimler Company made an agreement whereby the more luxurious Daimlers would be fitted with sleeve-valve engines. The finest

example of this collaboration, which was to last for many years, was the Daimler Double-Six V12 of 1926. This car had a seven-litre sleeve-valve engine, and the Royal cars were converted to take the new engine, although the King bought five new Double Sixes in 1931.

Destroyed in practice

Not only Daimler, but many other European and American makes adopted the silent and flexible Knight engine, including Willys and Stearns in America, Panhard, Mors, Voisin, Peugeot, Clément and Mors in France and Minerva in Belgium.

If their performance was a trifle leisured, the silence of the new "valveless" engines was much appreciated, and other inventors sought to rival the Knight designs, among them the slide-valve Imperial from Belgium, and the rotary-valve Itala.

Between 1911 and 1915 numerous models of cars with "valveless" engines were offered, with outputs of up to 50 horsepower. Itala even raced their *avalve* unit in 1913, but their efforts were not crowned with success. If a motorist of the day had to have a car with poppet-

King George V enters his impressive Daimler in 1910.

Even the dog takes part in the great day when the first car is delivered! A 1902 Brush.

A 1912 Delahaye. 10-12 H.P. 1,593 c.c. four-cylinders, high-tension magneto. The body is made of wood.

A rotary-valve Itala driven by Nazzaro in the 1913 French Grand Prix.

Two great veteran cars. Above a splendid, 1909 six-cylinder, 7,046 c.c. 40/50 H.P. Rolls Royce "Silver Ghost". Below — the 1912 3,615 c.c., 15.9 H.P. Hispano-Suiza.

valves, the six-cylinder engine was always smoother than a twin or four. The enormous popularity of this type of engine around 1908-1910, and the large number built, can only partly be explained by its undoubted technical advantages, such as increased silence and the sense of power which it has always given to drivers. On the other hand the six-cylinder engine was far from perfect, suffering as it did from whip and torsional deformation in the crankshaft, which was too long and complicated for the production technology of the day.

Ahead of their time

Among other multi-cylinder layouts were the V8 De Dion of 1910, which was produced only a few years after the abandonment of the single-cylinder formula to which De Dion had been faithful for so long; Winton's double-four engine; an overhead valve V12 by Marvel-Schebler in the United States; the narrow V6 of Delahaye and the V4's built by Aries in France. These engines never went into quantity production, however, as they were ahead of the mass-manufacturing techniques available at the time.

From 1910 onwards the motor car began to acquire a number of accessories which were of secondary importance but which were essential to its efficiency and comfort. First there was the windscreen wiper which, when it arrived, made obsolete all the complicated arrangements for maintaining some visibility in case of rain.

In America the bumper began to appear, born of the necessity of protecting the car as more and more vehicles used the roads. In Europe it was not adopted until later, because the need was hardly so acute. "Safety" glass was also introduced at this time; it was a type which consisted of glass and Celluloid.

Unfortunately it was considered a mere luxury for a long time, and as such was reserved for the more expensive cars. It was not until the late 1930s that its fitting became generally obligatory, and then only for the wind screen.

At the end of the first decade of the century great strides were made in carburation, a constant problem for engine designers. In this period around 1909 it was appreciated that the carburettor had to be cured of its many weaknesses; it caused many stoppages and required too much maintenance. The necessity for frequent blowing through the jets and continual cleaning of the float chamber was sometimes due of course, to the problems

In 1909 Sizaire and Naudin were still building single-cylinder engines. This was a 1½ litre.

A 1908 Lanchester with a 2,470 c.c., four-cylinder engine, three epicyclic gears, footbrake operating on the rear wheels and hand-brake by disc also on the rear wheels.

Vauxhalls in the 1914 Isle of Man T.T.

of preventing the contamination of the fuel by dirt and dust.

Important progress was made, however, by two French industrialists, Maurice Goudard and Marcel Mennesson. In 1910 they decided to devote themselves to the design and production of more advanced types of carburettor to replace the primitive devices manufactures still usually fitted in the most inaccessible place possible. The name of their product, Solex, was decided upon after a competition, and appears to have no particular meaning.

The success of the new company was assured from the start and about the same time a second major manufacturer of carburettors was born, the British concern, Zenith. These two have remained among the largest producers ever since.

The difficult problem of four-wheel brakes was also nearing solution at this time by modification of existing systems. In theory, the need for braking all four (or three) wheels had been known from the beginning of the century, but it had been held to be impossible to brake the front wheels efficiently in practice because of their steering requirements. The difficulty was not in transmitting braking force to the wheels, but rather in ensuring that this force did not change the position of the wheels, cancelling out the efficiency of the brakes and creating new dangers.

Braking difficulties

The problem consisted of the need — as can easily be seen today in the light of experience — to design steering geometry which was mechanically effective and able to keep the effects of steering and braking separate. This goal was finally achieved in practical and effective form in Scotland by Henri Perrot, though many before him, including Maybach, had tried and failed. Perrot helped to design the first car with four-wheel brakes which were considered safe; they were produced by the company for which he worked, Argyll.

The adoption of four-wheel brakes was extraordinarily slow, nevertheless, in part due to the prejudices of manufacturers, and in part due to fear of their customers' attitudes. These early motorists feared front-wheel skids. Progress in pneumatic tyre design was also slow. Their performance had been adequate for years apart from two major defects — their short life and the frequency with which they punctured. Before the First World War they had an average life of less than 2,000 miles. Improvements effected by the use of new materials and

A 1909 Bianchi 20-30 H.P.

better construction of the cover of the tyre were only to come later.

On the other hand, punctures were made less of a headache by the general adoption of detachable rims, fixed to the wheel by a number of bolts (it has been recorded how the 1906 Grand Prix was decided by the use of such a device for the first time by the winning Renault).

A most important step forward, when the whole wheel became removable, was due mainly to the British manufacturers Sankey and Rudge-Whitworth. It was due to Michelin, in the years immediately following, that the first wheels were produced in pressed steel.

1911 Bedelia 8 H.P. with front mounted V twin engine. Bore and Stroke 82 × 100 mm. Capacity 1,056 c.c. Ignition by h.t. magneto. 2 speeds, no reverse. Belt drive. Weight — 462 lb.

Leather face mask, goggles and gauntlets — almost a return to the middle ages. Danny Druce at the wheel of "Mooneyes".

HOT-ROD RODEOS

There is perhaps more than an ocean between Europe and America from the point of view of motoring competition. The differences are well known not only so far as the kinds of cars, tracks and racing regulations are concerned, but also in the attitude of the public. This does not mean, of course, that there can be no point of contact between these two worlds or that drivers cannot take part in races on the other side. Indeed, there has been a considerable increase in such activity in recent years with European drivers and cars at classic U. S. events and American drivers in Europe.

Little resemblance

There is, however, one type of motoring competition which has only recently begun to be popular in Europe — "hot-rodding".

Hot-rodding — it is the official, if somewhat illogical, term — describes quarter-mile sprints from a standing start. For this purpose specially developed vehicles are used which bear little resemblance to any other form of land vehicle.

Hot-rodding should not be considered the prerogative of a small group of rich devotees in the U. S. On the contrary, it is practised by tens of thousands of people, mostly young.

They work rigidly within the regulations of their appropriate federation, the National Hot Rod Association. These regulations have 72 different sub-classes of vehicle according to capacity and weight, and are grouped together in eight major categories, as follows:

Stock cars, which are derived from standard cars and to which only certain limited modifications may be made to increase safety. By accurate tuning they can have considerable acceleration. Stock cars are the only ones in the Association which run distance races on the trace.

Road cars, which are production vehicles considerably modified for sprints but still legally capable of road use. There are three categories of these.

"Moderate" competition cars, which are again derived from production cars but to which modifications are not limited by the need to keep them legally suitable for road use.

Competition cars, similar to the above but even more highly modified.

Experimental cars, or prototypes.

European-type sports cars.

American Mickey Thompson, dragster champion, in action behind his car's smoke screen. Its engine develops 1,000 H.P.

The principal modifications made to a standard production car consist of chopping and channelling, or of lowering the roof and the interior of the car until it almost touches the ground.

In addition to these eight categories which still preserve some resemblance to motor cars, there are two other categories: the "dragsters" and the "fuel dragsters".

These are vehicles built exclusively for quarter-mile acceleration competition. They are of distinctive appearance, with two light small wheels in front, two very large wide ones at the rear and often a parachute for braking. Everything that is inessential for acceleration is eliminated or reduced to the minimum. The chassis consists or two simple tubes; front suspension is rudimentary and rear suspension does not exist. There are brakes only at the rear. The driver sits well back over the rear axle.

Although great liberty is given to dragster builders — who are often the drivers themselves — the vehicles still have to conform with certain requirements as to weight, wheel base and track.

A typical "Hot Rod".

Special tracks

The "fuel dragsters" are a special category, the most esoteric of all. Any sort of fuel is permissible in these machines. These vehicles use fuels such as nitro-methane, and are always liable to explode. The engines are usually uncooled and sometimes without lubricant, to reduce loss of power to the minimum. Engines are switched off as soon as possible.

Hot rod competitions take place on special tracks all over the United States. The most important are at Daytona and Bonneville Salt Flats, where even the backroom boys of big companies go, often finding something interesting among the bright ideas of the builders.

The vehicles run in pairs, with the front-wheels lifting sometimes as much as two feet amidst clouds of smoke from the rear, caused by slip between tyres and the surface.

The skill of the driver in getting full power from the engine and using it immediately at full power is best exhibited by the way he controls the wheel spin to achieve maximum adherence.

Young people who take up hotrodding and drag racing in America work miracles of improvisation, often picking up parts cheaply from motor junk yards.

The races themselves present a scene typical of modern American entertainment. With their profusion of bright colours, publicity, designs and symbols of every type they are the rodeos of the present-day mechanical age.

From zero to 190 m.p.h. in eight seconds! Tony Nancy's dragster takes off. Below the same vehicle brakes by parachute.

These Mercedes six-cylinder cars raced in 1913. Lautenschlager drove the car on the right and Salzer the car on the left. Below a 1912 French six-cylinder — the 35 H.P. Renault.

In the period 1910 to 1914, vital years in the evolution of the motor car, the first attempts were made to solve suspension problems. Here, too, there had been earlier efforts but it was only in 1912 and 1913 that hydraulic shock absorbers went into general production.

Road-holding and stability over rough surfaces were also improved by lowering the centre of gravity, though this process took some time to crystallise. None the less, some firms did experiment with underslung frames, which passed under the axles, before the First World War. The best known exponents of this theme were the French Stabilia and the American Underslung on the other side of the Atlantic.

Back to open-top

There was apparently a move back in the direction of the open car. This dominated the motoring scene in early days, but formal carriages came into fashion with wealthy owners as the automobile gained wider acceptance. Open sporting cars were, however, very popular immediately before the war.

Aerodynamic styling, child of the new and rapidly developing field of aeroplane design, began to influence the motor car. It influenced the design of the "torpedoes", open cars which were relatively long and low and whose name gives an idea of explosive power. This picture of the 1910-1914 motor car would not be complete without acknowledging the work of the coachbuilder. The car manufacturer himself frequently supplied only the chassis, and the client selected the type of body he wanted and arranged with the coachbuilder to make it.

In practice, the waiting time for chassis meant that details were settled with the coachbuilder before his small army of highly skilled specialists could start work. This included, of course, the details of design and shape of the body and also the choice of metals, leather, fittings and colours.

Skilled craftsmen

Timber, too, played an important part in the interior of the car, in the widest variety of types from walnut to maple, from mahogany to elm, from beech to oak. The care with which this wood was selected and its seasoning carried out is shown by the perfect condition of the wood-work of many of these veteran cars existing today.

After a long period with the expert joiners and leather workers, the body passed to the skilled metal workers, who carefully built up the panelling, including external bolts and rivets, which were often plated or polished. All the vast number of fittings were mounted by hand, including the lamp brackets, windscreen, toolbox, running boards and spare wheel supports. Nothing was hurried and craftsmanship was all-important. Finally

the whole went for painting; perhaps as many as 16 coats were applied by hand in colours chosen after long discussion with the client.

One last visit to the lighting specialist, whose products of gleaming brass and crystal gave the finishing touch, and the car was on its way to the customer. The bill would be extremely high, as was inevitable for work which had occupied a number of specialists for weeks. But the "belle époque" of the motor car was drawing to a close. On the other side of the Atlantic, mass production was an accomplished fact. Ford had made gigantic strides in this respect and had provided the opportunity for thousands of Americans to own their first car.

In Europe, quantity production was at the half-way stage. Already some manufacturers were producing some part of their production by large-scale methods, fitting standard bodies and supplying a complete machine.

About this time a new sort of car was born which was to have a short life. This was the cyclecar. The manu-

A Nazzaro "Type 3" of 1914.

The 1908 Austin racing car built for the Grand Prix. It had a 9.7-litre six-cylinder engine based on the firm's contemporary 60 H.P.

facture of light vehicles was not new to Europe, and in fact *voiturette* racing had been a recognised part of the calendar since 1906. The reasons for the development of the cyclecar were, however, very different from those that led to the voiturette.

In addition to a substantial increase in the price of petrol, new taxes and fiscal charges in many countries were an incentive for manufacturers to produce vehicles less expensive to run. There were still thousands of potential motorists in Europe who could not afford even

A German production car. The 4-8 H.P. Opel "Doktorwagen" of 1908.

A 1903 Cadillac Model "A" with single-cylinder engine. Its catalogue advertised, "Price of the runabout $850. Extra for brass lamps, horn and the picnic basket".

the cheapest product of the day, and a substantial drop in price would open up a new market for manufacturers. This was a factor which Ford already appreciated and which Herbert Austin and others were to exploit.

Cyclecar prospers

The manufacture of cyclecars mushroomed throughout Europe in the years immediately before the First World War mainly because the motor car had reached the state of development similar to that of the electric car in the 1880s. As in the period three decades earlier, the basic problems had been solved and components such as engines, transmission and running gear were now universally available to the chassis builder.

Most cyclecars were built by people with little experience of car design or manufacture. Generally, they were simple, crude, uncomfortable and probably dangerous. The engine was usually that of a motorcycle of about one-litre capacity, and air-cooled. Transmission was by chain or even belt. Bodywork was reduced to something minimal and often bath-shaped, into which were fitted two crude seats; often one was placed behind the other with the driver in the rear. Braking was inadequate even for such light vehicles. Reverse gear and clutch were non-existent, and steering layout had much in common with a child's pedal car.

These vehicles were not to be produced for long, though there was to be a brief second wave of popularity after the First World War; these minimal vehicles also had a short vogue in the U.S.A. in 1915 and 1916.

Unlike the light, simple, "real" motor cars which existed alongside them, cyclecars had negligible performance. In their favour was one psychological factor. They introduced the possibility of a self-propelled vehicle to many people who otherwise would have been excluded from motoring. Thus they helped to create the conditions which enabled Austin, Morris and others to offer a satisfactory solution to the problem.

1905 Benz "Tourenwagen" 40 H.P.

Ricotti's torpedo and an American "Dream car" More than 50 years separates them.

PIONEERS
OF
AERODYNAMICS

In the early days of motoring, designers were usually concerned with the straightforward problems of function. The problem of aerodynamics received little consideration. It was only in the 1930s that the first tentative attempts were made to adapt coachwork to penetrate the air. Yet this is one of the ways, and by no means the most difficult, of obtaining the increase of performance and speed for which designers have always been looking.

There were, nevertheless, a few isolated efforts in earlier times to built aerodynamic cars. First was that of Jenatzy, the Belgian who became a racing driver. In modifying his Jeantaud electric vehicle, the "Jamais Contente", he took full account of aerodynamic problems and made it in the form of a marine torpedo. In doing so, however, he disregarded the comfort of the driver who had to insert himself in the most uncomfortable position for his record attempts.

The "Jamais Contente", however, was not a motor car in the real sense of the term. A remarkable vehicle ordered by Count Marco Ricotti in 1913 from Alfa Romeo and the coachbuilder Castagna certainly was. This was torpedo-shaped and could hold six. This unusual car, with which Ricotti made a number of speed attempts, had a door and four windows in each side. The front of the vehicle was formed mainly of a large curved windscreen.

Droplet of water

The engine was a 40-60 H.P., four cylinder 6,082 c.c. which gave the standard model a maximum speed of 78 m.p.h. Ricotti was able to achieve about 87 m.p.h. in his version. But, almost inevitably, the car was never put into production.

A somewhat better fate awaited the "Tropfenwagen" (droplet car) designed in Germany in 1921 by Rumpler, who took advantage of a mass of data derived from the practice with aeroplanes. His studies led him to the same conclusions as Ricotti: that the best shape was that of a drop of water falling freely in air, the front rounded and then tapering away to the tail.

But as Ricotti had to use an available chassis and so built a very large vehicle, Rumpler started from scratch and was able to modify many of the features of a normal car. The body conformation demanded the use of a layout in which the engine was immediately behind the passenger seats. This meant that there could be a short drive shaft, but longer linkages on gear change and clutch were necessary.

One headlamp

To remain true to the concept of aerodynamic form, Rumpler designed a fully enclosed body which covered the wheels. For the same reason there was only one headlamp, in the centre of the nose, and the mudguards were reduced to horizontal fins.

The "Tropfenwagen" had a better commercial fate than Ricotti's car. It was in limited production for a few years.

Today the science of aerodynamics is one of the major concerns of the car designer. Ironically, the missile-like shape of the modern high-speed racing car is, in a sense, a return to the earliest days of the record-breakers.

The Opel Kadett coupé L., designed to satisfy "sporty" tastes with the comfort of a saloon, which the Opel "Puppchen" 4-8 H.P. of 1913, below, was also intended to achieve. The "Puppchen" had a four-cylinder engine and could reach 40 m.p.h.

CHAPTER SIXTEEN
HAND PUMPS AND PUNCTURES

The beginning of the second decade of the century experienced one of those pauses in motoring which was to occur from time to time, and there was a general decline in racing interest.

This decline of interest is most clearly exhibited by the fact that the most important European motor race, the French Grand Prix, was suspended from 1909 to 1911. The reasons were complex in nature: economic, political and perhaps of habit.

Racing magic fades

The car had lost the "magic" of its pioneering years, but had yet to gain mass support. Some historians see the drop in popularity as being due in part to the growing interest in aviation, which was competing for public attention, though this is unlikely to have had a major effect.

The pause was not to last for long and interest was to revive before the outbreak of the war.

The French Grand Prix of 1908 was again held on the Dieppe circuit, but it was run to a new formula. Instead of being based on fuel consumption, it demanded that bore be limited to 155 mm. for four-cylinder machines

and to 127 mm. for six cylinders. This dubious restriction — which was to be imitated in other races, as indeed it had already been anticipated — was the cause of the "monsters" with exaggerated piston strokes. This led to very high bonnets.

This elongation of the stroke brought about by the new formula was not, however, the only technical innovation in the race. With increasing engine power, lubrication was becoming a more acute problem and

Theodore Roosevelt, back left in the picture, was the first president of the U.S. to use a car for official purposes. Olds is driving the car at Lansing in 1907.

many cars in the 1908 G. P. were equipped with large hand pumps, which the mechanic (who was still an obligatory member of the team) had to operate continuously throughout the race to maintain the supply of lubricant.

The race itself was interesting from another technical point of view, in that it was marked by an extraordinary number of punctures. Power and speeds had notably increased in the past few years but the pneumatic tyre had made little progress. Thus, as in an earlier period, the number of punctures became a deciding factor.

In the race eight French makes, three German (Mercedes, Benz and Opel), two Italian (Fiat and Itala), two English (Austin and Weigel) and one Belgian (Germain) took part, while Napier were excluded because their cars had Rudge Whitworth centre-lock removable wheels which the organisers considered too dangerous. The American company, Thomas, was also represented. One of the French cars had an engine with one of the first overhead camshafts.

Careful tactics

Fiat's hopes of repeating the success of the previous year were dashed when first Lancia, then Wagner and Nazzaro were forced to make long pit stops. The tyre disasters soon began with the two Benz of Héméry and Hanriot, joined by Lautenschlager's Mercedes and Rigal's Clément. The punctures continued, and when Rigal had 19 (a record for the race) he retired!

At this point Lautenschlager, Mercedes' chief tester and

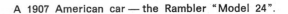

A 1907 American car — the Rambler "Model 24".

250

1909, the first Hudson.

an experienced racing driver who knew that there were no more spare tyres in the Mercedes' pit, began his very intelligent tactics. He accelerated down the straights but took corners gently, the point where most tyre wear occurred. His adversaries were less careful and Lautenschlager won by a large margin at the high average speed of 73 m.p.h. Second and third were the Benz of Héméry and Hanriot.

The victory at Dieppe was a triumph for the 120 H.P. Mercedes, designed by Paul Daimler, Gottlieb's son. The engine was a four-cylinder in-line with bore and stroke of 155 mm. × 170 mm. giving 12,781 c.c. For the first time the Grand Prix itself had been preceded by a race for voiturettes, light touring cars.

Long-stroke engines

This represented official approval of a type of competition that had been popular for some years, as the kind of cars which took part were based on standard production machines. This type of race had begun in 1905 when the French paper "L'Auto", aware of the tremendous publicity value of the great capital-to-capital races, has decided to organise a race for cars weighing less than 700 kgs. (1,540 lbs).

The race, called the "Coupe des Voiturettes" was run in 1906 and won by a single-cylinder Sizaire-Naudin. It was the first occasion on which the "stroke" formula was used (90 mm. for two-cylinder cars and 106 mm. for single) and, as with the larger cars, it led to the use of a large number of long-stroke engines. Among the

The fearsome front of a 1907 Darracq, with Morgan body.

251

many manufacturers to support this formula between 1905 and 1910 were Hispano-Suiza, Delage, Lion-Peugeot and Isotta Fraschini.

In 1908, the touring car race at Dieppe was won by Guyot in an interesting Delage with a single-cylinder engine of 100 mm. × 150 mm. bore and stroke with four sparking plugs and a double flywheel. This singular vehicle had been designed by the young Louis Delage, who had once worked with Peugeot, and an ex-school friend, Némorin Causan. This was excellent publicity for Delage, who was to have great success in the future, beginning with the period 1910 to 1913 when nine series of his famous "AB 8" were produced.

Source of ideas

Another interesting touring car present at Dieppe in 1908 was the Ariès which had four valves per cylinder and desmodromic actuation. For many years these races were a fountain of ideas, not all successful inevitably, but the source of many major and minor improvements.

In the subsequent story of the touring car, or voiturette, the 1910 two-cylinder Peugeot should be mentioned. In this car the long-stroke design went to unprecedented exaggeration — 80 mm. × 280 mm. As time went on, four-cylinder engines became more and usual and a new name was to be found among the manufacturers, that of Bugatti, who had set up his own factory at Molsheim in 1908.

The Grand Prix was not run in 1909 because of the lack of entries, 40 being the minimum number required by the Automobile Club de France. To this was added the high cost of preparing a large-engined racing proto-type, which already bore little or no resemblance to the ordinary production car. The touring car race proved to be much more useful to the manufacturer, as did a third type of event initiated by the Germans — the long-distance road rally.

Such rallies were run in Germany from 1905 to 1910, and this period may be considered in two parts — 1905 to 1907, which included three events in the Herkomer series, and 1908 to 1910. In these latter years there were three more trials sponsored by Prince Henry of

The Cadillac factory in 1912.

1913 Le Zèbre phaeton has two seats and a single-cylinder engine. Top speed — 22 m.p.h. Below a 1912 Delanaye.

Prussia, Kaiser Wilhelm II's brother, who was a keen motorist and took part in the last event. This race, incidentally had no individual classification. The famous Vauxhall sports car took its name from this series.

The races were held over ordinary roads in Germany and Austria-Hungary over a distance of 1,200 to 1,500 miles and lasting a week. Two distinct categories were envisaged for racing cars and touring cars respectively, but the latter were more important. As the series of Prince Henry Cup races went on more and more regulations were made to ensure the specifications did not deviate too far from that of standard touring models. Thus coachwork had to be painted and the body had to weigh at least 15 per cent of the total. Many famous owners took part in these races, and the winner of the 1910 event was Ferdinand Porsche in an Austro-Daimler of his own design.

Different formula

The first "post crisis" edition of the French Grand Prix was held in 1912, although there had been a rather poor affair the previous year at Le Mans.

The 1912 race was run to a formula very different from its predecessors. It was run over two days, with a break, for a total of 1,540 kilometres (960 miles), again on the Dieppe circuit. This event was run concurrently with the Coupe de l'Auto for light cars of up to 3-litres'

A 1913 two-seater Clément-Bayard tourer, having three speeds. Solex carburettor.

capacity, and only five of the entries all told retained the immense power units favoured in the past. Some of the competitors in the Grand Prix proper favoured much smaller engines.

It was clear from the start that there was going to be a fight between the 14-litre "old-fashioned" Fiats and the "small" 7.6 litre Peugeots. In fact, the race was to be a battle between brute force and advanced design. The Fiats were driven by Bruce-Brown, an American, and De Palma, an Italian-American, and Wagner. The Peugeots had relatively high revving engines (2,200 r.p.m.) and an interesting cylinder head design with twin overhead camshafts and four valves per cylinder. At first the Fiats had the advantage, but then both Bruce-

Brown and De Palma were disqualified for irregularities and the race was between Wagner and Boillot, the leading Peugeot driver.

The Peugeot won and it marked not only a worthy sporting achievement but also the victory of brains over brawn, of technical skill over capacity. Another significant result was the position of three of the four Sunbeams which came in third, fourth and fifth after Wagner, a compact group of cars of only three litres! These performances marked the end of the exaggerated monsters and brought Grand Prix racing back to rational limits.

For the 1913 Grand Prix a new venue was chosen, the 20-mile Picardy circuit, a group of roads near Amiens

1908 French G.P. The Clément-Bayard team lined up on the track, all "135 H.P.s" driven by (L to R) Rigal, Gabriel and Hautvast.

including a narrow eight-mile straight. For the racing car category (there were also races for cyclecars, and motorcycle combinations) 29 circuits for a total of 580 miles were envisaged. This time there was a new formula with two main requirements — fuel consumption not to exceed 20 litres per 100 kms. (13 m.p.g.) and weight to be between 800 and 1,100 kgs. (1,760 to 2420 lbs.). At this race, too, Peugeot appeared with cars capable of embarrassing all their opponents. These were versions of the previous year's cars but with cylinder capacity reduced to 5,650 c.c. Delage had an unusual car with horizontal overhead valves which led to exhaust pipes higher than the bonnet, and there were rotary-valve Italas.

Into the canal

The race quickly turned into a battle between Peugeot, Delage and the Sunbeam team whose cars were, as usual, beautifully prepared. These Sunbeams all had six cylinders. An unusual accident to Guyot's mechanic occurred when he was run over by their own Delage, having jumped out too soon at a refuelling stop. This left the Peugeots in command of the situation. Boillot and Goux finished in that order at 72 m.p.h., having consumed petrol at the rate of about 16 m.p.g. Lee Guinness, one of the Sunbeam drivers, ended up in one of the canals which ran parallel to the road.

Perhaps even more interesting than Boillot's victory was the performance of another Peugeot, a new three-litre designed by the Swiss engineer, Henry, which could reach about 105 m.p.h., thus being capable of beating

machines two and three times its capacity. Henry was to have a major influence on engine design up to the early 1920s.

The last pre-war Grand Prix in 1914 was also one of the most spectacular. The public was to see on this occasion the battle between a famous and idolized driver and a team working together to a perfectly prepared plan. It is probably not coincidence that the former was French and the latter German.

The man was Boillot, winner of the two previous Grands Prix, and the team was Mercedes, organized to the point that it was later referred to as "track militarism" (it

K. Lee Guinness at the wheel of the Sunbeam which won the 1914 Isle of Man T.T.

Still at Dieppe in 1908. The Renault team of 100 H.P.s with Szisz, Caillois and Dimitri (L to R).

Georges Boillot comes out of a bend in the 1913 French Grand Prix.

should not be forgotten that The Great War was about to begin and there were political undertones to everything, including the race itself).

Neither the public nor the competitors were apparently conscious before the race began of such implications even though there were signs of nerves among the French teams on the eve of the race, with Delage changing first his carburettors, then the system of valve mechanism on his cars, while Peugeot changed their tyres.

Although up to the last moment there was little to indicate the relative potential of the competitors — 34 out of 37 entries were built to the same formula of four cylinders with overhead camshafts — shortly after the race began on the triangular circuit at Givors, near Lyon, it resolved itself into a battle between two makes. It was soon apparent that neither Delage nor Sunbeam represented a major threat; the main battle was to be between Mercedes and Peugeot. The first move was made by the Mercedes driver, Sailer, who had agreed with his team to be the "hare".

German supremacy

He set off as fast as he could go, using all the capabilities of his car and forcing Boillot to chase after him. In the meantime, the other three Mercedes drivers, Lautenschlager, Wagner and Salzer, kept a distance behind, making certain they did not lose their key positions but also not forcing their cars. On the sixth lap Sailer, as might have been expected, dropped out with a con-rod through the cylinder — but his effort had not been in vain. Boillot went into the lead to the delirious enthusiasm of the crowd, but his machine had been over-stressed in the early part of the race and as his three pursuers gradually increased their pace he began to lose ground.

On the 18th lap Lautenschlager took the lead and on the last lap Boillot's engine, by now running on three cylinders only, broke a valve and dropped out of the race. Boillot was in tears.

Lautenschlager's clear-cut victory at an average speed of 65 m.p.h. was repeated more dramatically and lastingly in the 1930s. This race also saw the first, unsuccessful, appearance of a car which was to have great success after the war. This was the Fiat "S 57/14 B", a four-cylinder 4,492 c.c. car with three valves per cylinder and an output of 135 B.H.P., which was capable of over 80 m.p.h.

Change of circuit

Though the Grand Prix de France was the peak of motor racing in Europe before the First World War, it was obviously not the only race. Among the lesser races in Europe, at first run to widely different formulae but

These three cars were photographed in the 1964 Prescott hill climb. From top to bottom, 1913 Lanchester, 1914 T. T. Sunbeam and a 1913 Argyll.

BOTTLED GAS TO PUSH BUTTON

SCAT claimed that their cars were the only ones in Italy with "automatic starting".

If the complete structure of the motor car has undergone a drastic change during the past 70 years of its existence, so has each of its component parts.

It would be possible to write a long story about every such component, but it is the intention here to comment on the development of electric starting, since its consequences were so significant. For instance, it is not too much to say that it made motoring practicable for women, who before this might have made occasional appearances at the driving wheel. But they would always have to be accompanied by a willing and probably muscular male ever ready to prostrate himself with exhaustion in his efforts to get the machine started or re-started.

One can hardly blame the ladies, since to use a starting handle was a matter requiring great strength and often courage, as there was the possibility of a broken wrist or slipped disc.

It is impossible to state the exact date of the introduction of electric starting. In fact, the early histories of most motor car accessories and components are somewhat confused and inadequate, whilst many of the early cars which have survived and which are equipped with such a device probably had it added in later years.

One fairly reasonable theory gives credit to an American inventor, Charles Kettering who, in 1911, had an electric starter, which he had designed himself, fitted to his Cadillac.

Compressed gas or air

What is certain, however, is that the electric starter was generally accepted only after many European and trans-atlantic manufacturers had tried numerous other solutions to this particular problem.

One of the many methods involved a device which temporarily connected the conbustion chamber of a cylinder to a compressed gas bottle, the pressure from which forced down the piston and caused the crankshaft to turn. The complications of such a system were many and explain the wide variety of solutions.

If exhaust gases were used to charge the bottle (a solution that was relatively simple from a manufacturing point of view) it created a dangerous and evil-smelling source of poisonous gas. If compressed air were used, both a compressor and a reservoir were necessary.

Safety device

Furthermore, if the engine had a single cylinder, a safety device was necessary to permit the compressed air to enter the cylinder only when the piston was past top dead centre, to avoid the engine contra-rotating. If no such device were fitted, it was necessary to turn the engine over by hand to the right point. If, on the other hand, the engine was of a multi-cylinder type, a distributor was necessary to pass the air only to the cylinder in which the piston was past dead top centre. There were also other technical obstacles, particularly the problems of sealing the compressed air lines when the engine was running normally and of fitting a third valve. The complexity of these problems finally defeated even the most obstinate opponents of electric starting, who were dubious about electrical circuits in general (with some reason, considering the frequency of breakdowns).

The most difficult problem with electric starting was, in fact, to ensure only an intermittent connection (i.e. at the moment of starting) between the starter motor and the crankshaft.

This was solved first with the Bendix drive and, more recently, by electro-magnetic means. The push button starting of an engine has now reached such a stage of perfection that few motorists today could imagine what was involved for the pioneers of 70 years ago.

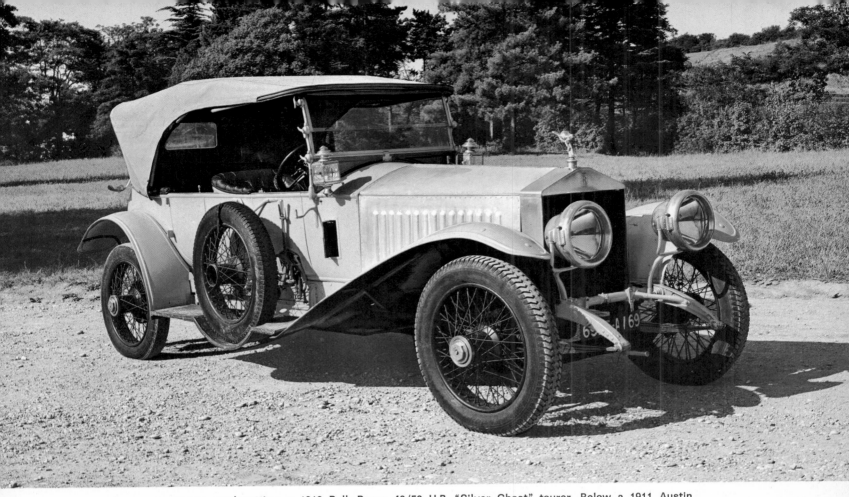

In an appropriate rural setting, a 1913 Rolls-Royce 40/50 H.P. "Silver Ghost" tourer. Below a 1911 Austin.

becoming more and more similar in style, was the Targa Florio in Italy, which went into a decline in the years immediately before the war.

From 1912 to 1914 the race acquired both a new circuit and a new name, being run on the coastal roads of the island for a distance of 650 miles and being called the "Tour of Sicily". The difficulties of the new course in 1912 attracted a respectable number of entries, 26 in all, including two Americans. The race was won by an Englishman, Cyril Snipe, in a SCAT car, at an average of 26 m.p.h. The low speed is an indication of the difficulties of the course, but it is also true that the competitors did not over-exert themselves. It is said that when the Englishman reached Sciacca he was so tired he decided to have a couple of hours' sleep. His mechanic persuaded him to continue, and the fact that he won suggests that other drivers had a similar nap.

Vincenzo Lancia, who was driving a 60 H.P. Mercedes, had an unusual accident. Blinded by the sun, he turned left when the road turned right and mounted a railway running parallel to the road. Not surprisingly his machine collapsed.

Different conditions

In Europe, the greatest number of races were in France, which before the First World War was undoubtedly the

The start of a race at Silverstone in 1957.
A scene that even the owner of the very futuristic-looking 1912
racing Singer pictured below could not have envisaged.

leading nation in motor racing. But races were held almost everywhere, even in Central Europe and in Russia, where the Moscow-St. Petersburg event attracted many of the well-known manufactures. Races were also held in Scandinavia, where the most important was from Gothenburg to Stockholm.

In Britain during the early days of the century the most important series of races was for the Tourist Trophy. At first the event was run on a fuel consumption basis in the Isle of Man. The winner of this 200-mile race in 1905 was J. S. Napier, on a two-cylinder Arrol-Johnston. The second race in the following year consolidated the reputation of Rolls-Royce, being won by C. S. Rolls. The third race was a victory for Rovers. That was the year when a class of heavy cars was handicapped by making them carry "aerofoils" to *increase* wind resistance.

In 1908 a horsepower formula was introduced and since most engines had a bore of 4 inch., it became known as the "Four Inch" race. The winner was W. Watson, with a 5.8-litre Hutton, which was really a Napier. Though from then on until 1914 Brooklands track was the goal of most sporting motorists, the T.T. was run

Two cars on the way to the start of a race at Brooklands.

again in that year in the Isle of Man over a distance of 600 miles. It was spread over two days and the victor was K Lee Guinness (of KLG fame) in a Sunbeam.

The 1914 event was for racing cars, in spite of its title, but this innovation was discontinued. In the race W. O. Bentley drove the smallest car, a French D. F. P., which influenced the design of the original Bentley.

It was not until 1922 that the race was held again, the winner being the Frenchman Chassagne with a Sunbeam, although Sir Algernon Guinness won the 1½-litre event with a Talbot-Darracq, driving without goggles in the blinding rain.

In 1928 the R.A.C. secured the Ards circuit, outside Belfast, and the series took on a new life. The first race was won by Kaye Don with a Lea-Francis, and was the start of a long run of events — from then until the second war — which attracted many of the most illustrious drivers and successful cars of the era. Winners included Caracciola, Nuvolari, Black, Whitcroft, Dodson, Dixon, Comotti and Gerard. These were the great years of the MGs and the sports-racing Rileys.

Ards had to be abandoned after the 1936 race, when

Bruce-Brown and De Palma, the Fiat drivers, ready for the start of the 1912 French G. P.

In 1911 this Renault bus travelled in the jungle.

a car ran into the spectators. But the excellent Donington circuit was available in time for the 1937 and 1938 events, which were now almost on Le Mans lines and were for sports cars little different from those available to the general motorist.

It was 1950 again before the T.T. was in the calendar, with a long series of events to the present day with the exception of 1956 and 1957.

1909 Daimler "Piccadilly" phaeton, with Knight double-sleeve-valve engine.

The 1914 Fiat S 57/14 B.

1938 Buick experimental "Y".

LABORATORIES ON WHEELS

A car of the future has as much fascination for motorists as the veteran of the past. In 1938 General Motors asked Harley Earl and C. A. Chayne to design an experimental car, the "Y", for Buick which supplied ideas built into 1942 and later models. At the end of the 1940s the same two men were asked to design experimental vehicles for Buick and Cadillac.

Both these cars incorporated many experimental suggestions which it was later considered useful to try and General Motors appropriately called them "laboratories on wheels". A condition of their design was that they had to have styling which would capture the imagination of the public and which would meet with the long-term forecasts of the companies' engineers.

Servo-assistance

These were the first two "dream cars" and were christened "Le Sabre" (Cadillac) and "XP-300" (Buick). For publicity, they were sent together to Europe and then toured the United States, where they attracted great interest.

The mechanical elements were common to both cars. Apart from the special 3½-litre V8 engine, the most striking feature at the time was the extensive use of servo mechanisms — for the windows, the radio aerial and the hood, which went up automatically when rain started to fall.

The bodies of the two cars, however, were different, though both had common elements of what might now be considered bizarre taste. The "Sabre" was a huge roadster, low and heavy-looking from the bulbous front to the long rear fins. The "XP-300" was smoother but on the same general lines. The body was built in light alloy with much decoration.

Both had panoramic windscreens, an idea which had safety as well as styling advantages and which was soon reproduced on various Cadillac production models. Some models, in particular the Eldorado, used other ideas taken from the two prototypes.

So far as the feasibility of many of the ideas incorporated in the "dream cars" of Earl and Chayne are concerned they can be said to have kept their wheels firmly on the ground.

A gas-turbine Firebird.

A 54

A Citroën of the DS and ID series and, below, the first Citroën, the Model "A".

CHAPTER SEVENTEEN
CLASSIC IN THE RED DUST

Among the major American motor races were some that were "classics" by European standards. One of them was the second Vanderbilt Cup, which was run in 1905 on Long Island. The "European" character of these races was a reflection of their origin, which began as an attempt to import the Gordon Bennett type of race to America.

The 'great bear'

Once again there was the usual strong contingent from the old world, including Darracq, De Dietrich, Panhard, Mercedes and Fiat. In the American ranks, however, there were some innovations. Alongside "normal" machines — the Locomobile, Matheson and the Pope-Toledo — there were some unusual vehicles such as the air-cooled eight-cylinder in-line Franklin driven by Winchester, a Premier which had a bonnet nearly 10 feet long and the first front-wheel-drive racer of all, the Christie with transversley mounted engine and a complicated system of transmission which caused it to move along in a somewhat zig-zag fashion. The crowd at once christened it "The Great Bear".

Of the U.S. cars, only Tracy's Locomobile ended in an honourable position. The rest of the race was dominated by Europeans. Victor was Héméry in his "light" 80 H.P. Darracq, which won at over 60 m.p.h. Second was Heath in a 120 H.P. Panhard. Behind Tracy's Locomobile came Vincenzo Lancia's Fiat, Szisz in a Renault and then Nazzaro and Sartori in Fiats. In tenth place was Louis Chevrolet, also in a Fiat.

Billy Knipper in a Keeton at Indianapolis in 1914. Below, Victor Demogeot in a Darracq at Daytona Beach in 1906.

The Vanderbilt Cup was to be dominated by Europeans for many years to come. In the 1906 race, in spite of frantic American efforts to make up the technical deficiencies demonstrated in 1905, Wagner won in his 110 H.P. Darracq; while speeding across an unguarded level crossing, he had missed a train by a hair's breadth. In the same period motoring in the U.S. and Cuba introduced a different sort of competition — typically American, although foreigners took part.

This consisted of straightline speed record attempts on sand in certain suitable localities such as Florida. Representatives of European manufacturers were frequently seen there, especially from France and Italy.

In 1906 Fred Marriott recorded 127 m.p.h. at Daytona with a Stanley Steamer, and was travelling still faster when his car exploded during a further attempt in 1907.

Home-made cyclone

In the same year the race between Los Angeles and New York ended in victory for a man whose name was to appear frequently among the lists of successful drivers in America before he was killed in practice in 1908 — Emanuele Cedrino. He raced in a Fiat imported from Italy, but in future years he was to use a machine built by himself from components, which he called Fiat-Cyclone. Ralph de Palma, in effect Cedrino's successor, averaged nearly 75 m.p.h. at Savannah during the first American Grand Prize in 1908.

American industry, so advanced in series production, was unable to make racing machines that could compete with those of Europe. This was true even though many race regulations put heavy limitations on European entries, which were not able even to take part officially and could enter only in the name of some American client. All the same, 1908 saw the first American victory in the Vanderbilt Cup — that of Robertson's Locomobile at just under 65 m.p.h. on the modified Long Island circuit, which now included an eight-mile stretch of the newly opened "parkway".

The most interesting American race in 1909 was probably the New York "Motoring 24 Hours", one of the first of a type of race which was quickly to become popular in America. In Europe they were to develop much more slowly. The winner was Raffalovich in a Renault.

G.P. Mills at the wheel of the winning Humber in the 1907 Isle of Man T.T.

According to reports at the time, this European victory was due not only to the merits of his car (to whose preparation the French company had devoted particular care as it was about to attack the American market and wanted some favourable publicity) but also to a "secret weapon". This was mounted at the last moment, and gave Raffalovich an advantage over the other drivers. It consisted of straight mudguards mounted just behind the front wheels to protect the driver from flying stones. This hazard nearly always appeared after a number of laps and drivers had to be very cautions when close behind other cars.

In fact, the photographs of the race show this Renault without mudguards at the beginning of the race, though they were shown at the end.

In 1909 the first race at Crown Point, Indiana, was organized by the Chicago Automobile Club. The race was to be for the western United States what the Vanderbilt Cup, before its migration, was for the east. The race was won by Louis Chevrolet, in a Buick, which towards

Even from the earliest days, racing cars differed greatly from production models, as can be seen in this photograph of Grillon at the wheel of a Hispano-Suiza in 1913.

A Hudson in San Francisco after an attack on the U.S. trans-Continental record in 1916.

A 1914 STAR.

the end was running on only three cylinders. Credit for the victory, however, should also go to William Crapo Durant, future founder of General Motors, who at that time was head of Buick and who planned his team's tactics shrewdly.

Free grandstand view

The Crown Point race did not, however, have the success its organisers wanted, largely because of one drawback. As the specially built circuit had a length of 30 miles, anyone who wished could watch the race without paying to go in the grandstands.

But this was a lesson for the rival organisers of the race held at Elgin which, unlike Crown Point, was to run for many years and become one of the most important in America. It was run on a triangular course inside the town; the organisers persuaded the owners of houses and of land around the circuit to sell tickets for the race — and this time they succeeded in getting half the entrance money themselves.

The Elgin race, first run in 1910, was held until 1933.

About to enter their 1912 Newton. Below, Boillot leans out of his Peugeot during the 1914 French Grand Prix held at Lyons on 4 July. Peugeot used storm tyres after days of heavy rain, but a brilliant sun dried the track and the French cars were at a disadvantage compared with the Mercedes.

The 1912 racing Aquila Italiana.

A 1913 D.F.P. "Type B".

GIOVANNI AGNELLI AND FIAT

When Fiat was founded in 1899 Giovanni Agnelli was little over thirty years old, having been born on the 13th of August 1866 at Villar Perosa not far from Turin. In 1892 he gave up his army career to devote himself to his estate at Villar Perosa, of which town he was elected mayor. (From that day onwards the chief citizen of Villar Perosa has always been an Agnelli).

His interest in industry, however, soon led him to give up the rather limited activity of his estate and seven years later, together with a group of Turin notables, he founded Fiat. Agnelli was by no means of a humble origin, but of the group he was certainly the least well known and the least rich. In spite of this, within a few months he became the leader and from then on kept a firm grip on the reins of the undertaking, right up till his death on the 16th of December 1945.

It has been written that Agnelli, in moving the first Fiat workshops from Valentino first to Lingotto and then to Mirafiori, was following an historic route which took the capital of Piedmont to its present day boun-

daries. It can be said that Agnelli and Turin grew together in the first half of the twentieth century. Rarely has there been such reciprocal affinity between place and man.

From his youth Giovanni Agnelli had been impelled to produce for the world that essential and universal instrument, the motor car. Where he copied, he copied in a logical and far-sighted way. Like Henry Ford he was not interested in originality or innovation in his cars. To Faccioli, his first Engineering Manager, he said. "I don't want inventions, only mechanisms and methods already tested by others". To his friend Michele Lanza, an amateur builder of motor cars, he said, "You don't build for sale. I do!" He was a series-production man in what was still a craftsman age — a man who felt instinctively that industry was to become the basis of world economy.

From the first decade his factory began to dominate the industrial life of the city. In 1906 he created RIV, to produce ball races and shockabsorbers, and thereby

Fiat 500 L - 2 door saloon, 4 seats, 2 cylinder, 499.5 c.c., air-cooled rear engine, 18 b.h.p. DIN, 60 m.p.h.

Fiat 124 Special - 4 cylinder, 1,438 c.c. front engine, bore and stroke 80 x 71.5 mm., 70 b.h.p. DIN, 4 speeds. 93 m.p.h.

125 Special - 4 door, 5 seater saloon, 4 cylinder, 1,608 c.c. front engine, twin o.h.c., 100 b.h.p. DIN, 5 speeds, discs all round with servo, twin hydraulic circuit brakes. 105 m.p.h.

850 Special - 2 door saloon, 5 seats, 4 cylinder, 843 c.c. rear engine, 47 b.h.p. DIN. Disc brakes at front. 84 m.p.h.

124 Coupé - 4 seats, 1,438 or 1,608 c.c. front engine, 90 and 110 b.h.p. DIN, 4 or 5 speeds. 106 or 112 m.p.h.

created a new and profitable industry for his mountain village, Villar Perosa, where he established the factory. Other makes were born there, to flourish for a while and then disappear. On the eve of the First World War there were more than twenty besides Fiat and Lancia. They ranged from Itala to Chiribiri, from Scat to Ceirano, Aquila, Temperino, Rapid and others, but in general they lacked a sound financial basis and could not survive.

It has been justly observed that the story of Fiat is that of modern Italy. Forty years ahead of his time, during the First World War, Agnelli put forward and developed the idea of a United States of Europe. The more progressive countries were to integrate their production techniques with those less fortunate. In fact, the problem of depressed areas was confronted on a supra-national scale.

In the meantime Fiat's industrial growth and concentration led to an analogous concentration of employees, creating social changes and problems which were not

Giovanni Agnelli and his grandson Gianni in 1940.

without dramatic repercussions on the company. In the critical period when Fiat workmen occupied the factories, Agnelli said he would still be the boss even in the theoretical case of the socialisation of the company. Later he offered a co-operative form of management of the company, which was not however accepted by his suspicious employees.

In those years he met Henry Ford in Detroit and in an interview on American radio in 1935 he said, "The American automobile industry represents the first major example of industrial rationalisation and an exceptional field of technical experience. I myself, visiting some of your great factories, have seen the level of efficiency achieved by the American automobile industry. And I will not conceal from you that I attribute a good part of the success of our motor industry to the fact that our engineers and technicians have been able to maintain contact with your manufacturing development."

Strong in his ability to choose exceptional subordinates

Dino Coupé and Spider - V. 6, 4 o.h.c., 2,418 c.c. front engine, 180 b.h.p. DIN, 5 speeds. All independent suspension. 130 m.p.h.

— one has only to think of the most outstanding of these, Vittorio Valletta — Agnelli once said that Fiat was a "Co-operative Society of Men" who offered their active contribution to the management of the company to ensure the continuity of its progress.

This continuity was in fact assured in 1945, when Agnelli died, by the presence of Vittorio Valletta. His work is witness to Fiat's expansion — from 25,000 cars built in 1946, to 250,000 in 1956 to 1,400,000 in 1967, the year in which Valletta died.

To-day, seventy years after its creation, another Giovanni Agnelli is the head of Fiat, by far the largest motor vehicle manufacturer in Italy, the second in Europe and the fifth in the world. Total invoicing in 1968 was almost one thousand million pounds.

The original capital of 800,000 liras has grown to 130,000 million and Fiat today comprises:
— 30 factories, mostly in Turin
— 30 main branches in Italy and over 11,000 service centres throughout the world
— 168,000 employees
— Fiat automobile production and assembly units in Austria, Spain, Germany, Poland, Turkey, South America, Africa, Asia and New Zealand. Under the famous contract of collaboration with the Soviet Union, the new motor car factory on the Volga is nearing completion and will have a capacity of 600,000 vehicles per year. Recently an agreement has been made with Citroën and Ferrari, and Lancia have been acquired in addition to O.M. and Autobianchi which have formed part of the group for some time.

Fiat 130 - 4 door, 5 seater saloon, V. 6, 2,866 c.c. front engine, 140 b.h.p. DIN, automatic, servo brake. 112 m.p.h.

850 Sport Coupé and Sport Spider - 4 cylinder, 903 c.c. rear engine, 52 b.h.p. DIN. Disc brakes at front. 93 m.p.h.

We shall finish this brief survey of seventy years, with a quotation from the press conference held by the President of Fiat, Giovanni Agnelli, grandson of the founder, during the International Motor Show at Turin in October 1969.

"This year sees the seventieth anniversary of the founding of the company. In that time Fiat has built 15 million vehicles, has employed more than half a million people, exported 5 million vehicles, produced 500 models and over 450 engine types. While in the past we were concerned above all with building motor cars and building them well and cheaply, I believe that in future we must not limit ourselves only to the manufacture of vehicles, but that we must concern ourselves also with the kind of society which the motor car has created, with the way in which the car is used, with traffic flow and the way of life which the motor car has produced."

The Fiat factories at Mirafiori (Turin). The first Mirafiori factory was opened in May 1939 and by the end of that year employed 22,000 people. The Mirafiori factories are on a site of 625 acres with a covered area of 13,000,000 square feet.

A shrouded start at the new track at Indianapolis in 1909 before the famous 500-mile race was introduced two years later. Number 34, a Buick, won the 100-mile race. The day before another Buick had won the 250-mile race.

For a substantial time it had a function for American motor racing equivalent to that of Indianapolis.

The 'Indy' is born

This famous 500-miles race, the principal American motor race, took place for the first time in 1911. The winner was Ray Harroun in a six-cylinder Marmon "Wasp" in front of Ralph Mulford in a Lozier; third was David Bruce-Brown in his Fiat — the car with which he was to win the American Grand Prize in the same year. The winner of the "500" had a rear-view mirror for the first time, and the publicity for the idea led to their swift adoption throughout America.

At Indianapolis a number of races had been held — two of them three-day races — when the track was half built. The construction of this track, marked for many years by its unique pagoda-like tower and built outside a city having many connections with the U.S. motor industry, was due to the efforts of an enthusiastic racing driver, Carl G. Fisher.

His project was clearly inspired by another circuit on which he had run a number of times, Brooklands. To

Indianapolis prestige has always attracted European companies. René Thomas in 1920 at the wheel of a car whose builder, Ernest Ballot, is the severe looking gentleman in the straw hat.

build his track, beginning with the difficult operation of buying the land, Fisher associated himself with three others, James Allison, Frank C. Wheeler and A. C. Newby. The first was an engine manufacturer who was to become well known in America as the builder of an aero-engine for the American forces. The second sold petrol and the third was the president of a small motor company.

Brick track experiment

By the time the track was finished the partners found they had spent a million dollars against initial estimates of about half that sum. Among the major difficulties they had encountered was that of the paving of the track, wood having been rejected as a material. Most American tracks at that date were of wood but as speeds became higher this became less and less suitable; and Fisher, who was always the dominant personality in the group, chose Macadam. The first surface was of this material.

It proved unsuitable, however, because of its rapid wear and Fisher had the idea of using brick and the track was rebuilt in this unusual way. Wear was no less than with Macadam; there was also a cloud of red, abrasive

The 1914 Opel which took part in the 1914 Grand Prix at Lyons.

The 1906 Maxwell. This American company built cars from 1903 to 1923. It was bought by Walter P. Chrysler.

1915 Dodge.

either he changed the surface or they would not compete. This was clearly unrealistic. On the one hand, it was obviously impossible to re-pave the surface on the eve of the race. A drivers' strike seemed equally unlikely in view of the high value of the prizes involved (this was a feature of Indianapolis right from the beginning). Fisher therefore offered the drivers a compromise. Instead of many races culminating in a 250-mile final, there would be just one race — of 500 miles.

The compromise was immediately accepted.

Apart from their technical significance, the Indianapolis races of the past half-century have provided American enthusiasts with an unrivalled spectacle.

Much is more folklore than motoring, but an incident in 1912, the second year of the race, illustrates the attitude of drivers and public.

One of the competitors, Dave Evans, skidded at high speed against a protecting wall in front of the grandstand. His machine shot into the air and another car passed clean under it without being touched. Evans fell heavily but at once jumped to his feet and waved his clasped hands above his head like a boxer, receiving a huge ovation from the crowd. Immediately afterwards he fell unconscious to the ground. He was seriously injured and was a long time in hospital. Indianapolis was like that even then.

dust which penetrated even under the cars' bonnets. These difficulties led to the introduction of the 500-mile race, a formula rare in America in those days when races were usually over 100 or 200 miles. The drivers, worried about the dust, gave Fisher an ultimatum –

Elegant and in harmony with its surroundings. A 1916 twin-cylinder Perry.

A 1908 Adams.

A 1908 Unic 12/14 H.P. It was built by
Georges Richard after he separated from
Brasier. The name derives from his policy
of building only one type of car. Unic now
forms part of Simca.

The 1913 edition was won by an European, Jules Goux, in a 7½-litre Peugeot. When leading early on, he had to stop at the pits because of tyre trouble and restarted in thirteenth place. He then drove a daredevil race and, notwithstanding the efforts of his competitors, took the lead again and held it to the end.

Seeing the verve with which Goux drove there were many who held that the race was won not only by the qualities of the car and its driver, but also by the French champagne which flowed freely in the excited pits and which Goux was seen to sample at every stop. Goux returned to France not only with the usual mountain of dollars but also with a young American wife.

Repeat performance

Goux's coup was repeated with interest in the 1914 500-mile race by four Frenchmen. The only American in the race in a position to oppose the Europeans was the veteran Barney Oldfield, who could achieve only fifth place in a Stutz. The race was won by René Thomas in a Delage after an exciting contest with the other three. Duray gained second place — surprisingly, as his Peugeot was a three-litre normally used in touring car races. Guyot in the second Delage was third and Goux, unable to repeat his previous year's victory because of more tyre trouble, was fourth.

Naturally the performance that most struck the public was that of the "little" Peugeot, which had maintained the formidable average of over 82 m.p.h., only slightly below that of the winner.

Although not possible in Europe, motor racing continued in America in 1915 and 1916. Both the 500-mile races of those years were won by European cars. The first was won by a Mercedes driven by De Palma, which gave him some revenge for the occasion in 1912 when his machine, also a Mercedes, broke down near the finishing line.

On that occasion De Palma and his mechanic pushed their heavy car for a mile towards the finishing line before being overtaken by the other cars. In 1916 the Indianapolis 500-mile race was won by an Italian, Dario Resta, in a Peugeot.

This was the last racing activity in the U.S. before that country was plunged into war, and the story of the motor car may be considered to have now completed its first cycle.

Beginning with the early pioneers, there had been gradual technical evolution and the laying of the foundation of large-scale production. With surprising rapidity, the motor-car had developed from an expensive toy for the rich into an essential concomitant of everyday life.

End of an era

The races in Europe and the U.S. provided spectacle and competition, the occasions for sporting rivalry and the meeting-place for those in the car industry concerned with technical improvements of all kinds. In little more than a decade, it had become an entertainment for a wide cross-section of the public.

The war called a halt to this; the car itself was called to the battlefronts of Europe. It was to return in civilian life to play an ever-increasingly important role as a method of transport.

Sir John Briscoe's 1911 Coupe de l'auto Delage.

The Daimler Sovereign is a high-quality car that embodies years of experience. Below—the 1906 side-valve Daimler with chain drive and 35 H.P.

CHAPTER EIGHTEEN

AMERICA FORGES AHEAD

The First World War had a relatively marginal effect on industry in the U.S., while that of Europe was to suffer the effects of the war for many years. The opportunity to experiment and test led to developments, industrial and technical, which assured the United States of a prominent position after the war.

Radical differences

The years immediately before the war had seen an interesting change in the American industrial picture. In addition to Ford and Buick (the latter being the most important part of General Motors), a third large manufacturer came to the fore. Overland was an old company whose fortunes, after some difficult years, began to pick up when John Willys, already president of American Motor Car Sales, joined the company. In 1907 he became president of Overland and made a number of improvements to production, possible because of a private agreement he had with the Pope Company of Toledo, Ohio. A short time later the company changed its name to Willys-Overland and moved to Toledo.

In 1908 4,000 vehicles were produced, and five years later Willys-Overland, with 37,000 vehicles, was in sec-

ond place between Ford (107,000) and Buick (28,000). The commercial policy of these three largest American companies differed radically one from another, though

Checking the petrol level.

perhaps it would be better to say that Ford represented a unique case and it is therefore difficult to make comparisons.

In 1913 the price of a Ford T in the four-seat "torpedo" version was only 440 dollars and there was even a two-seater "roadster" at 390 dollars. The cheapest rival product was an Overland at 780 dollars.

Offer refused

An industrial concern as important as General Motors could not accept the position indefinitely, especially since they had been pushed into third place by a relatively small company such as Willys-Overland.

The first attempt to improve the situation was of a financial nature — the offer by Durant to Ford to form a huge car manufacturing complex. The offer was refused by Ford; this marked the beginning of Durant's decline, and shortly afterwards he was replaced by Charles W. Nash, his former colleague and last president of Buick.

A view of the assembly line of Dodge Brothers.

A 1904 Siddeley.

It was Nash who was to engineer General Motors' recovery. Between 1912, when he became president, and 1916 when he left to form his own company by buying Thomas Jeffery's plant, he instituted a number of reforms.

Above all, he incorporated in General Motors a group of companies manufacturing components and accessories, already amalgamated as the United Motors Corporation. He also decided to launch the maximum possible sales attack on Ford, using as the spearhead one of his companies, Chevrolet, which so far had been relatively neglected.

1905 Buick model "C". This car had a flat twin engine. The catalogue says "Price 1,200 dollars, 22 H.P. guaranteed .... a car that overcomes any hill. Two forward speeds and reverse. Simple but built to last!".

1912-13	1914	1915
1916	1917	1918
1919	1920	The Chevrolet production from 1912 to 1920. The 1916 model is the famous "490".

The acquisition of Chevrolet by General Motors improved the firm's standing, but before this they had already made great strides with the "Baby Grand" of 1914 which boasted overhead valves, a solid chassis, and a conventional three-speed gearbox with central change. Even better was the "490" of 1916, which rivalled Ford's prices at only 490 dollars (though electric lighting cost another 60 dollars).

Meanwhile Nash had gone to work within General Motors, creating Buick's subsequent image of middle-class luxury with a six-cylinder model introduced in 1914, though a "four" was still available. General Motor's other makes, in ascending order of price, were Oakland's six, Oldsmobile's six and vee-eight, and Cadillac's vee-eight.

The famous "490"

When Nash became president of General Motors it left vacant the presidency of Buick. This was given to Walter P. Chrysler — another exceptional man — whose name was to be perpetuated by a great motor company. As technical director of the American Locomotive Com-

The Rover 20 H.P. that won the 1907 T. T.

1917 Kissel 6 cylinder. Kissel production, which went on until 1931, was known for its "European styling".

pany, Chrysler had joined Buick in 1911. Even though he was to become senior vice-president of General Motors, his most important work came later.

He then moved on to Willys-Overland in 1920 to save it from imminent failure, showing remarkable commercial qualities. Some years later he was to use these qualities to some effect in saving another company, Maxwell-Chalmers, with which he began an association on a personal basis in 1924. This association was to result a short time later in the birth of the Chrysler Corporation.

Numbers fall

In addition to the three great manufacturers, an immense number of smaller ones were working. In 1915 there were 170. In the space of a few years, however, they were to be reduced to about 10; this was inevitable as other manufacturers adopted Ford's mass-production techniques to stay in a market where craftsman production, and consequent high price, were less and less in demand.

In 1914 548,000 motor vehicles were built in the United

1918 Nash "681".

1914 15 H.P. Napier with 2,684 c.c. four-cylinder engine.

1919 Essex roadster.

1912 Oakland "Colonial Coupé". This was considered outstandingly beautiful at the time. The coupé body was interchangeable with the roadster.

States; of these 412,000 were produced by the ten largest companies. Thus, though the closing of so many companies was distressing, it was economically inevitable. This was shown by the fact that even what would be considered relatively large companies were having to accept offers from the giants in order to avoid a slow and miserable decline.

It might seem a paradox that in such a position other companies, such as Nash and Chrysler, could be created. In reality, though, the prospects were bleak only for those who — by dint of personality or out-of-date factories — were unable to adapt themselves to the times. Another reason, ultimately the determining factor for many companies, was the rapid change in the general concept of the motor car when a vast extension of the motorway network permitted higher performances.

Some cars had maximum speeds of around 40 m.p.h., which was acceptable in 1914 but was non longer so by

1913 Renault type AX two-seater tourer.
1,205 c.c. twin. Top speed 40 m.p.h.

1918. To meet these demands the manufacturer had to re-design not only the engine but the whole car, including suspension, steering and brakes.

A particular role was played by the company set up in 1914 by the brothers John and Horace Dodge, who had been associated with the Ford Motor Company and subscribed one-tenth of the capital, being responsible for the engines of Henry's cars. Their acceptance of Ford's offer, severely criticised at the time by their friends, paid them — when they severed their connection with Ford in 1919 — something like 25 million dollars against the 20,000 of their original investment.

Copied by competitors

Even before then, the dividends they received had enabled them to set up their own factory equipped with the finest machinery. It permitted them to design a "car of the future" in collaboration with their chief designer, Flanders, and a company named Budd, which specialised in the welding of steel sheet. The success of the new Dodge, built from 1914 onwards, was great. By 1915 production was 45,000 and two years later it had been doubled, largely owing to the lasting qualities exhibited

The tools of the trade. Below, one of the first test tracks in the world — that of Dodge near Michigan. The track is laid in wood.

1908 Stearns model 45/90. Six cylinders, 90 H.P. Below a 1909 Chalmers.

BIG BUSINESS IN MINIATURE

Exquisite working miniature models of transport and machinery have been built by craftsmen from the earliest times, but it was not until 1934 that the cast model car and lorry came to the market in volume. Even then the new toys were hardly regarded by their manufacturers as playthings (or collectors' pieces) in their own right; they were intended to give added realism to model railway layouts.

Frank Hornby had been making more and more elaborate train sets since the early 1920s. One of them, Meccano Set No 21, was embellished by six cast models comprising two cars, two commercial vehicles, a tractor and a tank. This was Set No 22 and is the reason why these very first Dinky models carried the same number.

Range increased

The models were crude by current standards. They were cast in an alloy of high lead content, which did not lend itself to the sharp definition achieved today. Nor were the models intended to be replicas of particular makes, although the first cars bore a resemblance to the S.S.1,

which preceded the Jaguar. In the matter of scale, the models did not always accord with the scale of the train set of which they were intended to form a part.

As the years went by, the Dinky range was greatly enlarged and the quality of reproduction and detail improved. Immediately before the last war there were some first-class military vehicle models, including tanks with rotating turrets and chain tracks.

In the early 1950s new production techniques in diecasting were introduced. Lesney, with their splendid Coronation Coach, and Corgi ("the ones with the windows") were hard on the heels of Dinky. Better detail, better colour finish, and better running gear heralded a new era which today sees the production of fascinating models in their multi-millions, still within the pocket-money range of most children.

Die-cast model vehicles flow down production lines in much the same manner as the "real thing", but in almost unbelievable numbers. The design, engineering and marketing background is similar to that of the motor industry. There is, of course, a high degree of co-operation between executives of both industries.

It is essential that the toy-makers be well-informed on projected models, because the time involved in producing a new item is nearly the same as is required to evolve the real vehicle. Normally the toy factory will require between nine and 15 months to design, tool and test a new model before it can be shipped to the markets of the world.

A model car or truck must be special or exotic, and it is for unusual design features that engineers from the toy industry study the drawings supplied to them by the car-men and browse over new models at motor shows all over the world.

Mock-ups

When the model to be built is decided upon, dozens of drawings are called for. Then, as in the car industry, mock-ups in wood and brass are made by highly skilled craftsmen. It is at this stage that any alterations must be finalised the the tool-makers' patient work may occupy up to 30,000 man hours. Pre-production runs reveal any shortcomings and, with these corrected, the model is ready for volume manufacture.

Dozens of separate components make up the current model car, each an exquisite example of fine die-casting and miniature engineering. Steering systems, suspension, stub axles, track rods as well as chassis and body shells, flow in millions through the deft hands of the predominantly feminine assembly team.

Model of a Rolls-Royce 1912 Silver Ghost.

The painting operation alone is fascinating, from barelling, degreasing, phosphating to final stoving. Today's models are just as bright, durable and colourful as the cars they represent finally, every model is "road-tested" on a special ramp and those that fail to run straight are ruthlessly rejected.

Inventiveness in design has come a long way since the first of the cast models. Windows, interior trim, opening bonnets revealing plated engines, almost friction-free wheels — all have been developments which have kept the British industry in the forefront of world competition.

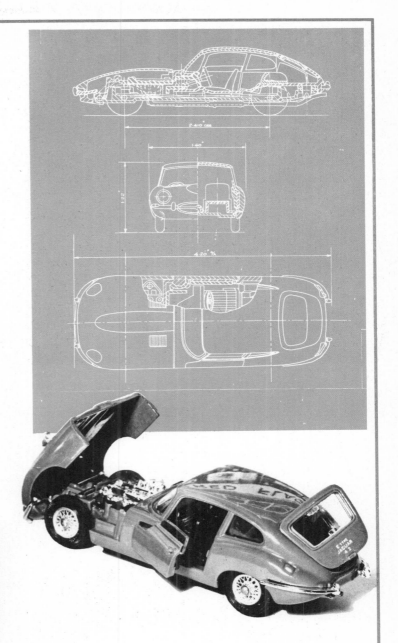

G. A. drawing and finished model of 4,2 litre Jaguar "E" type.

by the earlier models. One compliment to the success of Dodge cars was paid by their competitors, who copied them, even to the appearance. Both Dodge brothers died relatively young, in 1920, but the company continued its independent existence until it was absorbed by Chrysler in 1928.

Another important secondary company was Studebaker. The brothers Clem and John Studebaker's organisation had lived through the first decade of the century without great difficulties and without striking achievements, building both electric and i.c. engine vehicles, until they merged in 1911 with the E.M.F. Company (Everitt, Metzger and Flanders). From that time they produced only petrol vehicles.

Gold-plated show-piece

The next year their first four-cylinder model was built — in those days the number of cylinders served to define the degree of luxury of the car — and it was a success. The brand image that Studebaker adopted in those years was that of robustness and long life, and to demonstrate this the company exhibited a gold-plated chassis in 1916. Another U.S. firm which grew quickly was Hudson, formed in 1909. After trying various formulae, it finally specialised in six-cylinder cars, which were large and strong but of reasonable price — something half-way between a "cheap" and a "luxury" model. The most famous of these cars was their celebrated Super Six.

A less happy fate awaited another company, Maxwell, set up by Jonathan D. Maxwell. After working with Elwood Haynes on the latter's first motor car and building a number of twin-cylinder engines with Benjamin Briscoe, he set up on his own account to build cars with four-cylinder engines.

The failure of this venture caused him to withdraw finally from the motoring field in 1913, but not until he had made an important contribution to the motor car, as designer for Oldsmobile and other less important companies and as the inventor of a cooling system. The Maxwell was later revived by Flanders, along with the Chalmers.

"Orpham cars"

A typical American phenomenon of the years between 1915 and 1920 was represented by the assemblers, whose products were often known as "orphan cars". These were cars sold under a wide variety of names, to which their originators contributed some part of the bodywork, the radiator surround and the badge. They were built in some hundreds of small workshops all over the States, with components bought from specialist firms such as Continental, Hercules and Waukesha for engines, Borg and Beck for clutches and Timken for gearboxes and bearings.

At first they won a certain amount of public favour because of their low price and distinctive appearance.

Soon it began to be appreciated that such cars, which had no unity of design, might have faults such as an excellent gear change but a poor engine, or a transmission too weak for the rest of the car. The "orphans" gradually went out of existence.

Individually these companies had a short life, but as fast as one company died another was born and the public took some time to learn the value of the new one. The final *coup de grace* was given when the big manufacturers organised nationwide service, which the small companies were obviously unable to do. When these cars broke down they really became orphans; they were abandoned.

Also notable in this period was the rise of the American luxury car. Though such admirable vehicles as Packard, Pierce-Arrow, Peerless, Thomas and Locomobile had good followings, many wealthy Americans shopped overseas, buying Minervas, Rolls-Royces, Fiats, Delaunay-Bellevilles, and Renaults. The outbreak of war cut off these supplies, and henceforward all Americans had to buy American.

Of those who profited from this situation, at a time when the American gross national income was rising rapidly, the most successful was General Motors with Cadillac, which had been in the luxury market for a long time but with relatively little success.

In 1914, as the supply of European cars dried up, Cadillac was able to produce the V8 engine, underlining its indirect European ancestry. This was the beginning of a new production policy which led to 12- and even 16-cylinder engines.

The V8, however, remained the major Cadillac engine and formed the base for the commercial development of the company. This is shown by the fact that it sold — at

1914 Renault taxi. This was one of the famous "Taxis of the Marne" requisitioned by General Gallieni on 5 September, 1914, to rush troops to the front.

1913 Opel racer which would exceed 105 m.p.h.

prices of over 3,500 dollars — 47,000 cars from the end of 1917.

Parallel rows

Not only Cadillac benefited, however, by the changed situation in the luxury market. In 1915 Packard launched a "Twin-Six", a large 12-cylinder car whose engine, in addition to its high output, was very flexible and able to go from three to 38 m.p.h. in 12 seconds in top gear. It took its name from the fact that its 12 cylinders were arranged in two parallel rows of six, each being derived more or less from the old six-cylinder engine. There were differences, however, and the length of this new 6,800 cc V-12 engine was less than that of the previous six. The "Twin-Six" was an immediate success and over 35,000 were built, 10,600 of them in the first year.

Inevitably, the V-12 had imitators. National, Pathfinder, Austin-U.S.A., Hal, Haynes Enger and Kissel all built engines of this type. One of these, the Enger, had a curious device which permitted one bank of cylinders to be cut out when appropriate, in order to save petrol. A survey of this decade of American car production would not be complete without mention of two manufactures of sports cars which were to win an enormous popularity among the American public, and especially among the young. These were Stutz and Mercer. The first carried the name of Harry C. Stutz, an inventor

who headed first the Ideal Motor Company and then the Stutz Motor Car Company, both in Indianapolis. Stutz produced successive series of his "Bearcat", which was a technical anomaly for the period, as its engine had only four cylinders and side valves, a combination that had been given up by most makers of expensive cars. All the same, these cars were lively, mainly because chassis and body were reduced to the minimum. The most expensive model was a six-cylinder coupe.

The Mercers were technically even less forward-looking and their life was brief. Nevertheless, they had some years of success, particularly because of their showing in the 1912 and 1913 Indianapolis 500-mile races, when they took second and third places respectively. The Mercers were built in Trenton, New Jersey, and designed by Finley Robertson Porter.

'Souping up' engines

Many other American sports car companies first saw the light of day in this period. The so-called "orphans" were strong in this field, though many cars used in races were "souped-up" versions of standard models. The first car to become popular for this treatment was the Ford "T".

Because of its basic solidity and its resistance to mechanical breakdown, the car could be adapted for racing after many modifications, often only the chassis remaining. One of the best-known modifiers of the "T" was Louis

Only lifting the bonnet would indicate that this is a steam car, a 1911 Stanley tourer. Below a Gardner-Serpollet of 1906.

Chevrolet in the second period of his motoring career. Towards the end of the first decade a third generation of American sporting cars appeared, clearly inspired by the European cars which until 1916 were winning at Indianapolis. The most important feature was the adoption of overhead camshafts, a mechanism so far spurned by American constructors.

Hybrid cars

In certain cases the inspiration from Europe was taken to the point of direct copying. Such was the case of Premier, which built at Indianapolis copies of the 1914 4½-litre Grand Prix Peugeot. In 1919 Goux raced, in fact, in a hybrid machine, part Premier, part Peugeot. The brothers Duesenberg quickly distinguished themselves among the list of imitators and in later years some of the most admired American cars were to bear their name. Their first was a racing car in 1920, closely copied from the Delage.

The part-experimental activity of these smaller companies, often guilty of imitation but also initiating a design revolution in American motor car manufacture, was interrupted in 1929 with the first indications of the world slump in that year.

A typical example of standard components modified for competition. The Fiat-Abarth 2,000 which develops 230 H.P. Below — The Aston-Martin "Razor Blade" which also had its engine modified.

CHAPTER NINETEEN
PEACE BRINGS ITS PROBLEMS

The resumption of production by European car manufacturers at the end of the First World War was rapid in view of the tremendous difficulties which had to be overcome. The problems included lack of raw materials, disorganisation of transport, the necessity to rebuild ruined factories — and shortage of money. In such conditions, small companies often have advantages over large ones. This accounts for the fact that so many new firms were formed in Europe at that time; most, however, were not destined to exist for long.

In general, European cars between 1919 and 1920 were considerably different from those of the immediate pre-war years. Those manufactures who had intended to pick up production where they had left off were quickly made to feel the change in public taste.

Both bodies and chassis were lighter. All separation between driver and passengers had disappeared. The one-man hood, already regular equipment on the other side of the Atlantic, became a feature of open cars. So far as the mechanical components were concerned, the final disappearance of chain transmission and the cautious introduction of four-wheel brakes were the most important.

France once again took the lead in the quality of cars

1911 Opel 6/16 H.P. in which Ford influence is seen. Four-cylinder engine, magneto ignition. Below a 1909 Mercedes 45 H.P.

produced, though her dominance was not so marked as hitherto. A new name — Citroën — also made its appearance. His personality was to influence the whole French motoring world, and indeed, that of Europe.

André Citroën was the descendant of a family originating in Holland. As a young engineer from the Ecole Polytechnique, he had set up a small factory before 1914 to make a particular type of double-v gears whose patents he had bought in Poland. These gears (from which the company's sign is taken) enabled considerable power to be transmitted in silence, and were not superseded till the advent of double helical gearing.

He agreed with the brothers Emile and Louis Mors to manage their famous factory and to reorganise production, which was still much on a craftsman basis. His great industrial advance, however, came with the war when he proposed to the government a system for the mass production of shells. His proposals were accepted, and he built a new factory in the Quai de Javel, Paris, which extricated the French army from a grave crisis. It was the problem of reconverting the Javel factory that took Citroën back into the motor car field, after a short period making articles in mild steel.

Citroën was converted to the principles of Ford and

was determined to produce on a large scale. He therefore decided to concentrate on the production of one model only. So he sold the design of a second, a luxury car with a Knight sleeve-valve engine of 4-litres, to his friend Gabriel Voisin, who made it the basis of his future 18 H.P.

The car chosen by Citroën was a robust 1.3-litre four-seater designed by Jules Salomon, who had previously designed for Le Zèbre. The car was as light and spacious as he could make it, with a pressed steel body and a layout which made for easy maintenance. Top speed was 40 m.p.h.

The first appearance of the 10 H.P. "torpedo", or open tourer, was in 1919. The pressed steel wheels were made by Michelin. In order to attack a wide market and go quickly into full production, the model "A" was launched at the fantastically low price of 7,950 francs. This was quickly raised first to 12,500 and then 15,000 francs, thereby upsetting those customers who had been originally attracted by the lower price. In spite of this, the car was a great commercial success and by 1926, when the last of the original basic line was made, it had reached 500 a day.

Citroën's example and his great success in the 1920s was to have a marked influence on the big French and European manufactures, as he was the first to introduce mass production of cars to Europe.

Influenced by Model 'T'

Before this development, motor shows had begun again in 1919, and a number of new and interesting models were launched in France. Renault, who had also played an important part in war production making tanks and aero-engines, presented a new car. This was a four-cylinder 10 H.P. clearly inspired by the Ford "T", with which he replaced the glorious 9 H.P. of *Taxi de la Marne* fame.

In addition, a range of pre-1914 types was produced, the largest of which had grown up into the 9-litre 40 CV by 1921. Peugeot's range of production was also wide, from the luxurious 25 H.P. down to a cyclecar, the curious "Quadrilette", with two seats in tandem and 760 c.c. engine. Surprisingly, this car was to have considerable success when the seats were re-arranged side by side.

All the 1919 Panhard models save one featured the

Reputed to be the second oldest Bugatti in the world. Built in 1911, it can still reach over 35 m.p.h.

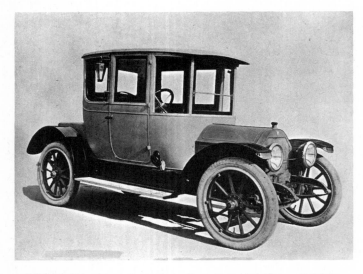

American car production, unlike European, expanded rapidly during the War. Above, top to bottom — Two Hudsons respectively of 1913 and 1917. Below — The company's range in 1920.

Knight sleeve-valve engine introduced before the War. Besides revamping the old models, one brand new car was introduced — a four-cylinder 16 H.P. whose engine, when doubled, was to form the basis of the famous 8-in-line 35 H.P.

Alongside these big companies were medium and small ones which were working hard to impose their new models on the market — Hotchkiss, Delahaye, Brasier, Bollée and many others. Apart from Citroën, new manufacturers included Farman and Voisin.

Mainstream makes

In England and Scotland during 1919 and 1920 there were as many as 90 motor car builders, the majority of them making decidedly "austerity" cars after the artificial boom times of war. There were, nevertheless, serious attempts at quantity production to meet the U. S. challenge, and these attempts were in some cases successful. By 1924, there were over 100 manufacturers.

Parallel to the introduction of new mass-production and luxury cars, there was also a boom in cyclecars. Almost everywhere in Europe, the tax authorities began to milk the motorist, usually on a basis of cylinder capacity and therefore of performance. Thus hundreds of cyclecar manufacturers mushroomed in those years, and even some of the big makers entered the field in case it might have a future.

These immediate post-war years have gone down in motoring history as the years of the cyclecar, but it would be wrong to judge the industry by the standards of those spindly, unreliable machines (among which the Morgan is perhaps the most memorable, and this be-

Continuity of style. The upper car was built in 1911 and the lower in 1921. One might think that they were of the same year. That of 1921 is the Renault type JM with 2,812 c.c. four-cylinder engine.

An 8 CV sports version of the early 1920s. Below a 1922 Maxwell charabanc.

cause it remained what it set out to be — a motorcycle on three wheels).

The era should properly be assessed on the mainstream makes such as the Austin, Morris, Riley, Clyno, Sunbeam, Talbot, Wolseley, Humber, Hillman Standard. Of these the fastest progress was made by the first two, and although Austin was slow to get going, he was making 100 cars a week by 1920, concentrating on a "mid-Atlantic" 20 H.P and then adding a 12 H.P.

It was Morris who produced the real sensation of the period. The "bullnose" Morris Oxford had been in production before the war, but in the early post-war years William Morris captured the low-price market so effectively that even as admirable a car as the almost competitive Clyno did not survive for many years.

Success stories were also being recorded by such firms as Rover, Hillman, Humber, Standard, Riley and Jowett, whilst considerable numbers of cars were being made by A.B.C., A.C., Angus-Sanderson, Bean, Cubitt, Palladium, Ruston-Hornsby and Star.

There were several makes of slightly better quality, and produced in lesser numbers, including Talbot, Sunbeam, Wolseley, Alvis, Armstrong Siddeley and Crossley. Some of these included thoroughbred sporting cars in their ranges. But the true "sportsters" of the age were the

The "T" in commercial use — a 1922 lorry. Below the Peugeot "Quadrilette", built in 1920. Four-cylinder engine, 3 speeds and reverse, multiplate metal clutch.

Bentley and the Vauxhall — the kings of today's vintage machinery.

The three-litre Bentley made its bow at the 1919 London Show and was a success once production problems had been solved. Though only two or three were made every week Bentleys went on to dominate the road race scene soon after.

The Vauxhall 30/98 existed as a prototype even in 1914, and small numbers were made during the war, between great batches of 25 H.P. military cars. Production proper got underway in 1919 and this side-valve E-type would do over 85 m.p.h. In later OE form, it was capable of 100 m.p.h., yet was docile when required.

Choice of monarchs

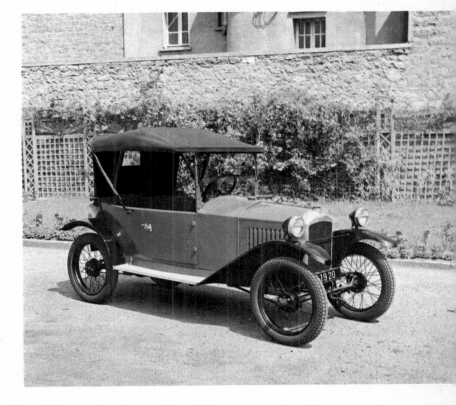

Among the out-and-out luxury cars were Rolls-Royce, Daimler, Lanchester, Leyland and — how many people remember — Guy. The classic Rolls-Royce Silver Ghost, virtually a 1906 machine but now with a self-starter, travelled on imperturbably into the early 1920s. Daimler was the choice of monarch and presidents, and its six-cylinder engine gave it a smooth and sophisticated performance. The great Lanchester Forty was another favourite of Royalty. Leyland's private-car connections are multifarious to-day, but this is the result of recent

A decorated Fiat Tipo 52 — this model was made from 1912 to 1920. Below a Fiat 501 tourer under load.

mergers; the Leyland 8 of the 1920s was a magnificent car but at £3,000 it was dearer than a Rolls, and not more than a score were made. The Guy was more realistic, and was almost unique among British cars in having a vee-eight engine. Smaller models were also made.

Other names of the period are Arrol-Aster, Arrol-Johnston, Storey, Argyll, Belsize, Beardmore, H.E., Horstmann, Deemster, Hampton, Swift, Albert, Straker-Squire, Enfield-Allday and Sheffield Simplex.

In Italy Fiat was predominant in the 1920s, not only because of its size but also because it was the only company in the country to follow an up-to-date production policy. This was based on a simple and robust product, capable of attracting a large market and of being manufactured on a mass scale. The car was the Fiat "501", designed by Carlo Cavalli, which was similar in some ways to the Citroën "A".

Though the "501" was only one of three models on which Fiat relied, the others being the "505" and the

"510" both introduced in 1919, it was the first European car built by modern techniques.

Its 1,460 c.c. engine developed 23 H.P. at 2,600 r.p.m. and there was later to be a sports version, the "501 S", which could reach 58 m.p.h. Other technical improvements of interest were a new cylinder head design, reduced dimensions of the engine, clutch and gearbox assembly and better carburation.

Production of the "501" ceased in 1926, by which time a very large number had been built. For a good part of its production life, it was built in the new factory at Lingotto, near Turin, which came into use in 1923.

Lancia production immediately after the war was concentrated on the "Kappa", a face-lift of the 1913 "Theta", which had been one of the first European cars with an electrical system built in rather than being treated as an accessory. Only the chassis was modified, and the engine remained the same four-cylinder five-litre. A new engine, a 12-cylinder o.h.v. 7.8-litre which developed 150 H.P., had been designed for the Kappa, but then Lancia decided he could not afford it.

Still elegant

Lancia's new production was to be seen, however, in the following years, first with the "DiKappa", a sporting version of the Kappa, and then with the "TriKappa", which used the chassis of the DiKappa but with a new V8 engine of 4,600 c.c. Top speed was over 80 m.p.h. Production totalled 850.

Other Italian manufacturers' new models included Bianchi with the "S.3", Ansaldo's tourer "4 C" with a 1,800 c.c. engine and a later sporting version, and models by Ceirano and SPA.

In Germany the immediate post-war models were of little interest. The older companies such as Benz and Opel produced austere four- and six-cylinder models, and Mercedes resumed production of their pre-war range.

Against the trend in Europe, 1919 marked the disappearance in Belgium of companies well-established before the war and at that year's Brussels Salon there were only the "three M's" (Miesse, Metallurgique and Minerva), and the Excelsior (with an interesting front suspension). In Holland Spyker built a six-cylinder powered by a German Maybach engine.

In Spain a number of companies were formed, notably Elizalde in Barcelona, which built sporting and luxury cars. These included an eight-cylinder car which was nearly 23 feet long, shown at the Paris Salon in 1921. A survey of Europe at this time might close with Czechoslovakia, where Skoda built Hispano-Suizas under lic-

The Lancia 8 cylinder "TriKappa". Above a spartan-looking 1911 Alfa 24 H.P. 4-cylinder, 4,084 c.c. engine giving 42 H.P.

Two 1923 1,100 c.c. Newton-Ceiranos built for the JCC 200-mile race.

___

An A. V. Monocar of 1921, a typical example of the minimal cyclecar as produced in Great Britain immediately after the First World War.

ence and there were other manufacturers such as Praga and Tatra; Switzerland with the Martini, Maximag and the Piccard-Pictet; and Austria with three major manufacturers, Austro-Daimler, Gräf and Stift and Steyr.

Of the great luxury vehicles among European cars, the Hispano-Suiza 37.2 H.P., which was presented at the Paris Salon in 1919, probably incorporated the largest number of technical innovations. They came from the brain of Marc Birkigt, the engineer from Switzerland whose nationality gave rise to the name of a company which united Spanish finance and Swiss technology.

This car had dual ignition by magneto and coil, an aviation-type twin-choke carburettor, four-wheel servo-operated brakes and superb suspension. Its many less obvious technical qualities included a crankshaft carved out of a single billet of special steel, which weighed 433 lbs. before machining.

Isotta Fraschini, too, were successful in the 1920s. They introduced their 5.9-litre Tipo 8 in 1919, enlarging the engine to 7.4 litres with the advent of the "8A" in 1925. The Isotta Fraschini was an imposing car, longer and heavier than either the Hispano-Suiza or the Rolls-Royce, but its original 80 b.h.p. engine could not match the performance of the former and barely that of the latter, whose Silver Ghost had been born in 1906 and was to remain in production until 1925. The Isotta had the advantage of eight cylinders against the six of its competitors, but is was not as silent as the Rolls.

The used car show at Crystal Palace in 1921. Below a 1914 4½-litre Grand Prix Piccard-Pictet rebodied after the First World War.

MINICARS

As long as engines were inefficient, baby cars had little chance of success. The De Dions of 1900-1905 with their high-speed single-cylinder power units combined 30 m.p.h. and reliability, but were very rough. Casting techniques of the period could not cope with the small "four".

A better combination of performance and economy was achieved by the tricar, a motorcycle structure with fore-carriage attached, which was both anti-social and uncomfortable. This gave way to the four-wheeled cyclecar, showing its motorcycle ancestry in its chain or belt drive, plywood bodywork, and noisy air-cooled vee-twin engine. It was fragile and unreliable, if faster than such

The unusual looking but practical Citroën "2CV".

primitive "big cars in miniature" as Peugeot's "Bebe" of 1913, strictly a two-seater and flat out at 35 m.p.h.

Even with conventional shaft drive, the cyclecar was not a sound proposition, and the three-wheelers which survived (in Britain especially) between the Wars were a halfway house between the sporting motorcycle and the small sports car, rather than true "minis". The first modern "baby" was Herbert Austin's Seven, a big car in miniature, even down to four-wheel brakes of a sort. With a 747 c.c. four-cylinder engine, conventional three-speed gearbox, and full electrics, it carried two adults and two children at 45-50 m.p.h., and was built under licence in France, Germany, and America, as well as inspiring Japan's Datsun. It formed the basis of all miniature car designs up to 1936 — apart from such small engine/large body solutions as the Jowett and the D.K.W. — but suffered from the inevitable growing pains, becoming a full fourseater and unnecessarily heavy. Weight increased by 25 per cent between 1933 and 1937. Overgrowth was also to affect later minicars. France's front-wheel drive Dyna-Panhard was a compact "750" weighing 12 cwt. in 1950: four years later it was a six-seater and 2 cwt. heavier It was left to Ing. Fessia of Fiat to produce a new idiom, with his "500" of 1936. The traditional front engine and rear-wheel drive were retained, but space was saved by the forward-mounted unit and dashboard radiator, and Fiat firmly kept it a two-seater. The result measured less than 11ft. from stem to stern, and could keep up with modern traffic; there were no motorcycle crudities, while independently sprung front wheels, synchromesh, and a fuel consumption of over 50 m.p.g. made it a best-seller.

Though the conventional small car survived the Second World War, it tended to grow still bigger, as witness Alec Issigonis's Morris "Minor" of 1948, but two new requirements now had to be met. The first of these, in impoverished Europe, was for a simpler, cyclecar-type vehicle, frugal enough to subsist in a world of rationed fuels: the second called for more compact dimensions as congestion supervened. This new cyclecar generation made liberal use of plastics and small two-stroke engines: three-wheelers, such as the British Bond, the German-Italian Isetta, and the German Messerschmitt, were common, but Spain's Biscuter, and another German offering, the Goggomobil, had four wheels. Bubble hoods, swing-up doors, and handlebar steering were among fea-

The Isetta, produced by B.M.W. with 250 c.c. engine in Germany was a success in the 1950s. But in Italy, where it was designed it found little favour.

regular small-car practice, but it was set across the structure with the four-speed gearbox mounted in the sump, and the result would take four people and their luggage, yet measured only ten feet in length and occupied an area of 47 square feet. The box shape might compare unfavourably with the curvaceous rear quarters of the 1936 Fiat, but the car not only caught on, but became a rally-winner as well. The east-west engine layout has been widely copied, and in 1967 it was applied by Honda of Japan to an even smaller device, a 354 c.c. air-cooled "twin" with 35 b.h.p. — five times the output extracted by De Dion from an engine twice as big in 1903.

Now that compactness has been achieved, the next step is a new type of commuter's car combining the layout of the better "bubbles" of the 1950s with fumeless battery-electric propulsion.

tures found in this phase, and some of these miniatures were quite efficient, though their crudity militated against long-term acceptance, and the Suez fuel shortage of 1956-57 was almost their swansong, albeit the Goggomobil survived into the later 1960s.

More important was a breach with convention — the "power pack", in which all mechanical components were concentrated at one end or the other. Citroen's legendary 2CV of 1949 — which was quite a big car despite its 375 c.c. flat-twin engine — had front-wheel drive, but though it represented a new minimum in capacity and output for the transport of four people, it was a money and maintenance saver rather than a space saver. Renault, Fiat, N.S.U., and Hillman, among others, opted for rear engines, but these posed problems of handling, and both Renault's 4CV and its immediate successors could be tricky on occasions.

Faced with the need to combine compact proportions, good handling, and adequate power in a four-seater saloon, Alec Issigonis came up with the B.M.C. "Mini" formula. The 848 c.c. four-cylinder engine was

Below: A Messerschmitt KR 200 of 1958 shows its aircraft cockpit characteristics.

By 1919 the big U.S. companies were using publicity photographs showing women at the wheel. This acknowledgement of the influence of the woman driver was much slower to reach European manufacturers.

The tragedy of the Isotta Fraschini, an excellent car, was that it was launched at the same time as the Hispano-Suiza — which was in almost every respect its superior — while the Silver Ghost and the later Phantoms had an aura of their own which not even the Hispano-Suiza could quite match.

There were inevitably other luxury cars, including the most expensive of all, the Farman, which had a special appeal in the world of film stars, with the somewhat ambiguous slogan "A car drives, a Farman glides". This company was, however, to abandon motoring to concentrate on aeroplane production.

Another was Voisin, who, like Rolls-Royce, Hispano-Suiza, Isotta Fraschini and Farman, used the experience gained with aero-engines. His "18" had considerable success, above all because of the silence of its Knight sleeve-valve engine. Delage, too, was producing luxury cars at this time.

Wartime ideas

So far as the sporting side is concerned, after the Armistice the first exploit of note was the speed record set up by de Palma at Ormonde Beach in 1919 in a 12-cylinder Packard at just over 150 m.p.h. A short time later the first post-war Indianapolis "500" was held. A strong American entry — including Duesenberg, Frontenac and Packard — was joined by a Peugeot, four specially built Ballots, from a factory which had just started car manufacture, and the machine which Goux built from a pre-war Peugeot.

The genuine Peugeot driven by the American Howard Wilcox again won, but it was to be the last European victory for many years. Goux's Peugeot-Premier finished a surprising third. For various minor reasons none of the Ballots finished the race but they were obviously advanced machines destined for success. They had been designed by Henry and reflected his ideas in the shape of such features as twin o.h.c. and four valves per cylinder: the aluminium pistons and dual-choke carburettors were obviously influences from war-time aero-engine design.

Winner goes backward

A French car was also victorious in the only other race of international interest held in 1919, the Targa Florio. Run in terrible weather, it was won by André Boillot in a 2½-litre Peugeot. The fastest lap was put up by Antonio Ascari in his first important race.

Boillot won in spite of a spectacular incident. Arriving at the finish at high speed he saw the road ahead blocked by spectators. To avoid an accident he braked, spinning around and crossing the line backwards. At the crowd's insistence an official made Boillot turn his car round and cross the line the right way — just as the other cars came thundering up.

Record breaking Sunbeam, 1000 H.P. with chain drive, two 12-cylinder engines. With this monster Sir Henry Segrave first exceeded 200 m.p.h.

The "Golden Arrow" built in 1929 to the designs of Capt. J. S. Irving. Its engine was a Schneider Trophy type Napier Lion 12 cylinder aero engine which gave 930 H.P. With this car Segrave raised his own record to 230 m.p.h.

Austin, from its establishment, was geared to producing a "car for everyone". Above, an Austin Mini in rural setting, and below a 1922 Austin Seven, with 747 c.c. engine, four cylinders, three speeds plus reverse and four-wheel brakes.

CHAPTER TWENTY

YEARS OF THE CHARLESTON

The years between 1920 and 1925 are among the most important in motoring history. It was in that period that, aided by a favourable economic climate in most countries, manufacturers finally moved from experiment to settled technique for car building. The age produced a breed of cars with the qualities of technical common sense, simplicity, robustness and excellent all-round performance; they have righly been given the name "vintage cars". The period for this includes cars built from 1919 to 1930.

Time of evolution

These were years of maturity for the motor car, though their drivers were going through an era of frivolity, as typified by the Charleston. Most of the car's essential features had been defined and brought to a high degree of efficiency and the "Vintage Years", so far as touring cars were concerned at any rate — it was different in the field of racing cars — were to be years of rational evolution rather than revolution. It was in these years that European and American cars were to diverge in types of vehicles produced. On the other side of the Atlantic, as mass-production soared, choice became limit-

ed, and the American with a desire to be different fell back on a wide range of body styles available on the chassis he favoured. In Europe, on the other hand, a wide variety of types of vehicle was produced, yet nearly all with the qualities that have made them "vintage".

The vintage car was quite different from its Edwardian predecessor. The chassis was lighter but rigid and, for the first time, all the four wheels were braked. Engines

were smaller and rotated at higher speeds following the introduction of aluminium pistons — a lesson learned from wartime aero-engine practice. Racing engines went as high as 4,500 r.p.m., compared with 2,500 r.p.m. before 1914. Gearboxes were now often mounted in unit with their engines, and coil ignition was on its way in. Carburation was efficient and trouble free. The steering was positive, if frequently rather heavy.

So far as bodywork was concerned, the motor car had now finally discarded its horse-drawn ancestry. Car design had a logic of its own. Styling was horizontal rather than perpendicular, and the bonnet line was carried through the scuttle and along the body. Saloon cars no longer had to accommodate vast headgear and were consequently lower and better proportioned. Exceptions could be found to these generalisations, of course. The Rolls-Royce "Silver Ghost" was one of the last luxury cars to adopt four-wheel brakes (in 1924), and later Vauxhall 30-98s had singularly ineffective ones,

but both of these were essentially Edwardian cars whose excellent qualities enabled them to live in the vintage era. Citroën, France's first mass-producer, replaced the 1.3-litre Type-A with a more powerful 1½-litre Type B, and strengthened their position in the market by introducing a taxicab variant.

Clover leaf

In 1922 Citroën presented what was to become one of the best known French cars of the period the 5 CV. Type "C", in one form known as the "clover-leaf" from its seating plan of two front and one behind. Unmistakable with its paintwork in lemon-yellow, the 5 CV was one of the first cars to be driven by women in any number. It had an 855 c.c. engine which developed 11 b.h.p. and top speed was around 42 m.p.h. Like the "B. 2" it was produced in open and cabriolet

Above, a 1926 Citroën taxi. On the left a Peugeot "163" tourer with four-cylinder engine capable of 37 m.p.h.

forms. This car was also manufactured in Germany under licence by Opel.

Citroën also produced other less important vehicles such as the "Caddy", a sporting version of the "B. 2" with unusual lines somewhat similar to the Labourdette "Skiff". It was not particularly successful. A certain number of tracked vehicles were also produced — the first for civilian use — and memorable journeys were made. They included the first crossing of the Sahara by car, and cruises across Asia. Renault, too, entered the field of cross-country vehicles but preferred to use six wheels instead of tracks.

In 1920 Peugeot was the second largest French manufacturer after Citroën, but its production consisted of largely outdated models.

1922 SPA "23 S".

Radiator replaced

Renault had been relegated to third place, not because of any shortcomings in its products but because the company had concentrated on "vertical" integration, producing in its own factories a high proportion of all the components used in its cars. Renault was also active as a manufacturer of tractors, railway engines, tanks and aero-engines. The Renault range was headed by the huge 45 H.P. which would do 87 m.p.h. and cost the enormous sum of 60,000 francs. Due to the competition from Citroën a strong and economical 6 CV was introduced in 1922 with a 950 c.c. engine. This car reappeared two years later as a four-seater, the "N N", which on the track at Miramas covered 10,000 miles at an average of almost 50 m.p.h. About this time the dashboard radiator, which had previously stood proud of the bonnet line, was streamlined out of sight, and the "coal-scuttle" bonnet was given a small frontal grille which later assumed a diamond shape.

The 5 H.P. Citroën "bateau".

A reunion of venerable cars at a Bentley Drivers' Club meeting.

The 1923 Vauxhall 23/60.

Among less important but technically interesting cars produced in France was the two-litre Georges Irat with many advanced features such as forced feed lubrication and an American Delco distributor; the sports cars built by Bignan and by Sizaire with overhead camshafts and advanced suspension; and the Omega-Six, a light 6-cylinder car. So far as Panhard-Levassor and Delahaye were concerned, they continued with their traditional models.

The Austin Seven

On the other side of the Channel, the most important event was the introduction of the famous Austin Seven which was to have, not only in Great Britain but all

In 1923, Chevrolet equipped a few experimental chassis with air-cooled engines, but it was not until 1960 that the company produced an air-cooled engine for commercial sale.

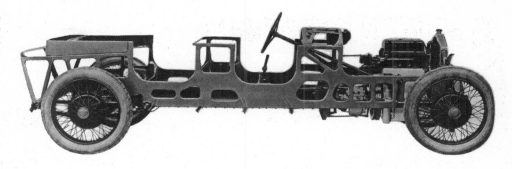

The "monocoque" construction of the Lancia "Lambda" which was one of the manufacturer's many revolutionary ideas.

over Europe, an importance comparable to that of the Ford "T" in America. It was, in fact, the first small car built in Europe which was available, if not to everyone, at least to a much larger public than hitherto. It had something of the appearance of a cyclecar, but there the similarity ended. It was made of the best materials and it was robust and well designed. The engine was famous for its long life and survived in production long after Austins dropped the model: manufacturing rights were taken over by Reliant of Tamworth, who fitted the unit in their private and com-

mercial three-wheelers. It had four wheel brakes at a time when the Rolls-Royce Silver Ghost did not, unusual in 1922 when it was launched. More than 250,000 were built.

Another successful English car, albeit a larger one, was the famous 1½-litre Morris Cowley built by William Morris, who had designed and put into production in 1912 the Oxford with an 8.9 H.P. White and Poppe engine. After the War the Oxford was produced with a 1½-litre Hotchkiss engine and the cheaper Cowley, introduced during the War, was made as an austerity

1923 Renault 3 - 4 seater, type KJ 1 with 951 c.c., 3 speeds plus reverse and 47 m.p.h.

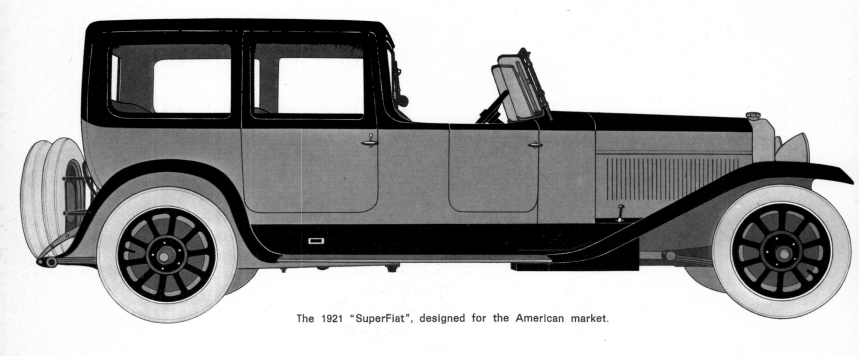

The 1921 "SuperFiat", designed for the American market.

The Fiat "509", the first Italian "utility" car and the first car sold in Italy on hire purchase.

version. These "bullnose" cars, so-called because of the shape of their radiators were a great success. A series of price reductions in 1922, combined with their sturdiness and reliability, and an excellent gearbox, earned Morris a respect and affection that was similar to that inspired by the Ford "T" in America.

In the luxury class, Rolls-Royce decided in 1925 to stop production of the Silver Ghost after 18 years of life. Since October, 1922, it had ceased to be their only model as the 20 H.P. or "Ladies' Rolls", had been introduced with a 3.1-litre six-cylinder engine. In 1925 a four-speed gearbox and four-wheel brakes were added.

From Ghost to Phantom

The most significant event for Rolls Royce in the period to 1925, however, was the substitution of the New Phantom or Phantom I for the Ghost. This, in effect, consisted of an improved version of the Ghost chassis but with an entirely new engine. Isotta Fraschini had introduced the eight-cylinder "A". This car, with the tremendous 8-litre 45 H.P. of Hispano-Suiza, were challenges that could no longer be ignored. A new Rolls-Royce chassis was also being developed but this was not to appear until 1929 as the Phantom II.

The new engine retained some of the characteristics of the Ghost, being an in-line six-cylinder in two blocks of three, but had a capacity of 7,668 c.c.

Bentley for his part had begun production of the 3-litre in 1921 but it was not until 1926 that production reached significant quantities. Daimler, ever faithful to the double sleeve-valve, brought out a 12-cylinder version, the double six.

Hire purchase introduced

Italian industry also made considerable technical progress in the period. Fiat presented, in 1921, the luxurious

1923 Alfa P. 1, six-cylinder, 1,990 c.c. engine which produced 80 H.P. at 4,800 r.p.m.

"SuperFiat" as a prestige car, particularly for the American market, but it had little success. It was a very long car with a V-12 engine. It had overhead valves and servo-assisted four-wheel brakes. This was the first Italian car to be fitted with a Delco distributor. The body work was modern in style. In 1922 the Fiat "519" was introduced but was not a commercial triumph. It was an O.H.V. six-cylinder. The most important Fiat model of the period was the "509" introduced at the end of 1924. It was the first Italian car for the mass market. This car was a great success, partly because Fiat introduced hire purchase for the first time. It was sold in four versions with a 990 c.c. engine, torpedo, spider, cabriolet and saloon, and its relatively low price at last took motoring from the exclusive sphere of the rich in Italy.

Also new in 1922 was Lancia's memorable "Lambda" with its independent front suspension and unitary construction of chassis and body. The vertical coil springs at the front were assisted by hydraulic shock absorbers. The bodywork was designed to eliminate a problem that was occupying the attention of manufacturers everywhere; this was the movement between body and chassis caused by the rough rouds. One of the solutions tried

1923 Morris Cowley.

A 1925 Morris-Oxford 14-28 h.p. saloon with 1.8-litre engine and front-wheel brakes, - Morris's first.

THE COUNT AND HIS "CHITTY"

A boys' book written by Ian Fleming, author of the James Bond books, tells the story of a fantastic motor car capable, among other things, of flying. The car was called Chitty Chitty Bang Bang, which has now given its name to a film. This name, usually abbreviated to Chitty, was also that of three real cars built at the beginning of the 1920s. These, too, were extraordinary, and belonged to a singular constructor and driver called Count Louis Zborowski.

Zborowski, known affectionately as "Zbo", was the son of Eliot Zborowski, a keen motoring enthusiast who was killed in 1902 in one of the early motor races. "Zbo" had inherited some remarkable qualities as an "inventor" of motor cars and his first Chitty saw the light of day in March, 1921.

His aero-engine car had a six-cylinder engine with the far from negligible capacity of 21-litres and followed his usual formula of putting a powerful aero-engine in a skimpy chassis. The car is reported to have consisted of a Maybach engine in a 1913 Mercedes "75" chassis. It would produce over 300 b.h.p. at 1,500 r.p.m. Each cylinder had four overhead valves.

It competed at Brooklands against other monsters such as the V12 Sunbeam and the Wolseley Viper, being frequently defeated.

Chitty II was similar in general conception to the first, with better weight distribution, and still exists in running order. It used a Mercedes chassis with an 18.9-litre Benz engine, and was once used by Count Zborowski, along with Chitty I, for a tour of North Africa.

Chitty III was a relatively smaller car with an engine of a mere 14,700 c.c. and the usual Mercedes chassis. Unlike its predecessors, this car had four-wheel brakes.

Zborowski built a fourth car in 1923 which, for some reason, was not called the "Chitty IV" but Higham Special, after the place where it was built.

50-litre spectacle

This was the largest car ever to race at Brooklands, having a 27-litre engine. It was raced against Mephistopheles, which was a reconstruction of Eldridge's Fiat. This latter giant had spectacularly blown up the previous May when racing against a Chitty, also wrecked before the end of the race. The reconstructed Fiat had a 21.7-litre Fiat engine and still exists.

The sight and sound of over twenthy-five-litres thumping around the circuit — though the "Higham Special" at 100 m.p.h. was revving only at 1,200 r.p.m. — was an impressive spectacle. With the disappearance of these monsters, racing became safer but undoubtedly less colourful.

Zborowski intended to build a fifth car to the same formula. Before he could do so he was killed in the 1924 Monza Grand Prix, when driving a Mercedes.

was the use of flexible coachwork, such as that of Weymann in wood and leathercloth. Lancia simply got rid of the chassis, hanging mechanical components on a semi-integral structure in pressed steel. This lowered the car's centre of gravity, enhancing stability but producing problems of style, especially as it was a new type of construction. Thus the first series Lambdas had a long horizontal look that was to be characteristic of later series.

The engine of the "Lambda" was derived directly from the "TriKappa", a 2,120 c.c. narrow V. 4, a type of engine layout which Lancia was to use frequently and still uses today in the Fulvia. It produced 49 b.h.p. at 2,350 r.p.m. and gave the car a top speed of 72 m.p.h. Alfa-Romeo, likewise, made their mark in the immediate post-war years: the company had been renamed after Nicola Romeo took over the old A.L.F.A. (Anonima Lombardia Fabbrica Automobile) which was itself the successor to the Italian branch of Darracq. Production was concentrated on sports cars; the first was the assembly in 1919 of the pieces of the "Grand Prix 1914", which had been hidden for the duration of the war in a medicine factory.

Monza winner

The most important of the Alfa Romeo cars was the "20-30 ES Sport" which could reach 80 m.p.h. It was also produced in a touring version. There was also a 3-litre six-cylinder, the "RL" which could achieve 70 m.p.h. in its touring version and 80 m.p.h. as a sports car, which was produced in various series until 1924, and there was an "RM" derived from the previous model.

Above — Salamano in a Fiat "805" in the European G. P. at Monza in 1923, in which he and Nazzaro took 1st and 2nd places. Right — two perfect models of an "804" and an "805".

The chassis of the Alfa 20-30 ES (1921 to 1923) four-cylinder, 4,250 c.c. engine developing 67 B.H.P. at 2,600 r.p.m.

Two of the surviving three Charron Laycocks. Both cars were built in 1921.

At the same time Alfa Romeo were preparing their first fabulous racing cars — the "P. 1" of 1923, with the 2-litre six-cylinder twin o.h.c. engine, and the 1924 "P.2" with a super-charged two-litre straight-eight engine. Designed by Vittorio Jano, the latter was to gain many victories for Alfa Romeo up to 1930, including the 1925 Monza Grand Prix, and the first world championship.

Among the lesser but old-established Italian companies of the time, one of the most active was the SPA. In seeking to attract a new clientele after the immediate post-war difficulties, SPA quickly launched four models, the "23", the "23. S", the "24" and the "24. S". They satisfied neither market, not being luxurious enough to attract the rich and too expensive for mass appeal.

Porsche design

German industry was known best in the earlier years for its racing cars, for which most of the credit belongs to Ferdinand Porsche. He had just joined Daimler and at once designed a 2-litre which performed brilliantly in the Targa Florio. Shortly afterwards, in 1924, Daimler and Benz merged into one company.

Count Masetti winning the 12th Targo Florio in his Fiat S. 57/14B after a long duel with Sailer in a Mercedes. It was the first time that German cars and drivers raced in Italy after the First World War.

One of the sensational racing results of this time was the victory of an American car, Jimmy Murphy's Duesenberg, in the 1921 Grand Prix de l'Automobile Club de France at Le Mans. There was particularly keen rivalry between the Duesenberg and the four Ballots, both types being 3-litre straight-eights. It was the only U.S. victory in this series, however, and the following year at Strasbourg the main competition was once again among European manufacturers. The reduction of the formula to 2-litre led to an effort to reduce weight resulting in some cars being particularly dangerous. This cost the life of the up-and-coming young Italian driver, Biagio Nazzaro, nephew of the legendary Felice. The latter won the race (15 years after his first victory in 1907) a few minutes after his nephew died when thrown on the track after an over-fragile rear axle broke. The winning car was a Fiat "804" with a six-cylinder engine, which averaged about 80 m.p.h. — a figure which was unthinkable only a few months before for a 2-litre. The quality of this Fiat was confirmed later in

Count Louis Zborowski at the wheel of an Aston-Martin in the 1922 French Grand Prix.

A type 172 BC 5VC Peugeot cabriolet with four cylinders, three speeds and multi-plate clutch.

the year when Bordino won in a supercharged version in the first Italian Grand Prix held on the new circuit at Monza.

1921 Horstmann.

Revenge for Fiat

The 1923 French Grand Prix was held at Tours and was particularly interesting, because of the wide variety of cars taking part. Fiat entered a 2-litre, supercharged, straight-eight. Delage had a 12-cylinder and Bugatti, whose cars had been having growing success in competition, appeared with three original if somewhat unstable models. Sunbeam had a supercharged six-cylinder, clearly inspired by the 1922 Fiat "804 s" and designed by Berta-rione, who had joined them from Fiat. One of these last, driven by Henry Segrave, was the winner. Segrave, of course, was later to take the World's Land Speed Record on three separate occasions — in 1926, 1927, and 1929. Fiat, defeated in France, had their revenge at Monza where their cars could not be beaten either by the Benz "Tropfenwagen" made under Rumpler licence, or by the "P. 1" Alfa Romeo. The winning driver was Salamano.

THIS SPORTING BREED

What is a sports car? One conceived for the pure joy of driving.

In the beginning every automobile was a sports car: the unreliability of the early primitives was enough to deter all but the most fanatical, and the super-enthusiast bought one of last season's racers. Even in 1910 the high-speed engine was largely undiscovered, and the recognised method of extracting more power was to build big Giants. Cars of ten- and fifteen-litre capacity were not unknown, and for all the charm of a big and lazy engine delivering a three-figure output at three-figure revs., it was less fun stopping such brutes, or keeping them in tyres. But if long-distance rallies such as the Price Henry Tour and the Alpine Trial bred high-performance machinery, voiturette racing bred high-speed engines, and even in 1914 we find cars like the 4-litre Vauxhall developing 75-80 b.h.p. and capable of 80 m.p.h. — whereas a decade previously such an achievement would have demanded more than twice the litreage.

Such cars were not for the many. Even in 1928 the enthusiast's beau ideal was still the 4½-litre Bentley, with effective four-wheel brakes, but still adhering to the old concept of a big, slow-turning power unit. Once again racing influence was felt, and on the Continent there was a trend towards smaller engines with forced induction, turning at 4,500-5,000 r. p. m., and requiring liberal use of the gears. Bugatti and Alfa-Romeo were offering 100 m.p.h. sports cars with less than 2½ litres under their bonnets.

Comfort was seldom considered. With good brakes and steering, and a delectable exhaust note, the enthusiast expected spine-jarring suspension and poor weather protection. Closed bodies were still too heavy, and the more elegant ones combined claustrophobia and foot-frying tendencies. The more advanced engines were apt to wet their plugs in traffic.

The 1920s saw a new line of development, the small, inexpensive sports car. Spiritual successor to the old cyclecar, it benefited from greater engine efficiency, and

Above: 1932 M.G. Midget. - Below an Austin - Healey Sprite.

offered 70 m.p.h. and 40 m.p.g. for around £250, in return for flimsy and uncomfortable coachwork, and expensive noises if one revved too hard. The French pioneered this trend, but by 1930 their mantle had descended upon Britain, whose M.Gs, Singers, and Rileys worthily upheld the tradition in more civilised fashion, giving less pecunious enthusiasts a lot of cheap fun.

The keen driver had something that would go by 1914, and ten years later he had something that would stop as well. The later 1930s saw an extension of the civilising process with cars like the legendary "328" B.M.W. of 1936. Here the twin objectives of 80 b.h.p. and 100 m.p.h. were attained on only 2-litres, together with the good ride conferred by independently-sprung front wheels, and more comfortable bodywork. The result was infinitely more tractable than the supercharged confections of an earlier era. The UK.120 Jaguar of 1949, though more sophisticated mechanically, was a development of the same theme.

Surprisingly the greater congestion and speed restrictions of the post-War world did not kill the sports car. Ordinary saloons now performed well: they were faster than the sporting machinery of 1939, and the public was becoming more selective. Further, there were new factors: better fuels, radial-ply tyres, and disc brakes, while the TC-type M.G. of 1946 had reintroduced fun-motoring to the U.S.A. By the middle 1960s Detroit had found a market for proper four-speed gearboxes with floor change, legible instrumentation, and "handling packages". Sales of half a million Ford "Mustangs" in the first eighteen months of production pointed the way, and as more and more motorists demanded more than mere transportation, the "sporting breed" underwent another change. The great cars of 1939 — B.M.W., straight-eight Alfa-Romeo, speed-model "4.3" Alvis, Delahaye "135" — where thought of as open models: their spiritual descendants thirty years later — Ferrari, Lamborghini, Aston Martin, E-type Jaguar, and the rest — were gran turismi, or closed, occasional four-seater coupés. If rear-seat passengers were sometimes cramped, the result was a vehicle equally at home in city or motorway. While most owners still preferred to shift for themselves, even the hairiest "GTs" could be had with automatic gearboxes, and the old-fashioned sports two-seater was all but extinct, except in the smallest and cheapest class.

More important still was the elimination of one of the great shibboleths of automobile design, the système Panhard — engine in front, gearbox amidships, and drive to the rear wheels. The success of the rear-engined Porsche was followed by mid-engined layouts such as Lotus's "Europa", Lamborghini's "Miura", and the 1½ litre British Leylad prototype. This made for lower and smoother silhouettes, better weight distribution, and (in conjunction with space-frames) lower weight.

What of the future? It is too early yet to predict the influence of either Wankel engine or gas-turbine, but one thing is certain. There will always be a demand for a type of car that will look different, handle better, and transport two people who want more than mere transit from A to B.

Above: the Triumph Spitfire. - Below: MGB GT.

From the start of motoring, spasmodic attempts were made to design bodies offering lower wind resistance. Only in recent years has the study become widespread and scientific. Above is an Alfa Romeo 2600 SZ, and below a 1909 Vauxhall "KN".

CHAPTER TWENTY ONE

THE DISTURBED DECADE

"Le Vingt Quatre Heures du Mans", the Le Mans 24 hours, the most celebrated of all long-distance races, arose almost by chance among three enthusiastic drivers. The journalist Faroux, Coquille, the French manager of Rudge-Whitworth, and Durand, secretary of L'Automobile Club de l'Ouest, decided to create a competition which would be a test of robustness and staying power of the cars involved. To this end they arranged to bring back into service, at their own expense, the old Sarthe circuit at Le Mans and to prepare some tough rules for the cars using it. They did not expect to attract much public interest, at least for the first year, but in the

The team of tank-bodied two-litre Bugattis which ran in the 1923 French Grand Prix at Strasbourg.

The first "all steel" Citroën.

Baron Manuel de Teffet at the wheel of a 1923 Alfa RL.

event they were pleasantly surprised. At 4 p.m. on 26 May, 1923, when the competitors set off, thousands of spectators were lining the circuit.

All the cars except three were "torpedoes" (open tourers) with sports engines, but strictly standard production models. The three exceptions were closed cars. In spite of the heavy rain, 30 cars finished. There was no winner because the organisers, perhaps from lack of confidence in their enterprise, had stipulated no precise regulations to decide a winner. However, the greatest distance, 1,380 miles, was covered by the Chenard-Walker, driven by Lagache and Léonard, at an average speed of 57½ m.p.h.; the fastest lap, at almost 67 m.p.h. was that of Duff and Clement's three-litre Bentley. From the beginning the Le Mans 24-Hour Race, fulfilled a useful function, and manufacturers were quick to recognise the publicity value of a good performance in this gruelling event. In 1924 another "24 Hour" was held at Spa in Belgium, a clear imitation of the French race.

By that year Americans had beaten off the European invaders at that other great long-distance race, the "Indianapolis 500". In 1920 the "Indy" was won by a Monroe built in the U.S. by Louis Chevrolet and driven by his brother Gaston, the engine being a copy of the Peugeot. The next year the victory was completely American because the driver was Tommy Milton and the car, a Frontenac, was entirely designed by Chevrolet; second and third places were taken respectively by a

Duesenberg and another Frontenac, instead of by Ballots as in the previous year. Meanwhile Gaston Chevrolet had been killed in a speedway crash when driving a Monroe-Frontenac.

In 1922 Jimmy Murphy won in a car built by himself, a victory he repeated the following year in an H.C.S. (Miller). The European entry in this race was heavy, partly because of the presence of Count Zborowski, the Bugattis (Ettore Bugatti was just beginning the most brilliant period of his career) and the supercharged Mercedes. The driver of one of these, Lautenschlager, dropped out of the race when his car hit a wall.

The 1924 race was won by a Duesenberg, but one of the points of interest was the entry of three model "T" Fords; these were heavily modified and ran as Barber-Warnocks. Henry Ford himself had encouraged the entry after the brilliant performance of one which had been entered the previous year. In these races, the name of Harry A. Miller, ex-carburettor specialist, was always prominent.

His first modern front-wheel drive racing car appeared in 1924: this had an advanced inboard braking system at the front.

From this car, built for Jimmy Murphy, was evolved a long line of f.w.d. vehicles. The racers apart, this design formed the basis of the famous L-29 Cord touring car, a breed now highly prized by collectors.

1927 Talbot Darracq G. P. and below 1928 1,100 c.c. Lombard

While European manufacturers were going over to flow-production methods in the early 1920s, design itself was undergoing further radical changes. One of the most important of these was the introduction of the low-pressure, or "balloon" tyre, after a number of unsuccessful experiments undertaken since the beginning of the century.

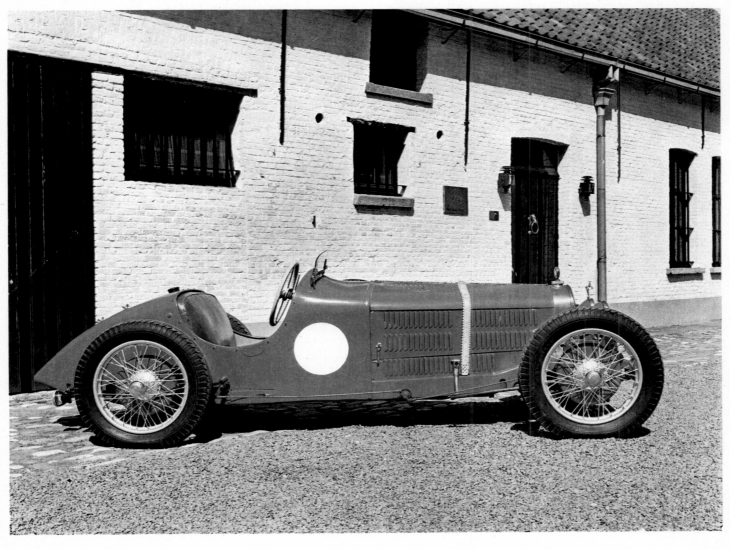

1924 Wolseley 11/22 H.P.

This was in part due to the way such tyres exaggerated the effects of uneven roads on the steering, an effect known as "shimmy". When these problems had been mainly overcome by modifying the suspension and steering box, balloon tyres quickly became universal. Apart from being more comfortable, these tyres were safer; the effect of a burst was less drastic than when the pressure was seven or eight atmospheres.

A great step forward was the adoption by most manufacturers, of four-wheel brakes. The same period also marked the first tentative application of brake servo mechanisms, built on a wide variety of principles and at the time limited to luxury cars. Some years later hydraulic braking was to be introduced.

Steel bodies

One important development, this time of a technological nature, was the adoption of the "all steel" body. This consisted of a structure of welded steel panels fastened to the chassis, resulting in a box structure considerably stronger than was possible with composite construction. Citroën were the pioneers, using this system in agreement with the Budd Manufacturing Company of America, on later editions of the "B. 2".

Finally, even the noise from a motor car in motion began to decrease. There were a number of reasons. Devices stopped the interminable squeak of the springs by means of pressure-greasing and gaiters; crankshafts were better balanced; gears were more precise. New oils and pressure instead of merely splash lubrication played an important part.

1921 Studebaker "Big Six Sedan".

A twin overhead-camshaft three-litre Vauxhall built in 1922.

One of the last Vauxhall 30/98s built in 1926 and derived from the Prince Henry three-litre.

Most of these changes were introduced gradually by manufacturers on models already in production, and 1925 to 1928 were mainly years of re-design and technical improvement for most companies.

Another "great" car of the period was the twin overhead camshaft "6C 1500" Alfa Romeo, designed by Jano to an unusual formula — six cylinders as in luxury cars, but with a capacity of only 1½ litres.

The new car was first exhibited at the motor show in Milan in 1925 but did not go into production till 1927. It was an immediate success and was produced in various versions until 1930. Its power ranged from 44 H.P. in the "normal" version to 54 and 60 in the twin overhead camshaft "Sport" and up to 84 H.P. in the last series, which were supercharged and could reach 97 m.p.h. The "6C 1500" had many racing successes, particularly in the open two-seater and tourer versions built by the coachbuilder Zagato.

Across the Atlantic Walter Percy Chysler started manufacture under his own name with a car that had some unusual features. At the time there had been a decisive change in taste. The public was tired of the "torpedo", the open tourer, and had opted for the "sedan", or closed saloon. The Hudson company was largely responsible for this revolution, having scored a big hit with their modestly priced four-cylinder Essex, a car of some performance by the standards of its day, and one which was offered with a closed "coach" bodywork at a price little higher than that of contemporary tourers. Even the largest companies had to review their production programmes quickly and introduce "sedans". The tourer was abandoned, and a new form of open car was to appear, the cabriolet or "roadster".

The only one not having to react immediately to the change in the market was Ford, well-entrenched with a model for which there was no price competition. But even at the moment when the giant of Detroit was recording an industrial triumph (20 June, 1925 - 9,000 cars built in 24 hours) the first signs of the rapid decline of the "T" were apparent. The Lizzie was given face-

1928 Alfa-Romeo 6 C 1,500 SS.

1926 Simca Violet with 500 c.c. air-cooled twin engine.

1930 Austin Seven special.

lifts such as wire-spoked wheels, lowered bodywork and a choice of colours, but in May, 1927, the last "Lizzie", No. 15,007,003, came off the assembly line. Her closest rival, the four-cylinder Chevrolet was having ever increasing success. It was the car which William P. Knudsen, the president of General Motors, had made the principal weapon in his attack. The build-up of the third big American company was rapid. Walter Chrysler, already known as a "company doctor", now introduced an advanced car with a high-compression six-cylinder engine of a type made possible by the advances in the quality of motor fuel.

Hotel exhibition

The organisers of the New York Show would not give Chrysler a stand so he exhibited the car in the Waldorf-Astoria. The public was favourably impressed by the elegant body, the interior finish, and the car's silence (the engine had seven main bearings and flexible mountings). The "Six" was an immediate success, a success then possible only in America; 106,803 were sold in the first year of its introduction at the competitive price of $ 1,625.

This excellent new "70" led the way to the meteoric rise of the Chrysler Corporation, soon to take third place in sales behind Ford and General Motors. The company set up branches in Europe and absorbed Dodge. Other aspects of the American scene in the 1920s were the diffusion in the luxury field of the straight-eight engine, the brief appearance of a luxury make, the Wills-Sainte Claire, and the last efforts by the supporters of the steam car.

The "straight-eight" engine was popularised by Ballot's racing success with a similar engine in Europe. Whereas in Europe production of such engines remained small in the early 1920s (Bugatti, Isotta Fraschini, Elizalde), in America considerable numbers of the type were produced right up to the early 1950s. The first of these to see large-scale production was the Packard "Single Eight" of 1923, which replaced the old established and more complex "Twin Six".

1930-32 Rolls-Royce Phantom II.

Steam has its day

The Indian summer of the "steamers" was due to the initiative and skill of an unfailing supporter of the steam car, Abner Doble. He began to build luxurious cars of this type in a small workshop in California. When Doble finally had to close down, less than 50 of these vehicles had been built — but one of them had achieved 125 m.p.h. In the European sporting events, 1924 was the year in which "Mephistopheles" gained the world speed record at Arpajon near Paris. (This record was the first event of world interest held on the new French circuit inaugurated on the occasion of the 1924 Paris Salon. The circuit was established after the French magazine "Automobile" held a referendum among the major world motoring personalities, resulting in a strong feeling in favour of a new circuit near the French capital).

The Fiat "Mephistopheles" in 1924 form was very different from its original guise, in which it is reputed to have exceeded 120 m.p.h. at Brooklands. The chassis was much the same, but lengthened. In 1921 it had lost two of its four cylinders in the course of a race — they literally came off — and Ernest Eldridge fitted a Fiat 22-litre aero-engine, the six-cylinder "A 12 bis" which produced 300 b.h.p. at 1,600 r.p.m.

Secrecy and triumph

The 1924 Grand Prix of the Automobile Club de France was held on the circuit near Lyons where it had been held ten years previously, though the track had been considerably modified in the meantime. It was in this race that the Alfa Romeo P. 2 made its first triumphal appearance in an international event.

Jano had previously run it in a race at Cremona where it had astounded the opposition (it had been built in great secrecy) by winning at almost 100 m.p.h. in the hands of a new racing star, Antonio Ascari. Ascari also drove in the French Grand Prix, when victory went to his team colleague Giuseppe Campari at an average of 71 m.p.h., a high speed in view of the circuit's famous S-bends and "devil's elbows".

Many of the cars in the race were supercharged, though second and third places went to two unblown Delages. Another point of interest of this race was the first appearance of the new sleek and elegant Type 35 Bugattis which embodied the best of Molsheim's design capabilities. In the 1924 race they did not have the speed to defeat their rivals, but from that year on they were to exhibit qualities of reliability and road-holding which were to enable them to win many races in future. The Bugattis also became the favoured car of the sporting enthusiast.

A 1925 three-litre Bentley.

The 1925 3,993 c.c. Sunbeam "Tiger".

The P. 2 repeated its success at Monza in the Italian Grand Prix, this time driven by Ascari. It was here that Count Louis Zborowski, of Chitty Chitty Bang Bang fame, was killed in his Mercedes.

This was the last year of the two-litre formula, which was then changed to 1½ litres and the minimum weight raised 50 kilograms. This was an effort by the authorities, who had become alarmed by the high speeds already possible, to reduce the danger to drivers.

The 1925 Grand Prix was run at Montlhéry for the first time. Also for the first time, the regulation requiring a mechanic to be carried in the car was abolished. This gave rise to the introduction of "pits", where the mechanic and his tools were now accommodated.

Victory went easily to the new supercharged Delage driven by Benoist. The Alfa Romeo team retired from the race as a mark of mourning for Ascari, who was killed when his P. 2 overturned after hitting a wall. The Delage victory was especially significant as it showed how a vastly complicated engine like the 12-cylinder, which revved up to 7,000 r.p.m., could run to the limit for hundreds of miles without stopping. This was a test of reliability that would have been considered impossible a short time previously.

Aerodinamic styling

The principal characteristics of the touring car in the years around 1926 may be summed up as follows: a more rounded appearance, which was a step towards aerodynamic styling, high bonnets with low windscreens, prominent rear luggage platforms with space for one or two spare wheels and pressed steel wheels. Wire wheels were almost entirely limited to sports cars.

From the technical point of view the major evolution was to come later, towards the end of the decade, when European cars adopted features recently introduced in America such as higher compression ratios — 7 to 1 became common — and higher engine revs, frequently reaching 3,500 r.p.m.

One of the more interesting cars of the period was the Citroën "B 14", a more powerful version of the "B 12". After initial difficulties due to reducing the weight of the chassis, the "B 14" became popular in France and was produced also as a van.

Peugeot, too, at last succumbed to the fashion for six cylinders, with the "12 Six". The new make of Lucien Rosengart, an ex-colleague of Citroën and formerly managing director of Peugeot, came out with a 5 CV, which was the Austin Seven built under licence with coil ignition. This was a great success. Hotchkiss reverted to six-cylinder cars with an excellent O.H.V. three-litre, and the Sizaire Frères had a Knight sleeve-valve engine and all four wheels were independently sprung.

1929 also saw the end of the vogue of the small French sports car, as typified by the Salmson, the Amilcar, and the Senechal.

In Germany the acquisition of Opel by General Motors in 1929 set that firm on the road to still greater prosperity, and a number of new four- and six-cylinder models were introduced. Mercedes redesigned the appearance of its car, and, under the guidance of Hans Nibel, it also returned to racing with Rudolf Caracciola at the wheel of a big supercharged SSK.

The ubiquitous Austin Seven was built under licence by Dixi, and later by B.M.W. (Bayerische Motoren

1924 Essex special roadster.

A 1919 Ford Model-T with Belgian "speedster" bodywork and below, a 1920 Peugeot.

Werke) who took over that firm. Another popular baby car was the Hanomag, a conventional side-valve four which had supplanted that firm's odd little single-cylinder "Kommissbrot' cyclecar".

In Italy Fiat replaced the out-of-date "501" by the "503" which retained the 1,460 c.c. engine, but had a high output of 27 B.H.P. It had a new "turbulent" cylinder head — introduced by Ricardo in England — to improve burning of the petrol and air mixure. Later Fiat added another model, the 2¼-litre "520"; from this car two larger versions were evolved — the "521" and the "525" — to add to the already wide range.

Lancia's "Lambda" was nearing the end of a long run and 1929 saw their "Dilambda" a big car with a four-litre vee-eight engine. It was capable of 75-80 m.p.h. Alfa Romeo in 1929 launched the glorious "6C 1750",

On the left a 1924 1½-litre Delfosse: on the right a 1931 Fiat 514 S.

1929 Alfa Romeo 1750 G.S. and above the six-cylinder supercharged Mercedes-Benz 7.1-litre S.S.K.L. of 1931.

The 1928 Mercedes-Benz SSK, supercharged and below a 1931 Opel six cylinder.

a development of the previous 1½-litre model that for many years was to be the pride — or the dream — of so many motoring enthusiasts all over the world. It was built in tourer, G.T. and sports forms, and later versions were supercharged.

In England the Riley Nine made its debut in 1926. This significant 1,100 c.c. sports tourer attracted the interest of J. G. Parry-Thomas, who was working on the "Brooklands" competition version at the time of his tragic death on Pendine Sands in 1927, while attacking the World's Land Speed Record on "Babs".

In the U.S. the Ford "A" had finally replaced the "T", and though its performance was up-to-date it clearly showed its ancestry. This four-cylinder Ford had hardly begun to win back its own market when the celebrated Chevrolet "Six" was introduced — more modern-looking, lively and silent.

With this car Chevrolet became the world's bestseller, despite the world economic crisis. The *marque* finally nosed ahead of Ford in 1931.

In the light car field the Studebaker Corporation had success in Europe as well as in America with the Erskine Six, named after the company's president — who committed suicide during the crisis — while Chrysler introduced a new four-cylinder car, the Plymouth, in mid-1928. Among the bigger cars Cadillac introduced a model with an unusual device — an all-synchromesh gearbox.

BUGATTI

Ettore Bugatti at the wheel of a 40/60 H.P.
Mathis-Hermés in 1907.

The personality of Ettore Bugatti is one of the most inspiring in the history of the motor car and for its versatility it recalls certain renaissance characters, bizarre and clever, not yet tamed by the tough routine of the techniques. It is enough to say that his name meant, for at least 30 years, the personification of the competitive spirit for the drivers challenged by him, a pillar of technical wisdom for all the European racing car enthusiasts, a fascinating mechanical designer's skill for the rich customers of his prestige cars.

This was all conceived from his unusually large head, inevitably covered by a bowler hat (worn at an angle depending on his moods; when in good humour at a rakish angle, when agitated pulled firmly over his brow). Constantly full of imaginative ideas and incapable of noticing the hum-drum irritations of everyday life: his carelessness was renowned.

At the age of 16 he planned and built a revolutionary

tricycle with two engines; at 46 he approached the Italian government in order to obtain the resources to build what could only be described as a "science-fiction semi-submarine" equipped with eight engines, with which he wanted to cross the Atlantic in 50 hours. Was he truly a person full of visions or only an incurable eccentric with numerous theories? The question can only now be asked as time appears to have erased many of the echos of his personality; this would never have been asked in his lifetime because all the motor world was admiring his incomparable insight and his confidence in planning engines and very efficient cars, capable of dominating the field in any race. Bugatti was born in Milan in 1882. The son of a well known goldsmith who was concerned in furthering in his two sons, Ettore and Rembrandt, their artistic tendencies.

Rembrandt was to become an ingenius sculptor (famous for his animal figures) — Ettore was unable to over-

9386 R 33

come the evercalling sound of the engine, despite the fact of his artistic background.

At the age of 16 he left the Academy of Brera to take a job at the Stucchi and Prinetti workshop where a member of the team was willing to give him carte blanche, having full confidence in the young man's potential.

By 1898 he had already managed to build his extraordinary double-engined vehicle, probably during his spare time as, by the following year, he had achieved for his employers a compact vehicle, that could truly be called an orthodox motor car which was also to be a commercial success.

However, in secret, he was still producing his bizarre ideas, which were to climax in a working "four-engined" machine. During this period he also was able to win a series of minor motor races most of the time in the original 1899 model, having already achieved the complete mastership of a true professional, fired by the spirit of youth.

In 1901 Bugatti produced his first real motor car, a 12HP four cylinder, which in some details carried the signs of his ingenius ideas: the cylinder head, for instance, was for the first time produced in one unit.

Baron De Dietrich, who owned a car factory in Alsace, noticed this up-and-coming young man, went to Italy and offered him a position and also bought his patents. Bugatti left Italy only to return many years later: he became a French citizen.

Three years later a short-lived company was formed between Bugatti and Emile Mathis, the Hermes Simplex. In 1907 the Deutz Motor Co. was founded which secured for itself the services of the gifted designer. His first achievement for them was a propelled vehicle with four cylinders with over-head camshaft and valves.

In the following year he won the the hill-climbing race at Gallion, in his new 1.5-litre engine, defeating "monsters" with engines of 15 litres!

In 1910 Bugatti rented a workshop at Molsheim in Alsace and began to produce on his own a "1400" called "Tipo 13" meant for racing. A the same time he prepared a very good commercial car which was immediately bought by Peugeot and produced in series under the name of "Bèbè".

Now started a period culminating with the outbreak of the First World War, when from the exuberant mind of Bugatti, came, little by little, marvellous mechanical characters, the stars of exciting races and successive victories, incredibly numerous (more than one thousand). From the "Tipo 35" to all the ones following, all originating from his first successful model. The history of these cars can be better followed elsewhere in The History of the Motor Car.

It will be enough to say here that the innumerable victories of the Bugattis, which the spectator could always recognise from the now famous "horse-shoe" radiator, were due to their exceptional stability and the extraordinary insight with which their engine had been planned: it had often unusual solutions (intake valves smaller than the exhaust valves, sparkplugs on the "cold side"

1913.

of the head) and pioneering details (Bugatti was the first to emphasise the utility of a super charger).

Meanwhile Bugatti imposed himself rapidly as the builder of splendid touring cars.

It is enough to remember the Royale — eight cylinders, 12,750 cc, $ 47,000, seven cars produced — and the famous and popular "Tipo 57".

As a conclusion of this brief portrait: Bugatti obtained all possible official recognitions. He was repeatedly invited to Italy to plan car and aeroplane engines for Diatto and Isotta Fraschini.

But personal tragedy overshadowed him and his success was in itself a kind of remorse.

His son Jean was killed testing one of his father's "Bolides".

Bugatti died in Paris in 1947 after a long illness.

1921.

1924.

1929 Bugatti. Below two Bugattis in the Boulogne four-hour race.
Chiron is in second place.

1929 Duesenberg "J" — an American high-quality car.

Bugatti supreme

The racing scene continued to provide plenty of excitement. Bugatti dominated the 1926 season when a 1½-
litre formula was in force. Most other manufacturers had
withdrawn rather than face the huge expense of re-design
involved in a change of formula. These Bugatti successes
culminated with wins at Monza (Sabipa-Charavel) and in
the French Grand Prix at Miramas with Jules Goux, and
served to create an atmosphere of fanatical support for
the cars among their many supporters. To be the owner
of a Bugatti at that time was indeed the pride of a
privileged few in Europe.

In 1927 the world championship, won the previous year
by Bugatti, went to Delage, who in the meantime had
developed the 1½-litre formula to the limit of its then
possibilities, extracting 170 B.H.P. with a supercharger
(in 1965, 1½-litre unsupercharged Formula I cars were
producing over 220 B.H.P.). The *marque* won the
French, Italian, Spanish and British Grands Prix.

For three year, from 1928, Grands Prix were run to a
"formule libre" with weight limits of 550 and 750
kilograms. As has occurred whenever the "formule
libre" has been in force, interest in Grand Prix racing
declined. In spite of this, many drivers later to become
famous, including Chiron, Nuvolari, Varzi, and Etancelin, participated.

Above a Fiat "520". Below the first B.M.W., built in 1928.

The faithful Type 35 Bugatti still won an impressive share of the laurels: among its victories were those of Williams at Comminges in 1928, and of Chiron at Monza the same year.

In 1929 — the year of the great U.S. slump which had effects all over the world, including European motoring — Britain led Europe in car production for the first time (235,000 vehicles in the year against 230,000 in France).

And 1931 saw the end of independent existence for two famous names, Bentley being absorbed by Rolls-Royce and Lanchester by Daimler. Some years earlier Vauxhall had been bought by General Motors.

Pierce-Arrow's big straight-eight of 1930 preceded the even more famous Twelve. Headlamps recessed into the wings were a styling feature still peculiar to this make.

The station wagon was born in America to meet the demand ot customers who needed a private goods/passenger vehicle. The value of such a car was appreciated much sooner in the U. S. than in Europe. Below, a 1958 Buick and above, the Citroën ID 19.

CHAPTER TWENTY TWO
THE LAST OF VINTAGE

At the depth of the Depression in America, there was an unexpected wave of super-cars. These included a 16-cylinder Cadillac, designed in secret by Charles Kettering in 1926 and launched in 1930; the 160 B.H.P. twelve-cylinder Auburn, the world's first V-12 to sell at less than $1,000; and 12-cylinder Pierce-Arrows and Lincolns. The last two had hydraulic tappets to ensure silence.

All these cars, however, remained one level below the fabulous Duesenberg "J", designed after the young industrialist Erret Lobban Cord had taken over leadership of the company. This car was the undoubted star of the American scene until it was supplanted by the even more striking supercharged 325 b.h.p. "SJ" in 1932, a car which cost Fred Duesenberg his life in an accident.

With regard to racing, 1930 was again dominated by Bugatti, even though Alfa Romeo re-entered the field with a redesign of the "P. 2" — modifications which mainly concerned the suspension and the body, which was now cut short to accommodate the spare wheel. Maserati, however, were making progress, having begun

345

The first Chrysler. Below the 1922 Nash model "46".

A 1922 6.6-litre Hispano-Suiza.

to build their own racing cars in 1926 after years of tuning and modifying Isotta Fraschinis. The French Grand Prix was won by Etancelin, with Sir Henry Birkin's sedate but potent Bentley four-seater tourer in second place. At Monza, however, Varzi was victorious in the new eight-cylinder two-litre Maserati.

In 1931 the monumental Mercedes "SSKL", the outcome of a number of successful predecessors, with its long bonnet and its chassis drilled for lightness, made its first impact in the German Grand Prix, driven by Caracciola. At Le Mans, however, the big German car was beaten by Howe's and Birkin's Alfa Romeo.

First Italian popular car

In France Citroën redesigned the "C 4" and the "C 6", improving the rubber mountings for the engines. In Italy an excellent light car made its appearance — The Fiat Tipo 508, or "Balilla", it enjoyed a huge sale, though the 508S, a sporting derivative, was made only in small numbers.

Launched as the first Italian popular car, the small three-speed "508" saloon and touring versions were shown at the Milan show in 1932. The cars had 995 c.c. engines and were capable of over 55 m.p.h. Fuel consumption was 30 to 34 m.p.g. A second version, introduced in 1934, had more curvaceous lines, a built-out boot, and a four-speed gearbox. The short-stroke engine made for long life, and the car's good reputation was inherited by its successor, the famous *Millecento,* introduced in 1937.

Equally famous was the little Fiat's contemporary, the Lancia "Augusta", a 1,194 c.c. saloon with the usual narrow-angle V4 engine. It had two American features redesigned for European use — a "free-wheel" which enabled the engine to idle while the car was running, and lubrication of the front suspension and steering joints by the engine oil.

Alongside their big cars, Hillman introduced the 1,185 c.c. four-cylinder "Minx", first of a line which has survived until the present day. Entirely different in concept was the M.G. (Morris Garages), a *marque* specialising in sports cars since 1924, when Cecil Kimber produced the first of this line. The first "Miget" was the M-type of 1929, but in the 1933 range were a new "Miget", the J2, and the even more important 1,100 c.c. six-cylinder K3 "Magnette"; which won its class in the 1933 Mille Miglia. Nuvolari also drove one to victory in that year's T.T.

In France Peugeot redesigned the "201" in 1932 and fitted independent front suspension, which was later applied to a new 1½-litre "301". Renault increased its vast range of cars with a relatively expensive straight-eight of some performance, the "Nervasport".

Citroën, having extensively modernised the Javel factory, had to forego the expense of designing new models and instead sought publicity by means of unusual endurance runs with Rosalie I, Rosalie II and Rosalie III ("Petite Rosalie"), which were based on the C 6 and the 8.

Also in France, Delahaye's engineering director, Weiffenbach, built the Superluxe, which he developed into the
"135" that was to become one of the finest sports cars
in the world, by fitting a six-cylinder engine into a new
chassis with independently sprung front wheels.

Across the Atlantic Ford was playing a series of commercial aces. First of all, in 1932, he launched a redesign
of the "A", called the "B". Two months later this car was
offered with an optional V8 engine with excellent characteristics — 65 b.h.p. at 3,400 r.p.m. giving 75 m.p.h.
in the saloon and over 80 in the roadster. Its success
was immediate.

Within a year the V8, which cost only $460 against
the $410 of the four-cylinder, had sold to the tune of
300,000 cars. Then Ford changed everything, replacing
the "B" and its V8 derivative with an improved and
modernised eight-cylinder car the Model-40. Nearly two
million were sold in three years.

The Birth of Ferrari

In 1933 the Scuderia Enzo Ferrari was born. The former
driver and mechanic took over the Alfa Romeo racing
cars, the company having officially withdrawn from racing. The "P 3", however, was not available to him and
he had to modify the old Monza, increasing capacity
to 2,650 c.c. and fitting a single-seater body in his well-
equipped workshop in Modena. Varzi scored the first
victory of the season at Monaco (this was the occasion
on which Nuvolari pushed his crippled car across the
finishing line) and then Campari won the French Grand
Prix at Montlhéry in the new 2.9-litre Maserati. After
this, Nuvolari left Ferrari and joined Maserati, taking
these cars to victory in race after race that season, apart
from the Ulster T.T. which he won in an M. G.

This caused Ferrari to press Alfa Romeo for the "P 3",
which he finally secured. With these cars — in the
hands of Fagioli and Campari — he won the races at
Pescara and Monza. Campari was killed the same day at
Monza in a subsequent race.

Revolutionary styling principles were applied a year
later to the first Italian true baby car, the Fiat "500"
which was known as "Topolino", or "little mouse", to
millions of Italians. This car was remarkable, apart from
its aerodynamic lines, for its solution to the problem
of making room for two people and their luggage in such
a little car. Among other features, the engine was
mounted over the front axle. The Topolino had a 570 c.c.
engine which produced 13 b.h.p. there was synchromesh
on third and top gears.

Shortly before the advent of the "500" H.T. Pigozzi
founded the Simca (Societé Industrielle de Mécanique
et Carrosserie Automobile) company in France to build
Fiats under licence, and the new model was produced
under the name of Simca-Cinq.

Among French cars of the time the Citroën 7 C.V. was
of considerable importance. This, with its successor, the
11 CV, was to have the longest production run of any

A 1932 Fiat "Balilla", which was for Italians what the Ford "T"
had been for Americans.

The 1933 FIAT "522 S" derived from the 1927 "520".

347

car, exceeding both the Rolls-Royce Silver Ghost and the Ford "T".

In 1934 Citroën was in a bad way financially, despite the publicity from the "Petite Rosalie" model in the previous year. Competition was keen and the company was short of money. It was clear that an outstanding new car was essential, but there was no capital available to design one. In a corner of the Javel factory was a prototype so unusual and so advanced, however, that the company had hesitated to launch it. The crisis, however, called for desperate measures. It was hastily put into production and launched as the 7 CV.

This was no ordinary car — the prototype even had automatic transmission — and was received enthusiastically, possibly even too enthusiastically considering its many teething troubles and defects. These were eliminated in later models of the 7 CV and in the 11 CV, which was derived directly from it. The models were popularly known by their main attribute, "Front Wheel Drive".

In 1934 it was courageous to launch a front-wheel drive car for mass sale and production, though the car had many advantages. The absence of a propeller shaft enabled the body to be lower and more spacious. The engine had overhead valves; the pistons and con-rods were of light alloy; and brakes were hydraulic. The whole car was light, under 2,000 lbs. The original 7 CV had a 1,302 c.c. engine, soon increased to 1,628 c.c.: from early 1935 there was also an 11 CV of 1,911 c.c. in short- and long- wheelbase forms.

The Citroën "11 CV" was produced in varying versions for nearly 20 years from the 1930s. It followed the famed Citroën "7 CV", which was the first car with front-wheel drive to go into mass production. The "7 CV" incorporated a vast range of other technical innovations. Above the Citroën B 14.

The American eight cylinder supercharged Auburn. 4,585 c.c. engine with three speeds, hydraulic brakes. Below the Napier Railton.

A single-seater 40 H.P. built by Renault specifically for performance records. In July, 1926, it broke the 24-hour record at Montlhéry by covering 2,587 miles at over 107 m.p.h. It had a nine-litre engine. Below a Chenard-Walcker at Le Mans in 1929.

The shadows of the political and economic crisis that was to lead the nations into the Second World War were already apparent when Rolls-Royce, abandoned the formula it had faithfully followed for almost 30 years and replaced the six-in-line engine of the Phantom II with the 12-cylindered one of the Phantom III. Legend says that the lettering of the radiator badge was changed from red to black as a sign of mourning for the death in 1933 of Sir Henry Royce.

At the 1936 London show, another splendid V 12, the Lagonda from the drawing-board of W. O. Bentley, made its debut.

In Italy, Fiat produced the Nuova Balilla or "508 C", which was a development of the original 508. This was, of course, the first of the famous Millecento line, a design which has survived to this day and is known

a 1933 1,496 cc. Frazer-Nash.

1933 Maserati 4 CM - 2000.

throughout the world. The new o.h.v. engine possessed performance, durability, and a modest thirst for fuel. The same model was made in France as the Simca "Huit", while Renault produced their Juvaquatre, inspired by the 1,100 c.c. Opel Kadett from Germany. Peugeot's new model was the aerodynamic "202", derived from the bigger "302" and "402" of 1936. Bugatti produced a number of variants of the "Type 57", the most powerful of which produced 260 b.h.p. Alfa Romeo introduced two new versions of the "6 C" series with 1,900 c.c. and 2,300 c.c. engines respectively. With Europe plunging into war, 1939 also saw another manufacturing boom in the American car industry.

The output figures themselves — over three million vehicles in a year — are impressive. But the most in-

teresting technical event was the introduction by Oldsmobile on a commercial scale of automatic transmission, the Hydramatic. Chrysler introduced the hydraulic clutch. Both were examples of development that were to influence American post-war manufacturing policies. From 1934 to 1937, the Grand Prix formula was based on a maximum weight of 750 kilograms, and in the absence of other restrictions outputs soared. The World Land Speed Record was raised to more than 350 m.p.h. by the out break of war.

In 1934 the most important races were again dominated by Italy, firstly with the Alfa Romeo "P 3", which Ferrari had enlarged to 2,900 c.c., and the "old" Maserati of the same capacity. Against these, the new 3,300 c.c. Bugatti "Type 59" had not enough speed. Already the Germans were returning to racing in strength, with Mercedes and the new Auto-Union, a company formed by the amalgamation of Audi, D.K.W., Horch, and Wanderer. These developments were due to the policy of Adolf Hitler. Ever eager to enhance Ger-

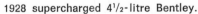

1928 supercharged 4¹/₂-litre Bentley.

The famous "P 3", a 1932 Alfa Romeo "Grand Prix" Type B. It had an eight-cylinder 2,654 c.c. engine with two superchargers.

many's prestige, he offered a huge prize to the German company that achieved the greatest number of victories in the next year's racing.

Grand Prix confusion

One outcome was the birth of Ferdinand Porsche's extraordinary "P-Wagen", a 4.4 litre V16 designed for Auto-Union with a 4,400 c.c. engine. On its first outing Stuck achieved 122 m.p.h. on the Avus circuit near Berlin. Varzi, Chiron, Guy Moll, von Stuck, Trossi (who

had once built his own front-wheel drive, radial-engined racing car) were the names most frequently heard in racing circles in 1934. The Alfa-Ferrari victories began at Monte Carlo with Moll, continued at Alessandria and Tripoli with Varzi and again with Moll at the Avus. Auto-Union made its first and unsuccessful debut there. After Von Brauchitsch's success at Barcelona, Alfa carried on with Chiron, Varzi and Trossi at Montlhéry. Only in the German Grand Prix did Auto-Union score a victory: Stuck was the driver on this occasion.

In the same year, 1934, Eyston and Denly in a Hotchkiss raised the 48-hour record to 153.470 k.p.h. at

1934 Auto-Union "P-Wagen" in the French G. P. of that year, one of its first appearances. Momberger is driving.

Montlhéry. Then it was put up by four Renault drivers in a "Nervasport" to 167.445 k.p.h., and again by the Delahaye team in a "135" six-cylinder to 177 k.p.h. (about 110 m.p.h.).

In Great Britain, Raymond Mays was meeting with great success: he was to become the leading driver for the new car, E.R.A. (English Racing Automobiles, financed by Humphrey Cook). So were Lord Howe, Malcolm Campbell, John Cobb, Kaye Don, George Eyston, Reg Parnell and Dick Seaman. Cobb won the Brooklands "500 miles" at 123 m.p.h. in a 23-litre Napier-Railton.

In 1935, German supremacy began to establish itself on the continent. Caracciola in a Mercedes won the Grands Prix of Monaco, Belgium, France and Spain while von Stuck in the Auto-Union won at Monza. Surprisingly, only at the Nürburgring in Germany did Alfa Romeo win, with Nuvolari.

1938 Type 328 B.M.W..

Montlhéry 1934. Achille Varzi at the wheel of a "P 3", follows Fagioli in a Mercedes. Below a 1935 Lagonda "Rapier".

For 1936, Alfa Romeo had prepared only two new engines, an eight-cylinder 38 litre and a 12-cylinder 4.4litre, while Mercedes had produced a completely new car, not fully developed due to the death of the designer Nibel. Auto-Union, like Mercedes, were achieving outputs around 500 b.h.p.; it was the beginning of a power race which culminated with Auto-Union reaching 650 b.h.p. in 1937.

The first race, at Monaco, was notable for a multi-car crash at the notorious chicane, involving Chiron, Farina, Trossi, Tadini and von Brauchitsch, in which no one was seriously hurt, and for spectacular spins by Rosemeyer and Fagioli. It ended in a victory for Caracciola in a Mercedes.

After Auto-Union had won at Nürburgring, where the young Rosemeyer earned himself the title of the "King of the Mists" for his command of the fog-cloaked circuit, they went on to a convincing win in the 1936

Trossi at the wheel of the car which he designed with Augusto Monaco. It had front-wheel drive and a radial engine.

1934 M.G. "Magnette" NE-type.

German Grand Prix in Berlin. Rosemeyer was again in first place and they had three other cars in the first six. Mercedes was thoroughly defeated.

Of the 12 Grands Prix, seven were won by Mercedes (four by Caracciola) and five by Auto-Union (four by the equally successful Rosemeyer). Ferrari disbanded his Alfa team and by 1940 had taken his first steps towards actual manufacture with the prototype "815" sports car.

The new 1938 Grand Prix formul was a confusing one. There was a relation between the rules governing capacity and weight, the latter regulations were different if a supercharger was fitted, and different capacity limits for blown or unblown cars. Mercedes and Auto-Union quickly took a lead with outputs around 400 b.h.p. This was due partly to their experiments with fuel, which was not restricted.

In addition to the eight-cylinder "308" prototype which produced 300 b.h.p., Alfa Romeo produced a 12-cylinder 320 b.h.p. and a 16-cylinder 350 b.h.p. Alongside these

1940 Alfa-Romeo 12 C 512 with a 12-cylinder 1,490 c.c. engine.

was evolved the 1½-litre "Alfetta" which was to dominate the early post-war Grands Prix. Maserati had a 32-valve, eight-cylinder supercharged model, which was to have great success at Indianapolis between 1939 and 1950.

The season began with the sensational defeat of Caracciola at Pau by Dreyfus in a Delahaye, and "maestro" Nuvolari was in a spectacular accident with his car in pieces and flames. But then again the familiar series of German victories began. Von Brauchitsch won the Grand Prix de Rheims, Seaman won at Nürburgring in a Mercedes and Auto-Union, with Nuvolari, won at Monza. In the meantime, Rosemeyer had been killed racing against Caracciola while trying to set up pure speed records for 3-litre cars on the Frankfurt-Darmstadt autobahn; Caracciola reached nearly 270 m.p.h.

The handsome Talbot "105" of 1934.

The famous E.R.A.s Remus and Romulus, in 1935 Romulus was bought by Prince Chula of Siam, who gave it to his cousin Prince Bira, a keen motorist. In Romulus, the latter won the 1936 Prince Rainier's Cup and the J.C.C. International Trophy.

1931 Eight cylinder Bugatti "Royale".

For the last season's racing before the war began, the Germans were again ready with new cars. Outputs were of 483 b.h.p. at 7,800 r.p.m. for the Mercedes (which used petrol for engine cooling as well, thus giving rise to a consumption of 2½ miles per gallon) and 485 b.h.p. for the "183" Auto-Union.

These outputs were achieved by the use of new two-stage compressors. Maserati were not far behind however with 450 b.h.p. Of the more important races, which were won once again by the Germans, the most exciting was at Rheims in the French Grand Prix where, against all expectations, the whole Mercedes team retired one by one with mechanical breakdowns after Lang had smashed the record in practice. Müller won in an Auto-Union after Nuvolari had led for most of the race.

The 1936 Mercedes 540 K Cabriolet and below the 1936 Simca-Cinq.

The only venues now possible for high-speed record work were deserts such as Bonneville Salt Flats in Utah and at Salt Lake City, the only place where the huge cars could run; Daytona and Pendine were abandoned. In 1935 Cobb, in his huge Napier-Railton, put up the 24-hour record to an average of 135 m.p.h. at Bonneville. Then Gulotta beat Cobb's average by a small margin in a Duesenberg only for Eyston, Denly and Staniland (in the Rolls-Royce aero-engined "Speed of the Wind") to put the record up to 141 m.p.h. It was to be five years later, in 1940 when the rest of the world was too busy to care, before Jenkins could raise the 24-hour record to 162 m.p.h. in his Mormon Meteor III; this was based on the Duesenberg but had a 750 H.P. Curtiss aero-engine. Jenkins went on to average almost 150 m.p.h. for 48 hours.

In 1938, Cobb returned to Bonneville in his Railton to set up the world's land speed record at 350 m.p.h., a speed that seemed fantastic but which was immediately beaten by Eyston in his 3,000 H.P. Thunderbolt at 357 m.p.h. The last word before the war, however, went to Cobb in 1939 with 369 m.p.h.

1936 S.S. Jaguar "100". The car could be supplied with a 2½ - or a 3½ - litre engine; the latter developing 125 B.H.P.

1947 Cisitalia Coupé Pininfarina. Examples of this Pininfarina masterpiece are preserved in the New York Museum of Modern Art and in the Turin Motor Museum.

WORLD STYLIST

The role of the Italian coachbuilder, stylist and industrial designer in the development of the motor car has become particularly important, especially after the Second World War when they moved from a craftsman-type organisation to series production. G. B. Pininfarina is universally recognised as leader of this "Italian School" of body design in both its aesthetic and technical aspects.

After a period of fruitful experience working with his elder brother Giovanni, the owner of the Farina factory,

in 1930 Pinin set up his own company and thus created a new school of body design bearing the marks of his own personality, artistic sense and ideals.

A broad glance over his designs reveals at once some of the most significant, such as the 1932 Lancia Astura saloon with the sleekness of a whippet; the fixed head coupé (one of Pinin's favourite themes) on the 1937 Aprilia chassis in which his surprising intuition produced aerodynamic lines years ahead of their time; and the open Alfa Romeo 2900 of 1939, judged to be the

Ferrari 512/S "Berlinetta Speciale", 1969.

Lancia Florida II Coupé, 1955.

G. B. Pininfarina between his son Sergio and his son-in-law Renzo Carli.

Alfa Romeo 3500 Super Sport, 1959.

Ferrari 275 GTB.

Ferrari 365/P "Berlinetta Speciale", 1966. A three seater with central driving position built expressly for Gianni Agnelli, President of Fiat.

finest expression of pure beauty in its day. Then, after the war, came that which is recognised as the initiator of a completely new style of body design — the Cisitalia coupé, which is preserved in the Museum of Modern Art in New York as "one of the eight most important cars in the world". It was from this 1947 Pininfarina design that the "new look" in body styling originated. Now famous throughout the world, the great Turin designer began to collaborate with major motor car manufacturers, designing the 1952 Nash-Healey, the Lancia Aurelia of the following year, the Peugeot 403 saloon (and subsequently all models, normal production or special, of that company), the Alfa Romeo Giulietta and Fiat 1200 sports, all Ferraris from 1952 onwards and various models of the British Motor Corporation. This activity of designing for large-scale production did not prevent the Pininfarina studios from continuing their interest in special models, many of which have become classics in the story of coachbuilding. Among these figure the PF 200 and the Florida (on Lancia Aurelia chassis), the Fiat-Abarth record breaker, the Alfa Romeo Super Flow, the Cadillac Eldorado coupé, the Ferrari Super Fast and the Fiat 2,300 Lausanne. It is a long list which has occupied Motor Show reports for over fifteen years.

During this period the "Carrozzeria Pininfarina" has grown to large-scale proportions. By 1956 the original factory in Corso Trapani in Turin had become too small and in that year the company moved to a modern factory in Grugliasco on the edge of the city (covering an area of over a million square feet with over 1,500 employees and an output of 150 units per day) to which later was added the Design and Research Centre, the heart of the factory. At the same time Pininfarina performed an act of wisdom and confidence — he gave over the running of the company to his son Sergio and his son-in-law Renzo Carli. While he maintained a close interest in the firm, most of his time he devoted unostentatiously to charitable works.

Forty years of design

G. B. Pininfarina died on the 3rd April 1966. He had had time to design the PF Sigma (a safety car which has been exhibited and studied in research institutes throughout the world and by, the United States Senate, and which is now in the Transport Museum at Lucerne, and which is referred to also elsew here in this History) and the first Dino "Berlinetta" shown at the 1965 Turin Motor Show. His spirit has been perpetuated however. Since his death magnificent designs continue to issue from the Carrozzeria Pininfarina — production coupés and sports cars, special designs, competition prototypes and study projects, built on the finest European chassis such as the Fiat Dino sports, the Fiat 124 sport, the Ferrari 365 3-seater coupé, the Alfa Romeo 33, the Lancia Flavia coupé, the Ferrari 512S coupé, more Peugeots, Austin-Morris and the Sigma Grand Prix, a major study in safety in Formula I design.

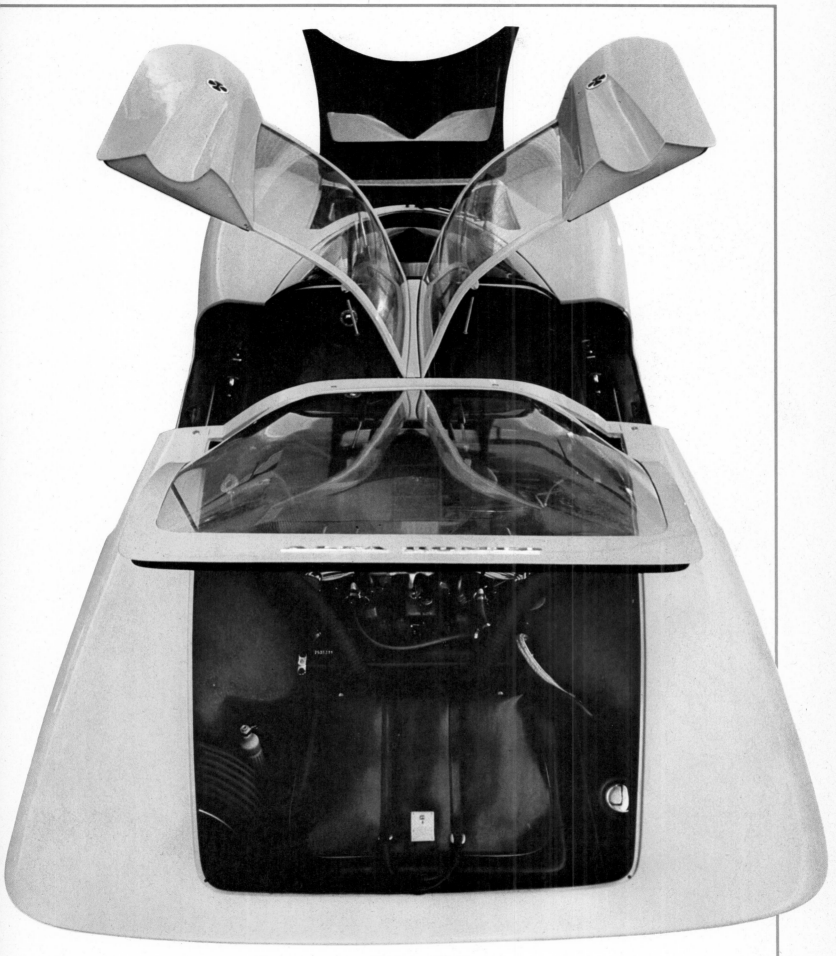

Pininfarina Alfa 33

The tracked Snowcat used by Sir Vivian Fuchs in his 1957 Trans-Antarctic Expedition is powered by a 5,300 c.c. Chrysler V8 engine. Below is a Renault "special purpose" vehicle of the 1920s.

CHAPTER TWENTY THREE
THE POST-WAR BOOM

The nearer our story gets to the present day, the more it becomes news and the less history, and the more difficult it becomes to decide whether a new development represents a fundamental change of direction or is just an interesting blind alley. The development work being done on means of propulsion for ordinary road vehicles is an example — will electric motors, turbo-jet propulsion, or rotary piston engines replace, wholly or in substantial part, the conventional i.c. engine.

We have therefore limited our account of post-war motor car development to those items which give a brief overall picture of trends in design and manufacture.

The story of European car manufacturing in the early post-war years is one of painful effort and fierce battles to get back on its feet in one way or another. In France, Ford at Poissy, Peugeot at Sochaux, Bugatti in Molsheim were either destroyed or badly damaged. But Simca was almost intact, while at Citroën only the records had been destroyed. Renault was struck by a second shock — nationalisation, following accusations of war-time collaboration against its head, Louis Renault, who had died in mysterious circumstances a little earlier in prison at Fresnes.

Somewhat less serious was the position of the British manufacturers, despite damage from bombing and "V" weapons, but with plant and machinery worn out. War had seriously damaged the Italian industry with the Fiat factory at Lingotto almost destroyed. Fiat there-

fore began the construction of a new factory at Mirafiore. Lancia and Alfa Romeo began to recover.

In Germany tremendous efforts were made to put factories back into working order. The job was particularly difficult for Daimler-Benz in Stuttgart and Opel in Rüsselheim, but less so for Ford in Cologne and Volks-

wagen in Wolfsburg, where fairly quickly the large-scale production was begun of the "people's car" which Hitler had promised so many years before. Things were different for B.M.W. in Eisenach and Auto-Union in Zwickau under Soviet occupation; these were to appear again later with new names and products.

In the U.S. the changeover from war to peace was rapid, and there was an increase in the number of cars on the roads from 24 million in 1945 to 61 million in 1955. Huge sums were spent on renewing plant and equipment, though the 1946 models produced were for the most part similar to those of 1942.

Returning to Europe, among the more interesting early post-war cars was the Renault 4 CV with a rear engine, the first product of the newly formed "Regie Nationale". This car, based on a design produced in secret during the war, had an engine of only 760 c.c., but was spacious and manoeuvrable.

At the same time, all over Europe, bubble cars and mini-cars made a brief appearance; these included the British Bond, Italian Isetta and German Heinkel. In Italy the

tremendous boom in scooters started some time later. The first post-war motor shows were held in 1946 and reflected the manufacturing position — most models were of pre-war design but a number of interesting prototypes were on show, even though they were not in production.

The indications of revival seen in 1946 began to be justified the following year, when the first post-war Geneva Show took place and the new Austins were outstanding among British cars. In the motor shows of 1947 there were numerous new prototypes but most production models were outdated.

Among these where a Bugatti 73C 1½-litre tourer, and Isotta Fraschini's last fling, the "Monterosa", with an eight-cylinder 3.4-litre rear-mounted V8 engine and hydraulic gearchange, neiter of which actually went into production.

A few months later Peugeot launched the 1.3-litre "203" which was a great commercial success with its inclined o.h.v.s. and high engine speed of 5,000 r.p.m. In 1948 the most important of American technical

The Alfa-Romeo 1952 1,997 c.c. "Disco Volante" (Flying Saucer). Above a 1947 Kaiser "Special".

Renault "Juvaquatre" with 1,003 c.c. four-cylinder engine. The first monocoque Renault. Below a 1948 Cadillac.

development was the spread of automatic transmission. General Motors's Hydramatic, already fitted to Cadillac and Oldsmobile, was joined by Buick's two-speed Dynaflow system, and (in 1950) by Powerglide, available on the group's cheapest car, the Chevrolet.

Chrysler's first fully automatic gearbox, the Powerflite, did not appear until 1953, while Ford had to build a new factory to supply automatics for his cars. The result was a massive switch by the American public to two-pedal motoring.

But not only in America was 1948 a year of innovation. In Europe new cars were introduced which were to play an important role in ensuing years.

In England a division soon became apparent due to the specialisation by some manufacturers in small and medium cars and others in G.T. models. In the former

category was the Morris Minor, redesigned by Alec Issigonis (future apostle of the transverse engine and Hydrolastic suspension), and the new Hillman Minx in scaled down U.S.-style, produced by Rootes Group. To the sporting category was added the first post-war Jaguar, the extremely fast (120 m.p.h.) "XK 120".

In Germany Heinz Nordhoff, an ex-manager of Opel, became head of Volkswagen and, aided by the Allied occupation authorities, began the mass-production of the famous "beetle" that was to make the company the largest manufacturer in Europe within six years. The four-cylinder Borgward Hansa was born at this time from the first entirely new German company to be formed after the war.

The most sensational novelty from the technical point of view in the year was the introduction of the new

1948 Panhard "Dynavia".

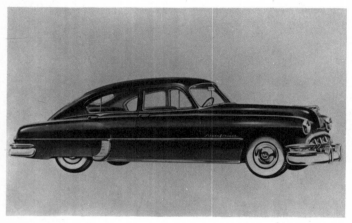

1950 Pontiac.

1953 Vauxhall Velox.

1956 Sunbeam "Mk III".

Taruffi's twin bodied, record breaking car.

version of the Panhard "Dyna 3CV" and the long-awaited economy Citroën "2CV". After the shock of its unusual appearance, the latter soon became popular on account of its remarkable robustness, spaciousness, excellent suspension, and the way its 375 c.c. engine would slog along all day. Its 2CV prototypes had been under test in 1938 and 1939.

In Italy the larger companies were not producing anything of great interest, but the fame of her coachbuilders was spreading throughout the world; among these masters of craftsmanship and design were Allemano, Bertone, Boneschi, Canta, Colli, Elena, Fissore, Ghia, Pininfarina, Savio, Scioneri, Superleggera-Touring, Vignale and Viotti. Italian stylists carried their influence outside their own country. Pininfarina's shape was adopted by B.M.C. in England, Michelotti served as a consultant to Standard-Triumph, and even some American cars reflected Italian influence.

In the racing field, nearly all the big pre-war races were back in the calendar by 1948, though the French Grand Prix had been held the previous year on a new circuit near Lyons; it was won by Chiron in a Talbot. The Italian Grand Prix at Monza in 1947 and the European Grand Prix at Spa were won by the "Alfettas" of Trossi and Wimille respectively.

The year 1948 was a period of considerable technical development, of rivalry between manufacturers and countries and also between the supporters of blown and unblown engines.

In the 1948 races, again dominated by the 1,500 c.c. "Alfetta", the name of the French driver Wimille stands out as the winner at Rheims and Monza, while his team-mate, Trossi, won at Berne in the European Grand Prix. Varzi was tragically killed in this race. At the same time the two-litre "166" Ferrari was beginning to make an impression.

Jaguar was upholding British prestige with new models and excellent racing results, as were Healey, Allard, M. G. and Bristol. One of Jaguar's triumphs, and one which boosted both production and sales, was the Mk VII saloon of 1951, using the XK 120 engine, which succeeded the attractive Mk V. Already, in 1949, Jaguar

Classically red — the 1951 Ferrari Formula 1 "G. P." and the Maserati 250 F of 1954. Both cars are in the Turin Motor Museum.

had made history by covering the sports car flying mile at 132.6 m.p.h. in Belgium with the XK 120.

The success of the new high-compression vee-eights from General Motors was followed by some advanced hemispherical-head designs from Chrysler incorporating hydraulic valve lifters. Studebaker also introduced a new vee-eight.

In 1949 Volkswagen reached its quota of production and was planning the improvements to be introduced to their "beetle" from 1951 onwards. The reconstituted Auto Union concern started production in West Germany at Ingolstadt, reviving the pre-war D.K.W. design with a transversely mounted, vertical-twin, two-stroke engine and front-wheel drive. Light two-stroke cars were also made by the Borgward owned Lloyd and Goliath works.

In Sweden, Svenska Aeroplan A.B. introduced the Saab 92, and the Volvo "444" was launched. In the U.S.S.R., parallel with the large scale production of heavy vehicles, four touring cars were introduced, the Moskvitch, inspired by the Opel "Kadett"; the Pobieda, a medium-sized saloon; the "Zim" six-cylinder inspired by Dodge, and the eight-cylinder "Zis 110" derived from the Packard. The 1949 racing year was dominated by the new Ferraris, after Alfa-Romeo had withdrawn their "Alfetta" as the deaths of Varzi, Wimille and Trossi in 1948 had robbed them of their drivers. Ferrari built three

A 1954 Austin A 30 2 door. Below the 1954 Jaguar D type.

kinds of cars — a 1,500 c.c. supercharged racing car for Formula I, an unblown two-litre for Formula II and another model for sports car racing. With these he gained many victories, including the first post-war Le Mans 24-hour race in 1949. Gordini also had some successes, as did a young Argentinian driver called Juan Manuel Fangio.

Production peak

The middle year of the century was also the year of a production record. World production in 1950 totalled 10,017,000 vehicles, a figure which was not to be reached again until 1955. The figures for the major producing countries were U.S. 8,003,000; Great Britain 783,000; Canada 390,000; France 357,000; Germany 306,000; Italy 127,000.

In the technical field, short-stroke or "square" engines were more common and petrol injection was introduced by some German companies on competition models. On 9 March the first real gas-turbine engined car made its debut on the track at Silverstone: the Coventry-built Rover "Jet 1" which reached over 85 m.p.h. The chassis was that of a standard "75" into which was built a 200 B.H.P. jet engine. Two years afterwards the car was developed to do more than 150 m.p.h.

1952 B.R.M.

Juan Manuel Fangio in a Ferrari in the 1950 Monza G.P. Below, in the same race, Farina and Fangio at the famous Lesmo curve.

1951 Fiat 1,400 with Siata body. Below two 1959 Austin-Healey 3000s.

The motor racing world saw the birth of a new Formula I car in 1950, this time in Great Britain. This was the B.R.M. (British Racing Motors) for which 160 British manufacturers agreed to co-operate to enable a Grand Prix car to be built which was capable of winning major races.

The initiative was due to Raymond Mays and Peter Berthon, designer of the old E.R.A. They produced an outstanding V 16-cylinder machine which had some success in the hands of Fangio, Parnell, Gonzales and Wharton. Indeed, the B.R.M. was developed to be the most powerful 1½-litre ever built, but it could not be called a truly successful car for a number of reasons.

The two most important were probably its intricacy, which made it unreliable, and its flat power curve. These disadvantages were being eliminated when the formula was changed. In 1953 B.R.M. was taken over by A.G.B. Owen of the Rubery Owen group and by the 1960s the B.R.M. was a very successful car indeed.

Vast scale investments

The next few years were a period of increasing automation and rationalisation in industry, and of the development of ancillary manufactures. All this required

1967 Volkswagen "Beetle". The shape is substantially that of Ferdinand Porsche's first design. Below the 1967 Fiat "124 Coupé".

investment on a vast scale, and inevitably the small manufacturers, who could not afford the increased tooling costs, were doomed to absorption or extinction. In some countries these concerns disappeared altogether. Meanwhile the world's motor-vehicle population increased by leaps and bounds: from just under 34 million immediately after the war to more than double this amount in 1951, and to a formidable 102,655,000 by 1956.

In 1952, the Morris and Austin companies combined to form the British Motor Corporation (B.M.C.) The first consequence of the amalgamation was the use of the 803 c.c. o.h.v. Austin A30 engine in the well established Morris Minor. Vauxhall launched the four-cylinder "Wyvern" and the six-cylinder "Velox" at moderate prices, while Ford of Dagenham continued with their existing range of cars.

European innovations

Ford launched the "Thunderbird" and Chrysler called in an Italian stylist. Three amalgamations took place in the United States — Kaiser with Willys, Nash with Hudson (to give rise to American Motors) and Studebaker with Packard.

Studded tyres improved the notable road-holding of this Citroën DS, seen on an icy road in the Monte Carlo Rally.

The Citröen Ami 6 and the 1962 Studebaker "Avanti".

In 1954 Citroën fitted hydro-pneumatic rear suspension on their 15 CVs which was to be more fully developed on the "D.S. 19". In the same year the French Ford company was taken over by Simca, and their eight-cylinder Vedette was continued under the Simca name. The next year Fiat built a gas turbine car which was capable of 150 m.p.h. In Germany Mercedes launched the "180 D", a version of their first post-war diesel-engined private car, the "170 D", but of more modern appearance and also the prestige sports cars, the 190 SL and the 300 SL. Many European manufacturers began to offer automatic transmission on some models.

Electronics take a part

Technical progress on the motor car has reached the stage in recent years that mere creation and even commercial success are not enough to pass into history. In a record of the motor car it is necessary to single out those which have in themselves contributed something to progress. In the case of present production, or most of it, judgment becomes a matter of individual taste. The greatest progress has been made not, as in previous years, in the adoption of new principles or previously unknown devices, but in the development of new production techniques and the use of new materials. So far as

The 1950 Studebaker "Commander" convertible

the former is concerned, the use of "transfer" machines, and automatic lathes (capable of performing a number of operations on thousands of components) and electronic devices for measuring tool wear and adjusting for it without human intervention, have led to greater engine silence, durability and strength. But such qualities were also present, it must be remembered, in the hand-built Silver Ghost of 60 years ago, though at greater relative cost. Better raw materials have contributed to the same result.

Such advances have also permitted the use of much lighter components, thus improving performance in relation to power. Specific horsepower (output per litre of engine capacity) has also increased notably, with the use of new materials allowing much higher compression ratios, and the speed and acceleration of modern cars have increased greatly in the last few years.

Particular items of progress have been the increasing use of overhead camshafts driven by toothed plastic belts.

The Ghia-Bodied Fiat N 500 "runabout" and below the Abarth 750 sports — a small car with G. T. performance.

The plastic era

Sodium-filled valves have been developed, and give a much better thermal performance. Dual-choke and multiple carburettors are increasingly common as is the use of petrol injection.

Greasing points have been reduced to a minimum by grouping, or by the use of "sealed for life" joints. Routine maintenance has been much reduced.

Basic components of the car have been improved. Iodine vapour lamps and asymmetric beams have made night driving easier. The use of toughened glass — safer than tempered — has increased safety. Radial-ply and tubeless tyres, with or without special treads, have also brought about improvements in the fields of safety and efficiency as has the widespread use of disc brakes.

Plastics are now used by the motor car industry on a large scale.

The Simca 1000 GLS, off the beaten track but with a welcome passenger. Below the ASA 1000 G.T. in the 59th Targa Florio.

One of the characteristics of the present day is the range of types and models offered by the large scale manufacturers. This has been made possible, while still preserving most of the economic advantages of a small range of models, by using similar production operations such as machining in different multiples. The manufacture of six-cylinder engines consists in effect of one-and-a-half four-cylinder units.

This is a particular aspect of a much more important tendency towards amalgamation going on, especially in Europe, as a necessity for survival in the face of the tremendous productive and economic power of the American giants. The alternative is elimination as has occurred with Studebaker-Packard in America. Among the more important of these amalgamations have been British Leyland in Great Britain (which has united the makes of B.M.H., Morris, Austin, Wolseley, Riley, M.G. Austin-Healey, Jaguar etc., with Standard, Triumph, Rover, Daimler etc.) Citroën and Panhard in France and Auto-Union and Volkswagen in Germany.

In Great Britain Rolls-Royce and Bentley continue to produce vehicles of great luxury and refinement and Jaguar unfailingly astonish the world with a series of luxurious saloons and high performance cars at prices which are remarkably low.

A whole series of medium-sized durable and attractive saloons are produced by the various members of British Leyland, which also produces two remarkable 2-litre

cars, the Triumph and the Rover, the latter being outstanding for its high quality, modern appearance and interesting performance. The most outstanding product of this group and of the British motor industry in recent years has been the amazing Mini-Minor, child of Alec Issigonis's fertile brain.

Abowe a Oldsmobile 442 hardtop. Below a 1967 Hillman Super Minx.

SAAB "96" 3 cylinder 2-stroke, 841 c.c. Top speed 80 m.p.h.

1961 Volga. 4 cylinder 2,445 c.c., 75 b.h.p. at 4,000 r.p.m.

In this same period the Rootes Group has been absorbed by Chrysler and has thus become the third large British motor company to become American owned, the others being Ford and Vauxhall, a subsidiary of General Motors. On the other side of the Atlantic the divergence with Europe has remained, with the emphasis on large capacity, low stressed engines in large bodies, which are often heavy-looking and finished with much chrome. The brief firtation with "compact" cars, intended as an economic measure to reduce European imports, is now almost a thing of the past.

Japanese invasion

In this period a third large industry has been developing in Japan with the rapid expansion of the "old" companies and the creation of new ones. Daihatsu, Hino, Honda, Isuzu, Mazda, Mitsubishi, Nissan, Suzuki and

Two versions of the Isuzu Bellett.

The Autobianchi "Primula".

Toyota are the names of the more important Japanese companies which are beginning to invade overseas markets.

Here are the tangible results of a never-ending quest for greater efficiency. The inventiveness and ingenuity of the designer, the skill of the production engineer, the craftsmanship of the factory, and the expertise and courage of racing drivers on the circuits have all contributed to the reliability, comfort, and ease of operation of the millions of cars in service on our roads to-day.

The motor car has come of age. In a man's lifetime, it has grown up from the perilous plaything of eccentrics to a comfortable means of transportation and one that has become an integral part of our civilisation.

One of the most exciting sports cars of the world: the Fiat Dino Coupé.

THE ROLLS-ROYCE
SILVER SHADOW

Introduced in 1965, the Silver Shadow has advanced technical specifications. Powered by an eight-cylinder 6,230 cc engine made almost entirely of aluminium with spun cast cylinder liners. Three separate hydraulic braking systems operate disc brakes on all four wheels, which have independent suspension. Automatic hydraulic leveling ensures constant riding height whatever the load. The transmission is by three-speed torque convertor fully automatic gearbox.

Incorporated in the suspension geometry is anti-drive characteristics on the front and anti-lift at the rear. There is also a "g" sensitive value in the brakes to reduce premature locking of the rear wheels. The interior is upholstered in top grain English hide and all-wool carpet covers the floor. The two front seats are electrically adjustable for height, tilt and backwards and forward movement. The windows are also operated by electricity, as are the selection of gears.

The Silver Shadow fully complies with all the worldwide safety and exhaust emission laws, and combines this with all the traditional qualities always associated with Rolls-Royce: comfort, silence, performance and reliability.

Over 50% go abroad

Current production is running at about 2,000 cars a year ($15\frac{1}{2}$% Bentleys, $84\frac{1}{2}$% R-R) and rising. Of these, more than half are exported, the bulk of them going to America. Switzerland, France and Australia are also good customers. About 84% of total production are standard Silver Shadows, the remainder Mulliner Park Ward coachbuilt cars of which, on average, nearly one a week is a Phantom VI. R-R reckon that about 83% of the cars sold in Britain are used for business purposes, 85% are owner/executive driven, and that the average age of ownership is falling. Two out of three customers have owned a Rolls-Royce before.   *

IN 1980 THE OTHERS MAY CATCH UP

The first Wankel Rotary Combustion (RC) engine coughed into life at NSU in Neckarsulm in 1957. Barely seven years later the first series production small car, the NSU Spider, powered by a single-rotor RC engine came off the production line. The twin-rotor Wankel RC engine and the NSU Ro80 car, weighing nearly a ton and a quarter, appeared three years later.

Meanwhile, Curtiss-Wright, in the U.S.A., produced various twin-rotor automotive Wankel RC engines, developing 185 bhp, without being able to secure a firm footing in the automotive field. Toyo Kogyo, one of the Japanese licensees, developed numerous single, twin, three and four-rotor Wankel RC engines for research purposes, but they caused the greatest stir in 1967 with their Mazda Cosmo sports car, followed by the R100 coupe which went into production in 1969.

Also in 1969, Mercedes-Benz publicised their experimental C111 sports coupe with a three-rotor Wankel RC engine which relies on fuel injection and develops 280 bhp (DIN) at 7000 rev/min., while making it clear that they did not intend to take this car into series production.

It is no coincidence that the cars actually in production are fitted with twin-rotor RC engines. Why? The engineers' answer is that they regard the twin-rotor concept as almost ideal in its simplicity of construction and it is particularly suitable for high volume production.

Doubling-up, so to speak, on the Spider engine design by both German and Japanese engineers has resulted in two engines which closely approximate to each other in size, low weight and power - bulk and weight about half that of a reciprocating engine of equivalent power; and power round about 130 bhp from a combustion chamber volume of only 1000 cc. One of the hardest things to define is the classification of an RC engine, but FIA, the authority which controls international

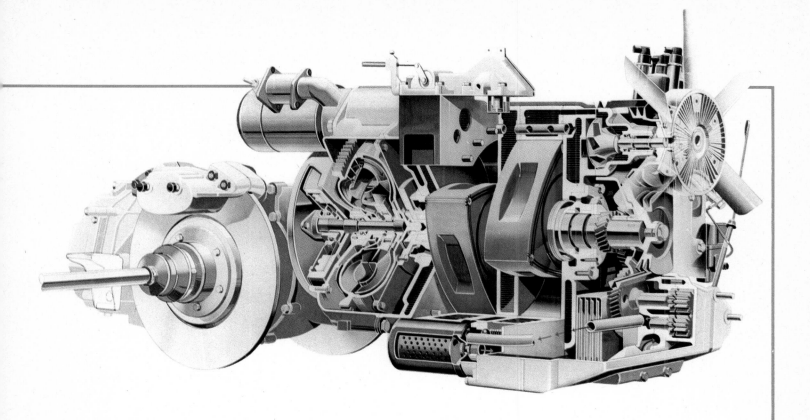

motor sport, has agreed that it is logical to classify it as twice the swept volume of a single chamber multiplied by the number of rotors - which makes both German and Japanese twin-rotor engines broadly equivalent to two-litre reciprocating piston engines.

The Wankel RC engine is not only compact, light and powerful. It is also comparatively cheap to produce; it is estimated that production costs amount to about 65 per cent of those of a six-cylinder and 90 per cent of those of a four-cylinder reciprocating piston engine developing the same power.

Moreover the twin-rotor engine is easy and simple to maintain, especially since the engine of the Ro80 requires no oil changes, only periodic topping up (not forgetting cleaning and/or replacing the filter elements of the oil filter and of the air cleaner-silencer). All the Wankel RC engines produced to date are sandwich-type constructions, the twin-rotor units requiring only two main bearings, and incorporating, therefore, rather short and rigid main shafts.

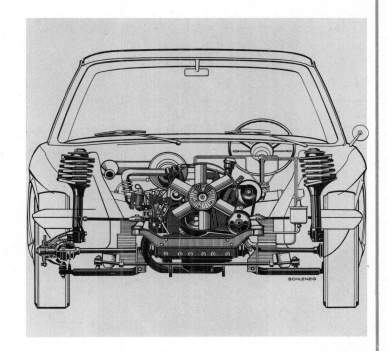

Comparing the performance

But the most significant advantage of the twin-rotor Wankel RC engine to the engineer, as well as to the driver, lies in the low vibration levels, which seem to diminish as engine speed rises. These are due to the low torque fluctuations and the absence of reciprocating masses. The importance of these torque characteristics was brought out in a recent study by a British consultant automotive engineer, Richard Ansdale, comparing the performance of the NSU Ro80 engine with those of two other powerful German cars - the BMW 2000 TI and the Mercedes 250 SE. Of particular significance was his comparison of shaft speed at which maximum torque is developed as a percentage of the speed at which maximum power is developed. This showed:

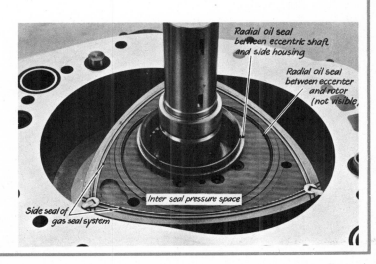

Radial oil seal between eccentric shaft and side housing

Radial oil seal between eccenter and rotor (not visible)

Inter seal pressure space

Side seal of gas seal system

Car	Percentage of speed	Percentage of Max. Torque at 1000 rev/min
NSU Ro80	82	87
BMW 2000 TI	62.1	55
Mercedes 250 SE	72.8	74.9

These figures indicate that over the current speed ranges Wankel RC engine performance characteristics may be tailored to suit the particular application (within limits) in the same way as the characteristics of the reciprocating piston engine are made to suit their applications. Most important of all, research into further development of the reciprocating piston engine yields diminishing results at increasing cost, whereas the Wankel RC engine, though already competitive with the conventional piston

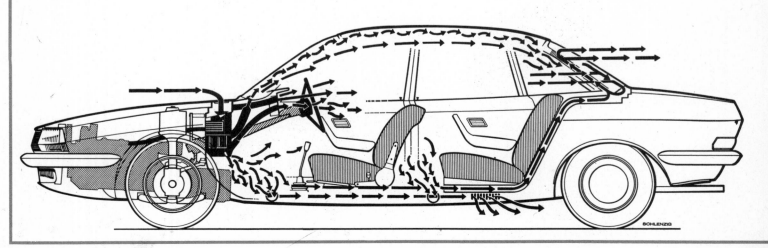

engine, is at the beginning of its performance potential. With any new engine (as with pharmaceutical products) allowances have to be made for unexpected side effects. The most persistent early problems of the Wankel RC engine were the chatter marks on the epitrochoidal bore, which were overcome by matching the apex seal materials to the bore material and finish. The current bore deposits of nickel and silicon carbide, with IKA (a particular piston ring cast iron) apex seals, ensure a satisfactory life for the NSU Wankel engine. The Mazda answer is equally satisfactory with a hard chromes bore and special carbon type apex seals; other combinations are being used and will continue to be developed.

The exhaust emissions of a Wankel RC engine were thought to present a very difficult problem, mostly by engineers unfamiliar with the combustion peculiarities of this type of engine. Their beliefs were disproved during the summer and autumn of 1969 when both the Ro80 and the R100 coupe passed the full 4,000 mile primary and 50,000 mile secondary emission tests in the U.S.A. as prescribed by Federal regulations for 1970. It should be emphasised that these results were achieved whit the same type of air pumps and emission control systems as are applied to the conventional piston engine. Research in progress in Britain and elsewhere is expected to reduce the exhaust emissions of Wankel RC engines to the stipulated levels without a lot of the paraphernalia now required for both reciprocating piston and Wankel RC engines.

These notable advantages assure a long life and increasing number of applications for the twin rotor Wankel RC engine. *

THE MOST ADVENTUROUS VEHICLE

The Gypsies, or more accurately the Romanies, landed in Britain in the 15th century; they were of low caste Indian origin and by tradition musicians and rug makers.

A typical Romany caravan is a one-roomed house on rather high wheels, with windows at the back and sides, and a door and detachable steps at the front. There is a rack (known as the cratch) at the back for carrying domestic articles of various kinds; and underneath the wagon at the back there is a cupboard (known as the pan box) which serves both as larder and as kitchen compartment.

The whole of the back par is occupied by a two berth sleeping space beneath which is a compartment with doors, and in this the children sleep. The lantern roof has coloured glazing and the windows have shutters and lace curtains.

The Gypsies expressed their individuality by painting their wagons in extremely distinctive colours and embellishing them with much wood carving.

A typical Searle Carawagon is a mobile lounge with four wheel drive, panoramic visibility from the ten toughened windows, and folding steps to each of the three doors. There is a rack at the front for carrying bulky luggage and underneath the wagon at the back are cylinders of gas for operating the cooker with grill and refrigerator.

Inside the wagon along the nearside is a storage unit incorporating a wardrobe, pumped water supply, folding table and storage for linen and personal belong-

ings. On the other side is a locker seat for three which pulls out to form a double bed for adults.

The elevating roof has long windows in stove enamel duraluminium panels beneath which children sleep in twin hamock bunks. The windows may have roller blinds and detachable flyscreens.

Just as the gypsy caravan with its huge wheels "four leg drive" was capable of travelling a long way from the beaten track, the Searle Carawagon with its four wheel drive and 8 speed gear box is capable of taking the adventurous owner anywhere from the local shops to the furthest corner of the African continent.   *

ALPHABETICAL
INDEX
OF NAMES AND ILLUSTRATIONS

THE NUMBERS IN BOLD TYPE REFER TO THE PAGES IN WHICH ILLUSTRATIONS APPEAR

ERRATA

The publishers apologise for the following printers' errors.

Page 57: Line 5, read Chenard-Walcker not Walker.

Page 101: Line 12, read Winton, not Wenton.

Page 143: Line 6, read Porter, not Poter.

Page 157: Title, read Johnston, not Jonston.

Page 264: caption should read 7,428 c.c. not 1,816 c.c.

Page 341: Line 54, read Innumerable.

PICTURE CREDITS

Abarth, Alfa Romeo, Ansafoto, Antony Nowarth, Aston Martin, Audie Photo, Austin, Austin-Healey, Autobianchi, Auto-Union, Bentley, Bizzarrini, BMW, British Petroleum, Brunaud, Civica Raccolta Bertarelli, Citroën, DAF, Daimler, Derek Livemore, De Tomaso, Eastern Press, Ediprint, ENI, Ewin Galloway, Farabola, H. F. Fergusson-Wood, Esq., Ferrari, Fiat, Ford, General Motors, Ken Phillip, Innocenti, ISO, Jaguar, Lamborghini, Lancia, Lotus, Mark-3, Maserati, Mercedes, MG, Montagu Motor Museum, Morris, National Benzole Company Ltd., News Blitz, NSU, Opel, Opera Mundi, Palnic, Peugeot, Photo Service, Porsche, Publifoto, Renault, Rochetaillée Motor Museum, Rolls-Royce, Rome War Museum, Rover, Royal Automobile Club, Saab, Shell, Sibilia, Simca, Skoda, Soblisky, Sunbeam, The Daily Telegraph, Triumph, Turin Motor Museum, Vauxhall, Volvo, Volkswagen, Votava.